CENTRAL ASIAN
SECURITY

CENTRAL ASIAN
SECURITY

The New International Context

Roy Allison
Lena Jonson
Editors

In association with the
Swedish Institute of International Affairs

ROYAL INSTITUTE OF INTERNATIONAL AFFAIRS
London

BROOKINGS INSTITUTION PRESS
Washington, D.C.

BROOKINGS INSTITUTION
1775 Massachusetts Avenue, N.W.
Washington, D.C. 20036
www.brookings.edu

The Brookings Institution is a private nonprofit organization devoted to research, education, and publication on important issues of domestic and foreign policy. The Institution maintains a position of neutrality on issues of public policy, and interpretations or conclusions in Brookings publications are solely those of the authors.

ROYAL INSTITUTE OF INTERNATIONAL AFFAIRS
Chatham House
10 St. James's Square
London SW1Y 4LE
www.riia.org

The Royal Institute of International Affairs is an independent body which promotes the rigorous study of international questions and does not express opinions of its own. The opinions expressed in this publication are the responsibility of the authors.

Library of Congress Cataloging-in-Publication data

Central Asian security : the new international context / Roy Allison and Lena Jonson, editors.
    p. cm.
"In association with the Swedish Institute of International Affairs." "Royal Institute of International Affairs."
Includes bibliographical references and index.
    ISBN 0-8157-0105-5 (pbk. : alk. paper)
    1. National security—Asia, Central.   2. Asia, Central—Foreign relations—1991–
3. Asia, Central—Strategic aspects.   I. Allison, Roy.   II. Jonson, Lena, 1948–
III. Utrikespolitiska institutet (Sweden)   IV. Royal Institute of International Affairs.
DK859.5 .C485 2001   2001000360
327'.0958—dc21   CIP

9 8 7 6 5 4 3 2 1

The paper used in this publication meets minimum requirements of the American National Standard for Information Sciences—Permanence of Paper for Printed Library Materials: ANSI Z39.48-1992.

Typeset in Sabon

Composition by Northeastern Graphic Services, Inc.
Hackensack, New Jersey

Printed by R. R. Donnelley and Sons
Harrisonburg, Virginia

Contents

Acknowledgments

This volume originates from a conference entitled Central Asia in a New Security Context, held in September 1999 and organized by the Swedish Insititute of International Affairs (SIIA) together with the Centre for Pacific Asia Studies and the Forum for Central Asian Studies at Stockholm University as well as the Department of Peace Research at Uppsala University. A wide range of international specialists contributed to the success of this conference, including the authors of most of the chapters in this book. The conference benefited greatly from the contributions by Barry Buzan, Ole Waever, Selcuk Esenbel, Sergei Gretsky, Klara Khafizova and Doulatbek Khidirbekughuli.

The conference was financed by generous grants from the Swedish Council for Research in the Humanities and Social Sciences, the Bank of Sweden Tercentenary Foundation and the Swedish National Defence Research Establishment.

A selection of papers from this conference were extensively revised and updated, and two new chapters were prepared to suit the themes of the book, using the administrative support of SIIA and the Russia and Eurasia Programme of the Royal Institute of International Affairs (RIIA). We are particularly grateful to Eve Johansson for her work in copy editing the manuscript and checking transliterations, and to Margaret May for advice on the publication of the volume and for liaison with the Brookings Institution Press.

The Central Asian and Caucasian Prospects project at RIIA provided research contacts and materials for writing several chapters of the book and helped to sustain the commitment to such a wide-ranging study.

ix

Chapters 8 and 10 were also prepared as preliminary research contributions for a project supported by the Economic and Social Research Council at the Russia and Eurasia Programme, RIIA, and the Department of Middle Eastern Studies of Manchester University, entitled Subregionalism and Foreign Policy Transformation: Russia and Iran in Central Asia (award ref. R000239137).

ROY ALLISON AND LENA JONSON
November 2000

Acronyms

BVO	Basin Management Authority
CAEC	Central Asian Economic Community
CAU	Central Asian Union
CEE	Central and Eastern Europe
CENTCOM	United States Central Command
CICA	Conference on Interaction and Confidence-Building Measures in Asia
CIS	Commonwealth of Independent States
CNPC	China National Petroleum Corporation
CPC	Caspian Pipeline Consortium
EAPC	Euro-Atlantic Partnership Council
EBRD	European Bank for Reconstruction and Development
ECO	Economic Cooperation Organisation
EPT	Environmental Policy and Technology Project
EU	European Union
EUCOM	United States European Command
FDI	Foreign direct investment
GDP	Gross domestic product
GIS	Geographic Information System
GNP	Gross national product
GUAM	Georgia, Ukraine, Azerbaijan and Moldova
GUUAM	Georgia, Uzbekistan, Ukraine, Azerbaijan and Moldova
ICAS	Interstate Council on Problems of the Aral Sea Basin
ICWC	Interstate Coordinating Water Commission
IFAS	International Fund for the Aral Sea

IMF	International Monetary Fund
IMU	Islamic Movement of Uzbekistan
INOGATE	Interstate Oil and Gas Transport to Europe
NATO	North Atlantic Treaty Organization
NGO	Non-governmental organization
OIC	Organization of the Islamic Conference
OSCE	Organization for Security and Co-operation in Europe
PfP	Partnership for Peace
PJC	Permanent Joint Council (NATO–Russia)
PKK	Partiya Karkeren Kurdistan (Kurdish Workers' Party)
PLA	People's Liberation Army
SACLANT	Supreme Allied Commander Atlantic
SVR	Foreign Intelligence Service (of Russia)
TACIS	Technical Assistance to the Commonwealth of Independent States
TRACECA	Transport Corridor Europe Caucasus Asia
TÜDEV	Turkic States and Communities Friendship, Brotherhood and Cooperation Foundation
UNDCP	UN Drugs Control Programme
UNDP	UN Development Programme
USAID	US Agency for International Development
UTO	United Tajik Opposition
WTO	World Trade Organization
XUAR	Xinjiang Uighur Autonomous Region

About the Authors

ROY ALLISON is Head of the Russia and Eurasia Programme at the Royal Institute of International Affairs in London. His publications include *Security Dilemmas in Russia and Eurasia* (co-editor) (London: Royal Institute of International Affairs, 1998); *Challenges for the Former Soviet South* (editor) (Washington, DC: Brookings Institution/RIIA, 1996); and *Internal Factors in Russian Foreign Policy* (co-author) (Oxford: Oxford University Press, 1996).

STEPHEN BLANK is Professor of Russian National Security Studies at the Strategic Studies Institute of the US Army War College. He has published over 140 articles on Soviet/Russian military and foreign policies. His books include *Imperial Decline: Russia's Changing Role in Asia* (editor) (Durham, N.C.: Duke University Press, 1997); *The Sorcerer as Apprentice: Stalin's Commissariat of Nationalities* (Greenwood Publishing Group, 1994); and *The Soviet Military and the Future* (co-editor) (Greenwood Publishing Group, 1992).

EDMUND HERZIG is a Senior Lecturer at the Department of Middle Eastern Studies at Manchester University and a Senior Research Fellow at the Royal Institute of International Affairs in London. His publications include *The New Caucasus: Armenia, Azerbaijan and Georgia,* Chatham House Paper (London: Pinter/Cassel, 1999); and *Iran and the Former Soviet South* (London: Royal Institute of International Affairs, 1995).

STUART HORSMAN has been a tutor in politics at the University of Sheffield and held research attachments at Bradford University and the Royal Institute of International Affairs. His research has focused on environmental and ethnic dimensions of security in Central Asia and he has published a number of articles and book chapters on these subjects. His doctoral dissertation was entitled *Security Issues Facing the Newly Independent States of Central Asia: The Cases of Kazakhstan and Uzbekistan.*

LENA JONSON is a Senior Research Fellow at the Swedish Institute of International Affairs. Her publications include *Keeping the Peace in the CIS: The Evolution of Russian Policy,* Discussion Paper (London: Royal Institute of International Affairs, 1999); *Russia and Central Asia: a New Web of Relations* (London: Royal Institute of International Affairs, 1998); and *Peacekeeping and the Role of Russia in Eurasia* (co-editor) (Boulder, Colo.: Westview Press, 1996).

ALEXEI MALASHENKO is a Senior Associate at the Carnegie Moscow Center and Professor at the Institute of Oriental Studies in Moscow. His publications include *Islamic Revival in Contemporary Russia* (in Russian) (Moscow Carnegie Center, 1998) and *Conflicting Loyalties and the State in Post-Soviet Russia and Eurasia* (co-editor) (London and Portland, Ore.: Frank Cass, 1998).

MARTHA BRILL OLCOTT is a Senior Associate at the Carnegie Endowment for International Peace in Washington and professor of political science at Colgate University. She has published numerous articles and books on Central Asian affairs. Her publications include *Getting It Wrong: Regional Cooperation and the Commonwealth of Independent States* (co-author) (Washington, DC: Carnegie Endowment for International Peace, 1999); *The New States of Central Asia* (Washington, DC: United States Institute of Peace, 1996); and *The Kazakhs* (Stanford, Calif.: Hoover Institution Press, 1987).

GARETH WINROW is Professor in the Department of International Relations at Istanbul Bilgi University. His publications include *Turkish Policy in the Caucasus* (London: Royal Institute of International Affairs, 2000); *Turkey in Post-Soviet Central Asia* (London: Royal Institute of International Affairs, 1995); *Turkey and Caspian Energy,* The Emirates Occasional Papers, no. 37 (Abu Dhabi: Emirates Center for Strategic Studies and Research, 1999); and *The Kurdish Question and Turkey: An Example of a Trans-State Ethnic Conflict* (co-author) (Newbury Park, London: Frank Cass, 1997).

GUANGCHENG XING is Deputy Director and Professor at the Institute of East European, Russian and Central Asian Studies at the Chinese Academy of Social Sciences in Beijing. His publications in English include 'China and Central Asia: Towards a New Relationship' and 'Security Issues in China's Relations with Central Asian States' in *Ethnic Challenges Beyond Borders: Chinese and Russian Perspectives of the Central Asian Conundrum* (London: Macmillan, 1998).

CHAPTER ONE

Central Asian Security: Internal and External Dynamics

LENA JONSON

ROY ALLISON

Introduction: the new international context

The dissolution of the Soviet Union in 1991 created five new independent Central Asian states and fundamentally changed the strategic configuration of the wider Central Asian region, although the implications of this geo-strategic upheaval could not be predicted with any certainty at that time.[1] The natural inclination of the rulers of the new states which joined the Russian-led Commonwealth of Independent States (CIS) was to maintain close alignments with and continue to depend on the former metropolitan centre, now represented by the new Russian state. This approach was both the product of their Soviet-era socialization and a reflection of the reality of their close and multi-layered integration with the Russian Federation—a meshing together which Russian leaders sought to preserve in many key aspects. The fact that former Soviet military forces and installations were scattered throughout the CIS Central Asian states reinforced the perception that the establishment of independent security and defence policies was a remote and unrealistic goal for the Central Asian states. This conservatism was not essentially shaken by the early and contrasting response to independence in other post-Soviet countries such as Ukraine, Georgia or the Baltic states, which sought to forge their identities through a struggle to establish autonomous foreign and security policies.

Against this background, it seemed likely to many analysts in Russia and the West in the early and mid-1990s that a Russia–Central Asia strategic axis would emerge, characterized by strong structural dependence of the smaller states on Moscow and centred on Russian alignment with Kazakhstan, a state with no natural boundaries to its north despite a borderline of over 6000 km with Russia and a large ethnic Russian population. This expectation was reinforced by bilateral treaties signed between the Central Asian governments and Russia on defence and military cooperation, which specified the functions of Russian and local military forces, offered Russia the use of local military facilities and in some cases even envisaged joint military doctrines or coalition forces.[2] All this suggested that Russia had the capacity and was sooner or later to establish a hegemonic security policy role in Central Asia, or might be capable of developing the CIS into an integrated economic and military union of at least Russia and the Central Asian CIS member states, either on a voluntary basis or as the result of various forms of subtle coercion.[3]

The prospects of this scenario being realized had sharply diminished by the middle of the 1990s, despite the formal conclusion of a plethora of bilateral and multilateral treaties. These agreements buoyed up Russian expectations that its strategic influence could be recovered in Central Asia, but most of them were never implemented, especially when they required significant Russian financial subsidies. In retrospect it can be argued that these agreements represented or became a form of public relations diplomacy. Similarly, a grand declaration by then Russian President Boris Yeltsin in spring 1994 that some 30 Russian bases would be set up in CIS states, mostly presumably in Central Asia and the Caucasus states, came to very little: Russia acquired access to a limited number of military facilities.

By the end of the decade the Russian effort to create a forward security zone in the southern CIS states was crumbling. Russia lacked the personnel to occupy the bases it coveted and the financial means to realize the various joint military tasks with CIS states necessary to establish a new strategic glacis to the south.[4] Russia's preoccupation with its internal economic crisis and the chaotic policy-making environment in Moscow, which allowed various interests to compete for influence and frustrated efforts to develop strategic directions in foreign policy, accelerated a process of Russian 'involuntary disengagement' from Central Asia in the political, economic and military fields.[5] This dissociation from the region has been apparent in the poor results of Russian efforts to maintain a multilateral, though mostly Russian-led, 'commonwealth' structure as well as in the uneven outcome of more pragmatic Russian efforts to sustain key bilateral relationships.

Russia is no longer able unilaterally to define the nature and extent of purported common interests with the Central Asian states, but such common interests exist and Russia remains highly influential in the region.[6] Indeed it cannot be assumed that a Russian withdrawal from Central Asia can be expected to take place as a linear development. The relative Russian weakness in the 1990s should be compared both with the strength and capability of the Central Asian states themselves and also with what outside powers are able to provide in the form of support and assistance in specific situations.

This relates to another crucial aspect of the strategic reconfiguration of Central Asia. From at least the mid-1990s the Central Asian states, except Tajikistan which was still embroiled in civil war, have actively sought to diversify their security policy relations and form new partnerships outside the context of the CIS or bilateral agreements with Russia. Through reducing their former dependence on Russia it became easier for the Central Asian leaders to assert distinct foreign policies and national security priorities. This has been reflected in the growing engagement in Central Asia of other regional powers—Turkey, Iran and China[7]—as well as the United States and other Western states. The prospects of exploiting the rich oil and gas resources in the Caspian region have attracted not only Western but also Asian investors and governments.[8]

From a strategic perspective analysts and officials in the West attached increasing importance to Central Asia's central location at the crossroads of Eurasia.[9] For example, former US official Zbigniew Brzezinski was sufficiently impressed by the shift in the external ties of the Central Asian states by autumn 1997 to call for a US strategy to 'consolidate and perpetuate the prevailing geopolitical pluralism on the map of Eurasia' in order to shape a new 'cooperative trans-Eurasian security system' in the future.[10] This clarion call to support geopolitical pluralism and to reconfigure Eurasian security is wholly at odds with Russian discussion of CIS 'integration' or more transparently of Russia as the key player in Central Asia. These options represent two clearly alternative strategic trajectories, although the constraints on the policies of the

Central Asian states and fluidity in the regional security environment means that both approaches influence Central Asian security decision making.

It may be argued that the active engagement of external powers in Central Asia is likely to contribute to peace and stability in the region and that contacts with the wider international community can enhance opportunities for the Central Asian states to develop their economies, build more democratic societies and resolve conflicts. However, this rationale for 'geopolitical or geo-strategic pluralism' has yet to be confirmed. Moreover, legitimate concerns can be raised that the manner in which regional powers engage in Central Asia can re-ignite old conflicts and give rise to new ones.

Regional powers carefully monitor the involvement of other powers in the fragile Central Asian states and assess the potential impact of new foreign ties on the balance within the region. The existence of a wide variety of internal sources of instability within Central Asia means that the potential for conflict is ever-present and the growing influence of foreign states and transnational influences in the region could deepen divisions within vulnerable societies. Foreign companies and foreign governments with agendas of their own could act as rivals, with deleterious effects on the interests of the states in the region. At the same time local groups or interests may be inclined to exploit the opportunities provided by the presence of external actors to the detriment of other states or groups in the region.

The purpose of this book is twofold: to analyse the changing security policy challenges in Central Asia since Russia became more disengaged from the region in the mid- to late 1990s, and to discuss the security policy relevance of the expanding network of relationships between Central Asian states and regional and international powers. The focus of the analysis is on instabilities which may generate conflicts between states. In this context we may define regional security as encompassing 'issues that increase the likelihood of conflict among states, or that promote instability within them and that, in so doing, increase the risk for foreign intervention'.[11] This definition requires us to identify those factors that give rise to such instability or conflict and undermine wider regional security. A basic assumption of this volume is that the effect of the engagement of external states in Central Asia depends on how such engagement interplays with the region's internal dynamics, and that the future strategic configuration of Central Asia will depend on how regional powers address destructive challenges as well opportunities for cooperation arising from within Central Asia itself.

Three specific questions will be addressed. How are conflictual or cooperative processes developing which are relevant for the security orientation of the region? How does the involvement of external powers affect the security dynamics of the region? And to what extent are security arrangements evolving which are capable of responding to security threats to the region? The last question highlights the crucial issue of whether the Central Asian states themselves are capable of overcoming threats individually or in concert, or if the assistance of external powers is required for efforts to maintain regional peace and stability. An important consideration is the extent to which non-traditional security threats that are internal to the region, which may lead to disputes between the Central Asian states, can be managed in concert with regional or external powers and organizations.

In assessing the Russian role in Central Asia a key question is whether Russia's influence has been so far reduced that it can no longer in any meaningful sense act as a security 'guarantor' for the Central Asian states. A concomitant issue is whether this role, which Russia tried to assume throughout the 1990s, can be adopted by any other state or group of states, or whether instead completely new security arrangements are evolving for the region. For example, is a new 'cooperative trans-Eurasian security system', as advocated by Brzezinski, in the making? If so, what would be the characteristics of such a system?

Central Asia as a regional security complex

To analyse the relevance of new forms of cooperation for Central Asian regional security and the effects of the interaction between external powers and regional security dynamics, it is useful to employ the concepts of a 'regional security complex' and 'security dynamics'. A security complex has been defined by Buzan as 'a group of states whose primary security concerns link together sufficiently closely that their national securities cannot realistically be considered apart from one another'.[12] The states in a regional complex are locked into common security concerns and linked each other in such a way that the actions of one state to advance its security are likely to have consequences also for other parts of the complex.[13] It is important to note that a 'security complex can exist and function regardless of whether or not the actors involved recognise it . . . they may well not see, or appreciate fully, the whole pattern of which they are a part'.[14] The states of a complex may be linked by security concerns, therefore, whether the leaders of these states recognize this condition or not.

It may be argued that the common heritage of the five CIS Central Asian states, as a fully integrated part of the Soviet Union under the security umbrella of that state, contributes to the formation of independent Central Asia as a regional security complex. Moreover, the Central Asian states make up a coherent system in geographical and cultural terms (represented by Sunni Islam and the Turkic language, except in the case of Tajikistan). In security policy terms it can be argued that the Central Asian region has its own dynamics, preoccupations and opportunities; although each state conducts its own specific national policy as determined by its own interests, their security policies are interconnected.[15]

However, it is not clear that there is sufficient commonality in security policy interactions across the whole of the vast region formed by the Central Asian CIS states—for example, between Turkmenistan and Tajikistan—to identify a security complex. Nor is it clear whether the definition of such a security complex should be confined to the borders of the CIS Central Asian states as cross-border interactions with a wider Central Asia become more significant. Which neighbouring geographical regions are clearly relevant for an analysis of Central Asian security policy and perhaps also for the integrity of a Central Asian security complex? Northern Afghanistan at least may be considered as lying within a 'wider' Central Asian security complex, although its role in exporting instabilities beyond the Afghan frontiers represents an immediate challenge to the security of Central Asian states. The northern and eastern parts of Xinjiang increasingly also appear to fit within such a wider Central Asian security complex, despite the efforts of Chinese leaders to insulate Xinjiang from cross-border instabilities. There are also security-relevant interactions across the Russian–Kazakh border, which could place regions in southern Russia in this wider complex.

Another question is the extent to which a Central Asian security complex—whether comprising just the CIS states in the region or defined in a wider sense—could incorporate the Caucasus region or parts of it. The Caspian Sea region links Central Asia and the Caucasus and offers an alternative geographical category. The region is increasingly defined by a network of new transport networks and pipeline projects. These geo-economic developments have attracted political commitments from large states, which in turn may have strategic relevance. It is certainly the case that the eight states of the Central Asian and Caucasus region are developing certain common concerns and shared objectives. As indicated in the chapters in this volume on Russian, US, Turkish and Iranian policy in Central Asia, these powers often regard the two regions as interconnected. However, the common concerns of the states in the two regions are largely an outgrowth of the new trade, transport and energy opportunities around the Caspian region and is it less clear how far they reflect security policy priorities or have security implications. Evidently geographical distance limits security-relevant interactions between countries such as Georgia and Tajikistan, although they both seek to contain instability within or on their borders linked to ethnic separatism and radical Islamic groups.

This ambiguity is shown in relation to the GUUAM grouping of states, which consists of Georgia, Uzbekistan, Ukraine, Azerbaijan and Moldova. A grouping of states so geographically dispersed can hardly be interlocked in their direct security concerns even if their leaders share various expectations and objectives which are sufficient to generate interstate cooperation on certain issues. Commonality in core security priorities would require closer geographical proximity than GUUAM offers. Certain common goals on energy development may provide a focus for cooperation between a core group of Georgia, Azerbaijan and Ukraine. But such cooperation is far from sufficient to create a security complex even in this subgroup of the GUUAM states.

It may be possible, however, to identify smaller subregional security complexes within Central Asia, which may have a negative or positive impact on stability. The Ferghana Valley, where Uzbekistan, Kyrgyzstan and Tajikistan meet, could offer a negative example of such an intricate subregional complex. The difficulty of containing instabilities within or bordering this valley to any one state was apparent during summer 1999 and 2000, when armed militants easily crossed local borders and precipitated subsequent military cooperation between the three states and Russia. Ethnic divisions and challenges by radical Islamic groups around the Ferghana Valley, which are linked to insurgency in Afghanistan, are becoming critical security issues for local leaders.

More positively, the Caspian Sea littoral and the sea itself (littoral states include Russia, Iran, Kazakhstan, Turkmenistan and Azerbaijan) could be viewed as an example of a potential security complex based on positive security interactions. The economic benefits from the exploitation and export of energy resources are likely to overcome competitive tensions and result eventually in an agreed demarcation of the Caspian Sea. This in turn could give rise to confidence-building measures for the sea, including some measure of demilitarization. But even more negative security policy outcomes would confirm the existence of a local security complex around the Caspian Sea.

The concept of a regional security complex enables one to examine the interplay between two levels of analysis—the local or national level and the international level of external powers active in the region—by focusing on the regional level. Buzan suggests that the main characteristics of a regional complex can be found in the lines of division between states and in the power balance between them. He uses the terms 'enmity' and 'amity' to describe the poles along the lines of division. Amity can be viewed as 'relationships ranging from genuine friendship to expectations of protection and support', while enmity can be understood as 'relationships set by suspicion and fear'.[16] Patterns of relations of these kinds reflect issues such as border disputes, interests in ethnically related populations, ideological alignments and long-standing historical links.

For the purposes of analysis in this volume the terms for the two poles representing lines of division can be modified to 'friendship' and 'suspicion', since 'amity' and 'enmity' are too stark for the Central Asian context. It is also clear that in Central Asia no single unambiguous one-dimensional pattern of dividing lines exists so far.[17] Instead, some states within the region have more in common and therefore are disposed to each other in a more friendly manner. Others do not feel such an affinity and view each other with a certain degree of suspicion or as competitors in some respects. A distinction can be made between structural and conjunctural patterns. Conjunctural shifts in relations between states follow from temporary political coalitions and should be distinguished from more structural alignments.

The power balance between states in the region reflects territory, population, economic strength and military power. In Central Asia there is a structurally in-built competition between Kazakhstan with the largest territory and Uzbekistan with the largest population and the largest military organization. This influences their alignments with other countries. To Kazakhstan, relations with Russia are particularly important since it borders Russia and has a large ethnic Russian population. Uzbekistan lacks borders with Russia (though the two states share some security concerns, for example over radical Islam) and feels more free to act indepen-

Figure 1. *The regional security complex*

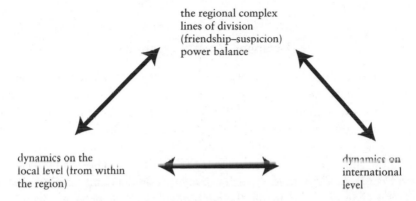

the regional complex
lines of division
(friendship–suspicion)
power balance

dynamics on the
local level (from within
the region)

dynamics on
international
level

dently, for example in developing programmes for military cooperation with Western countries. Its actual and potential influence in the region raises its importance for regional powers.

Changes in the regional system may be prompted by internal as well as external factors. With regard to internal factors, Buzan refers in the first place to shifts in the level of economic or military strength, which determines the power balance between states. Change in the regional system is also initiated when former dividing lines disappear as old conflicts are resolved, and new conflicts and new dividing lines may evolve in their place. External factors stimulating changes in the regional system mainly take the form of alignments by external powers within the region, which influence the power balance in the region by contributing to the economic or military strength of one state or group of states.

The interplay of internal and external factors results in a structure for interaction between states in the region and with external powers. What begins as interaction in the economic or even cultural field may develop into a mutual interest in developing cooperation in security and military affairs. An intensified network of contacts and exchanges may even foster common values and interests and eventually result in close security cooperation in the form of a 'security community' of states.[18] It is not a premise of this volume that such a 'security community' is a probable outcome in Central Asia, since competition between Central Asian states is deeply embedded. However, movement in this direction is possible. Cooperation in the economic and energy spheres is part of the analysis in subsequent chapters, therefore, since such cooperation is regarded as relevant in studying the reorientation of the security policies of the Central Asian states.

Regional security dynamics

To better understand the consequences of the engagement of external powers in Central Asia it is necessary to examine more closely the dynamics of the region with regard to conflict and cooperation and to consider the factors influencing those dynamics. One may distinguish between *cooperative* dynamics, which hamper conflicts, stimulate cooperation and strengthen peaceful relations between states of the region, and *conflictual* dynamics, which aggravate conflicts and tensions. Later in this chapter, in discussing the consequences of the engagement of external powers on security and security cooperation in Central Asia, a distinction is drawn on the one hand between *cooperative* and *conflictual dynamics* and on the other hand between *internal* and *external factors*, which differ according to whether they emanate from within the region or from outside it.

The interplay between the engagement of external powers in the Central Asian region and regional dynamics works in both cooperative and conflictual directions. As Russia no longer dominates the region, in the manner described by Buzan as 'overlay', regional dynamics in Central Asia have returned to the forefront. Not only may a potential for conflict within the region erupt into conflict between states, but the dynamics within the region may result in a reorientation of security policy and foreign policy preferences. These dynamics within the region make predictions about the effects of involving international actors and efforts at international cooperation uncertain. Internal developments in Central Asian countries could persuade their leaders to turn away from the outside world of investors and governments, or alternatively they could encourage them to invite international organizations, foreign companies and governments into an even deeper engagement with their states. For example, the possibility of widespread violent conflict in the region, perhaps commencing in the Ferghana Valley, cannot be precluded. This could result in efforts by Central Asian leaders to sharply reorient their policies towards Russia to gain close support from that state and could result in most international partners withdrawing from Central Asia.

Regional dynamics are often so strong that outside powers, when engaging in a region, tend to fall in line with the existing pattern of power relations and dividing lines between states of the region. However, as has already been noted, outside powers also influence the regional security complex. This can be done by influencing the conditions of the region, which affects the policy choices and policy making of the states there and results in a further chain of events. Moreover, the dynamics in the relations between external powers may spill over into the region, which means that rivalry and tension between external powers can be transferred into the region and thus influence regional dynamics.

However, a crucial issue is to determine which dynamics actually meet in the interplay between internal and external factors. An outline of the possible alternative outcomes is constructed here in the form of a diagram of the possible alternative outcomes of external powers' engagement in Central Asia and the consequent interplay with dynamics arising from within the region.

The dynamic interplay: alternative options for the future

The outline presented below provides four alternative security situations, each of which may generate different possible security policy responses. In analysing internal factors, the conflictual and cooperative dynamics of these factors will be discussed. The same can be done for external factors, which may also be conflictual or cooperative in their impact on other regional powers. Strong rivalry between external powers thus gives rise to conflictual dynamics between them.

This framework excludes situations where external powers have no influence at all on the region or such weak influence that the internal dynamics predominate. The possibility of such a situation should, of course, be recognized, as external powers may dissociate themselves from the Central Asian states because of the magnitude of the problems in the region or because their own interest in the region declines. The framework advanced, however, is only concerned with situations when there is certain and relevant engagement by external states and international actors.

Option 1: If the dynamics from within the region are mainly conflictual, external powers easily fall into line with regional divisions. If relations between external powers with an interest in Central Asia are characterized by rivalry, a situation will arise according to the first option. In this situation either one or several powers will develop close relations with individual Central Asian states. As a result the region will be fragmented and have deep divisions.

Table 1–1. *Future security options**

| | | Internal factors | |
		Conflictual dynamics	Cooperative dynamics
External factors	Conflictual dynamics	1	2
	Cooperative dynamics	3	4

*Numbers in the table are not measurements, but correspond to the options discussed below.

Option 2: If, on the other hand, dynamics in the region result in cooperation between Central Asian states while external powers are in a state of rivalry, a situation according to option 2 arises. If the Central Asian states are strong enough to manage to balance a diversified relationship with regional powers, the result may improve regional security at least on a temporary basis. This order would, however, be fragile and the rivalry between external powers may easily spill over into the region.

Option 3: If the external powers are prepared to cooperate in a situation where strong conflictual dynamics exist in the region, the powers may still be unable to exercise much influence because of the dominance of regional dynamics. If, however, the external powers are able to influence the security situation, conditions would be positive for a concerted effort to manage and resolve conflicts in the region. Their efforts would easily be undermined, however, by the lines of division in the region.

Option 4: If the regional dynamics are cooperative and the external powers are prepared to cooperate, new multilateral security frameworks have a chance to develop. The conditions for responding to challenges from within the region would be positive.

Internal and external factors of Central Asian security

The Central Asian states have a common legacy which provides them with the basis and potential for the expression of cooperative dynamics in the region. They share a common history, which precedes the period of Russian/Soviet domination and have substantial cultural commonality. The population is mainly Sunni Muslim and the language Turkic (except in Tajikistan). Central Asia is mainly cut off from its southern neighbours by high mountains, a geographic reality which has always hampered contact with peoples to the south. Decisions made during the

Soviet period provided them with a common interlocking transport system, energy grids and irrigation system for the use of scarce water resources (though the latter has become contentious). The Central Asian states also share similar problems in seeking to break with the legacy of the Soviet economic and political system, although their reform trajectories differ in pace and content.

Formal cooperation within the region has developed and even acquired an institutional format, although it is still rather weak and not all states in the region are active participants in multilateral structures for cooperation. For example, the Central Asian Economic Community (formerly the Central Asian Economic Union, created in 1994) excludes Turkmenistan, which has chosen not to engage in such multilateralism except on an ad hoc basis.

Other structures for regional cooperation include different regional powers and offer the means for such powers to promote their views or policies in the region—the Turkic Union (which includes Turkey), the Economic Cooperation Organisation (which includes Iran and Pakistan), the 'troika' (which includes Russia), the Shanghai Forum (which includes Russia and China), not to mention the CIS organization which still offers Russia access to Central Asia in various ways.

Despite the existence of cooperative regional dynamics in Central Asia it appears that conflictual dynamics are more deeply entrenched. After the dissolution of the Soviet Union there were fears that ethnic strife and conflict would spread through the complicated ethnic matrix formed by Central Asia. The fact that this did not happen is a notable achievement for the Central Asian leaderships. With the exception of Tajikistan, which suffered a devastating civil war during 1992–97, the Central Asian states managed to maintain relative stability. In her chapter in this volume Martha Brill Olcott points to the potential for conflict within the region and concludes that the risk of Central Asia turning into a highly unstable region is quite real but that this is not inevitable.

The risk of instability arises from the possibility that the underlying tensions and rivalry which prevail in the region will predominate. Olcott refers to competing national strategies pursued by Central Asian states in the economic and foreign policy fields. This dynamic of instability reflects the fact that these states are fragile and they are facing serious economic and political challenges at the same time as they are trying to consolidate their statehood. Deteriorating social conditions serve to heighten the atmosphere of rivalry between different ethnic groups and increase the prospects for tension between them. In these circumstances the lack of coincidence between ethnic and state borders creates a significant potential for conflict.

The potential of Islam in Central Asia is analysed in Alexei Malashenko's chapter. This is a factor of growing importance for Central Asian security and has a potential for cooperative as well as conflictual dynamics. Central Asian leaders fear the threat of an Islamist opposition from within their countries and the intrusion of international terrorism into the region. The bombings in Tashkent in February 1999 and the incursions of Uzbek Islamists into southern Kyrgyzstan in August 1999, and as far as Uzbekistan in summer 2000, indicate a potential for escalation to violent conflict with an Islamist label. The threat of 'Islamic fundamentalism' and 'international terrorism' has brought states of the region into cooperation not only between themselves but also with Russia. National policies in this regard also create problems with neighbouring states, for example, when the Uzbek security services have pursued Uzbek Islamists outside Uzbek territory. Malashenko also discusses the role of Islam in the foreign policy reorientations of Central Asian states, which has prompted closer contact with the Muslim world.

Water is a contested and strategic asset for the Aral Sea Basin countries —Kyrgyzstan, Tajikistan, Turkmenistan and Uzbekistan. Transboundary water management problems are a source of tension between these states. In his chapter Stuart Horsman emphasizes the seriousness of these frictions, although he doubts that they will lead to violent interstate conflict. He shows how external states such as Afghanistan and China may clash with Central Asian states over the use of water resources. However, Horsman also reveals how a variety of international actors have become involved in efforts to mitigate environmental security challenges in Central Asia.

The external powers included in this study are regarded as regional powers insofar as they engage in the region. The policies of Russia, China, Turkey, Iran and the United States in Central Asia are discussed in individual chapters. The new relations evolving between these states and Central Asian states can be characterized as resulting from: (*a*) *historical and cultural affinities*, which are reflected for example in Turkey's role in all the Central Asian countries except Tajikistan, Iran's role in Tajikistan, the Russian role in Kazakhstan, and are also based on Soviet experience throughout Central Asia; (*b*) *economic interests*, in the form of trade, investments and the exploitation of energy resources (for exam-

ple, Iran's evolving economic and transit trade cooperation with Turkmenistan and Kazakhstan; China's growing trade with Kazakhstan and
Kyrgyzstan; Turkish and US investments in the regional economies overall; and the energy interests of all the regional powers); (c) *security concerns,* which depend on the degree to which the security of the external
powers is directly linked to the Central Asian region: Russia, China and
Iran share borders with Central Asian states, which creates a direct interest in the region; and (d) *strategic interests,* which stem from the visions
of the regional powers about their role in Central Asia. The strategic
interests of external powers may combine goals such as maintaining the
status quo, denying the strategic access of other powers, or increasing
their own influence in Central Asia.

As Russian influence in Central Asia has declined the Russian Government has cast around in search of a policy to counter this trend. Lena
Jonson analyses the changes of Russian policy in Central Asia and assesses the options available for Russia in respect of security policy and
the broader goal of maintaining and enhancing its role and influence in
the region. Russia failed to create integrated defence and security structures in Central Asia in the 1990s and has withdrawn its troops and border forces from most Central Asian states, but it still seeks to maintain a
strong military outpost in Tajikistan. In the geo-economic 'Great Game'
related to energy resources and future pipeline projects, Russia retains
influence over Kazakh energy evacuation but has failed so far to deflect
the east–west routing of other Caspian region energy projects. Russia remains the main military power in Central Asia, but has far more limited
military access to the countries of the region than in the early 1990s and
is seeking new formulas for military cooperation with them. Jonson
raises the question whether the Russian leadership under President Putin
could reverse these trends and increase Russian strategic influence in
Central Asia.

In his chapter, Stephen Blank identifies the United States as the new
power in the region. Its growing interest in the region, he claims, is 'in
the highest degree strategic or even geopolitical and aims to enhance US
and not other states' influence. It combines all the traditional instruments
of power, superior economic potential and military prowess as well as a
commitment to integrating the area more fully into the west both in
terms of defense and economics'. He identifies the Caspian region, including Central Asia, as an important area of direct contention between
Russia and Western states. As the strategic stakes rise, he concludes, the

US and NATO regional engagement is likely to grow. Blank discusses whether the option of a US guarantee for Central Asian security is realistic and argues that Washington is overextending its commitments since its resources are not sufficient for this task.

Russia, China, Iran, Turkey and the United States all now link their national interests to Central Asia, but for some of these states events in Central Asia are of more direct concern to national security than to others. For China and Russia, which have long borders with Kazakhstan, the development and character of cross-border relations on the local level is highly relevant. Kazakhstan's borders with these powerful states is of particular strategic importance since these borders are perceived in Moscow and Beijing as the main potential gateway for instabilities from Central Asia into Russia and China. For Russia this perception of vulnerability has grown with its failure to maintain a forward defence zone bounded by Russian border troops on all the outer CIS state borders.

For China the vulnerability of Xinjiang is becoming a primary security concern. Separatism among ethnic Uighurs and Kazakhs and the support this may receive from across the border in Kazakhstan is monitored with great concern by the Chinese Government. China is also challenged by the spread of radical Islam in Xinjiang among the Muslim Turkic-language Uighurs. Guangcheng Xing argues in his chapter that China has been mainly interested in maintaining regional stability and the threat of unrest in Xinjiang has affected its policy in Central Asia. Against this background China has agreed to confidence-building measures and steps for military disengagement in the joint border region with Kazakhstan and Russia. China and the Xinjiang region have also developed into an important economic and trade partner with Kazakhstan and Kyrgyzstan. These countries are gradually becoming drawn closer into the Chinese geo-economic orbit.

After the collapse of the Soviet Union many expected that Turkey and Iran would assume a crucial political and in the case of Turkey economic role in Central Asia based on cultural or linguistic associations. This assumption underestimated the extent to which the Soviet period had left its imprint on the former Soviet Central Asian states. It was also unrealistic in terms of the economic resources Turkey could offer the region.

Iran initially tried to become a source of religious inspiration when an Islamic opposition movement developed in Tajikistan, but soon adopted a different policy. Edmund Herzig notes in his chapter that Iran, which borders Turkmenistan, has sought to maintain regional stability and made a substantial contribution to the inter-Tajik negotiating process which began in 1994. Today Iran is of growing importance as an economic partner for Central Asian states, especially for Turkmenistan, and could play a more significant role in the Caspian region as an energy transit state and consumer if the opposition of the United States to the regional engagement of Iran were to be moderated.

In his analysis of Turkey Gareth Winrow demonstrates how Turkey failed to live up to its ambitions in the early 1990s of playing a leading role in Central Asia. More recently, however, Turkey has become a key transit state for projects to exploit Caspian energy along an east–west corridor (bypassing Russia and Iran). Turkey's status as a member of NATO has increased its weight in its partnership agreements with states in the Caspian Sea region. It has pursued an agenda of bilateral military contacts and at the same time could be viewed as a vanguard state for NATO in Central Asia through the Partnership for Peace (PfP) programme.

Turkey is concentrating relatively more on developing relations with the states in the west of Central Asia, Turkmenistan and Kazakhstan, while its relations with Uzbekistan have been more unstable. Iran has most contact with Turkmenistan and Tajikistan. China in turn is mainly engaged with Kazakhstan and Kyrgyzstan, and the United States concentrates more on the principal states of the region—Uzbekistan and Kazakhstan. Russia has given priority to relations with Kazakhstan, Tajikistan and Kyrgyzstan (although it has given renewed attention to Uzbekistan since late 1999). This pattern of interaction between the Central Asian states and regional powers reflects the various interests of these powers as previously described.

A conflictual dynamic has developed, however, in the relations between regional powers engaging in Central Asia. Russia is particularly preoccupied with the growth of American influence in the region, and this concern is shared and openly expressed by Iran and China. Russian officials view Turkish involvement in the Caucasus states as a geopolitical challenge and are likely to consider the growth of Turkey's military links in Central Asia in the same light. The United States in turn is sensitive to Iranian involvement in the development of the Caspian region and to perceived manifestations of Russian leverage on Central Asian states, although the latter perception is often muted in official statements. China and Russia are already to some extent competitors in forging economic and political ties with the Central Asian states, despite the overall cordiality of Russian–Chinese relations.

This synopsis suggests that Central Asia is developing into a region of strategic rivalry, which is reinforced though not determined by competition over access to Caspian region energy resources and over the routes to evacuate these oil and gas supplies. It can be argued that the regional powers, particularly the most powerful—the United States, Russia and China—are predisposed to view the Central Asian region mainly as an arena for free competition. The rules of the game for these states effectively are zero-sum, despite the promotion of multilateral cooperation in Central Asia by various regional and international organizations.

In his chapter on US policy Stephen Blank cautions against accepting declarations by the US Government about the desirability and feasibility of 'win–win' policies in Central Asia, especially when referring to US and Russian involvement in the region. The USA's description of its goals is uncontroversial: to promote the sovereignty and independence of the Central Asian states, to encourage their transformation into democratic, prosperous and stable societies, and to facilitate conflict resolution. This can be done inter alia through a diversification in the trade, energy policies and security ties of the new states. Yet in fact such diversification is interpreted selectively in Washington so as to reduce or exclude Russia and Iran from energy and military–security arrangements in Central Asia.

The descriptions in the chapters that follow on the development of internal and external factors related to Central Asian security indicate the existence of conflictual dynamics within the region as well as between the regional powers. Consequently there is a danger that the Central Asian region will become fragmented along deep lines of division and the local states will turn to different regional powers for partnership or alignment. For the region to become characterized instead by cooperative dynamics a much greater effort is necessary by each of the regional powers to find common ground for joint approaches to security in Central Asia.

Evolving security arrangements in Central Asia

A variety of security arrangements are taking shape in Central Asia, which may be distinguished according to whether they are bilateral or multilateral and whether they are primarily military or non-military in character.

Russia still dominates the structure of bilateral military agreements which have been signed by Central Asian states, even if we discount those agreements which have not been implemented or have lapsed. However, as noted at the beginning of this chapter, such military cooperation with Russia declined sharply in the late 1990s. The trend in this direction is unlikely to be significantly reversed under President Putin since other Russian defence needs are likely to be accorded higher priority and the overall Russian resource base is not sufficient to maintain an effective forward security zone to the south underpinned by real military commitments. The main Russian roles are likely to be the continued provision or sale of some military supplies to Central Asian states, the use of the Russian military contingent in Tajikistan and coordination with the local states over anti-terrorist measures.

In these circumstances can the option of Russian security guarantees to the region be replaced by other arrangements? A variety of structures and frameworks for security policy cooperation with and in Central Asia are analysed in the chapter by Roy Allison. One possibility would be greater self-sufficiency of the Central Asian states themselves. However, these states have failed to initiate joint military cooperation in a form that would make them confident that they would prevail in conditions of violent conflict or insurgency within the region. A joint peacekeeping battalion of Kazakh, Uzbek and Kyrgyz forces has been formed, Centrasbat. But this has not been employed in combating armed militants in Tajikistan, Kyrgyzstan or Uzbekistan and it could not be used for any major military tasks. The armed forces of Uzbekistan, which are the strongest in the region, may be perceived as threatening by other Central Asian states, which would undermine the readiness to cooperate militarily too closely and especially in a subordinate role to Uzbekistan.

Another option would be the provision of security guarantees under certain conditions by another powerful non-Central Asian state. As Blank argues in this volume, in official statements the United States has shown some readiness to assume military obligations in Central Asia. However, Blank doubts both the determination of the US Government and its capacity for military involvement in this region. China has not indicated any desire or preparedness to offer security guarantees or significant military assistance to the Central Asian states. However, if one adopts a long-term perspective, the possibility that China might make such an offer, if it viewed it as necessary in order to ensure stability in the face of separatism in the Xinjiang region in western China, cannot be excluded. Both Turkey and Iran are unlikely candidates to become military guarantors for the Central Asian states. However, it is true that Turkey is training Central Asian officers and may step up assistance for Central Asian border forces. Low-profile forms of military assistance, and even the delivery of some military equipment, are likely to be part of the bilateral relations between the Central Asian states and all the regional powers, except Iran.

The most prominent multilateral military security structure involving the Central Asian states is the one based on the CIS organization. The 1992 Tashkent Treaty on Collective Security of the CIS states (a treaty which at the outset only excluded Turkmenistan among the CIS Central Asian states) created a formal system of collective defence, although it has only been activated for the limited purpose of consultations over threats from Afghanistan. Uzbekistan allowed its membership of this treaty to lapse in 1999. As noted previously, the CIS treaty structure has atrophied and most supplementary agreements on defence cooperation in the CIS framework have remained on paper. If it continues to exist will the CIS be a façade for Russian policy or can it still oversee multilateral coordination of policy among its member states on some security concerns, for instance, in countering terrorism?

If Russian-based or CIS-based structures are not regarded by Central Asian states as the appropriate format for future cooperation, the question arises whether any other state would be prepared to act as the driving force in a multilateral security structure for the region, or whether such a structure could be created without such a core state. Since the late 1990s some have characterized the NATO PfP programme as an alternative framework to the CIS for military cooperation in Central Asia as in other parts of the former Soviet Union. However, PfP membership can hardly offer a security guarantee and is distinct from NATO membership in this respect. Its functions are those of education, political consultation, confidence building and preventive diplomacy. It has also organized peacekeeping exercises in Central Asia but it seems unlikely that large scale peacekeeping or peace enforcement operations under the aegis of the PfP will be established in this region.

There has been growing interest among the Central Asian states as well as regional powers in creating and participating in security arrangements which are primarily non-military in function. These structures are most often of a consultative character, but in some cases suggest also that 'international regimes' are beginning to form.

A number of subregional or regional initiatives which have been principally sponsored by the Central Asian states can be identified. The Central Asian Economic Community (CAEC), established in 1994, is essentially a consultative framework and addresses security issues to only a limited extent. Kazakh President Nursultan Nazarbayev has proposed the creation of a Eurasian Union as an alternative to the CIS but this remains a Kazakh blueprint. Nazarbayev has also promoted an Asian version of the Organization for Security and Co-operation in Europe (OSCE)—the Conference on Interaction and Confidence-Building Measures in Asia (CICA)—while Uzbekistan has offered its own prescriptions for regional security. An initiative to declare Central Asia a nuclear-free zone, which began as a joint Uzbek and Kyrgyz proposal and was subsequently supported by all the CIS Central Asian states, represents an effort to create an international regime on this specific issue. Overall, one may conclude that such subregional structures, promoted in the first instance by the Central Asian states themselves, remain incipient or only declaratory and appear unable to properly address the security challenges and threats in the region.

There are other examples of multilateral security frameworks in Central Asia which have firmer support from regional powers and are directed at confidence building or the creation of a format for regional negotiations. These may offer small Central Asian states the opportunity to raise particular concerns as well as their own international profile. The multilateral format has helped to balance the foreign policy ambitions of strong states in a constructive direction, especially when regional powers have a clear interest in the stabilization of a region. The framework of the '6 + 2' negotiations over Afghanistan offers one example (this includes the states bordering Afghanistan plus the United States and Russia, and operates under the aegis of the United Nations). The Shanghai Forum is another example. This group of states, which held its first meeting in 1996, consists of China and the former Soviet states on its border—Russia, Kazakhstan, Kyrgyzstan and Tajikistan. It has reached important agreements on military reductions and confidence building and has become an established mechanism for consultations.

Central Asia is also a region of concern for the United Nations and the OSCE, which includes all the new Central Asian states as members. These organizations are engaged in the region through their efforts at mediation in the conflicts in Tajikistan and Afghanistan, through information offices in the Central Asian capitals, and through humanitarian aid. However, neither the UN nor the OSCE has demonstrated the necessary collective political will to act decisively in situations of violent conflict in

Central Asia. Peacekeeping in Central Asia under an OSCE or UN mantle is unlikely in the near future, especially in conditions of general insurgency or before a ceasefire (which may not even be obtainable) but should not be discounted entirely. Neither organization is in a position to offer any explicit security guarantees to Central Asian states.

The question remains whether there may be a more effective way of sharing tasks and responsibilities between different structures and frameworks for security in Central Asia that might contribute to the strengthening of regional security.

It is of crucial concern to the Central Asian region and to the outside world to analyse the possible security policy consequences of the growing engagement by regional powers in Central Asia. This volume seeks to identify the key issues that such engagement raises through analysing trends in the policies of regional powers and their interaction with the security dynamics of the region. An important objective is to distinguish between regional power involvement which promotes security in Central Asia and that which acts to undermine it. Equally important is the attempt to determine which structures, frameworks, and forums for consultation may best address the challenges to security in Central Asia.

Notes

1. For this volume the Central Asian region comprises Kazakhstan, Kyrgyzstan, Tajikistan, Turkmenistan and Uzbekistan. The term 'wider Central Asia' will also be used to indicate the areas of Russia, China and Afghanistan, which border the core Central Asian states and share sizeable ethnic minorities with them.

2. Roy Allison, *Military Forces in the Soviet Successor States,* Adelphi Paper no. 280 (London: International Institute of Strategic Studies, 1993), pp. 15, 54–62.

3. Mohiaddin Mesbahi, 'Russian Foreign Policy and Security in Central Asia and the Caucasus', *Central Asian Survey*, vol. 12, no. 2 (1993), pp. 181–215. The editor of a later work, arising from a conference in the mid-1990s, took the view that the emerging cooperative network between Russia and Central Asia 'is not similar to the old Soviet system' since 'it is based on mutual interests and needs rather than on a unilateral hierarchical arrangement'. Mehdi Mozaffari, 'The CIS' Southern Belt: a New Security System' in Mehdi Mozaffari, ed., *Security Politics in the Commonwealth of Independent States* (London: Macmillan, 1997), p. 29.

4. Roy Allison and Christoph Bluth, eds, *Security Dilemmas in Russia and Eurasia* (London: Royal Institute of International Affairs, 1998); and Roy Allison, 'The Military and Political Security Landscape in Russia and the South' in

Rajan Menon, ed., *Russia, the Caucasus and Central Asia: The 21st Century Security Environment* (Armonk, N.Y., M. E. Sharpe, 1999).

5. Lena Jonson, *Russia and Central Asia: A New Web of Relations* (London: Royal Institute of International Affairs, 1998).

6. Gennady Chufrin, ed., SIPRI, *Russia and Asia: The Emerging Security Agenda* (Oxford: Oxford University Press, 1999); and Martha Brill Olcott, Anders Åslund and Sherman Garnett, eds, *Getting It Wrong: Regional Cooperation and the Commonwealth of Independent States* (Washington, DC: Carnegie Endowment for International Peace, 1999).

7. On Turkey's and Iran's early engagement in Central Asia, see Alvin Z. Rubinstein and Oles M. Smolansky, eds, *Regional Power Rivalries in the New Eurasia: Russia, Turkey and Iran* (New York and London: M. E. Sharpe, 1995). On the development of Central Asia's trade relations with its southern neighbours see Richard Pomfret, *Central Asia Turns South? Trade Relations in Transition* (London: Royal Institute of International Affairs, 1999). On relations with China, see Mark Burles, *Chinese Policy toward Russia and the Central Asian Republics*, Rand Corporation, 1999, URL <http://www.rand.org/publications/MR/MR/1045/>.

8. John Roberts, *Caspian Pipelines* (London: Royal Institute of International Affairs, 1996); Ottar Skagen, *Caspian Gas* (London: Royal Institute of International Affairs, 1997); and Martha Brill Olcott, 'The Caspian's False Promise', *Foreign Policy*, summer 1998.

9. See, for example, S. Frederick Starr, 'Making Eurasia Stable', *Foreign Affairs*, vol. 75, no. 1 (1996); and Ali Banuazizi and Myron Weiner, eds, *The New Geopolitics of Central Asia and Its Borderlands* (Bloomington and Indianapolis: Indiana University Press, 1994).

10. Zbigniew Brzezinski, 'A Geostrategy for Eurasia', *Foreign Affairs*, vol. 76, no. 5 (September/October 1997), pp. 50–64.

11. Rajan Menon, 'Introduction' in Rajan Menon, Yuri Fedorov and Ghia Nodia, eds, *Russia, the Caucasus and Central Asia: The 21st Century Security Environment* (Armonk, N.Y.: M. E. Sharpe, 1999), p. 5.

12. Barry Buzan, *People, States and Fear*, 2nd edn (New York and London: Harvester Wheatsheaf: 1991), p. 190.

13. However, Buzan suggests that a regional complex would not appear if the region were dominated by a great power or a regional power—a condition of *overlay*.

14. Buzan, *op. cit.*, p. 192.

15. Mozaffari, *op. cit.*, pp. 7–9.

16. Buzan, *op. cit.*, pp. 189–190.

17. As observed by Mozaffari, structural enmity does not really exist in Central Asia. He writes: 'The existing disputes over minorities, territory and water resources (as between Uzbekistan, Kyrgyzstan and Tajikistan) are, after all, "normal" political disputes'. Mozaffari, *op. cit.*, p. 14.

18. Barry Buzan, Ole Waever and Jaap de Wilde, *Security: A New Framework for Analysis* (Lynn Rienner: Boulder, Colo., 1998).

CHAPTER TWO

Central Asia: Common Legacies and Conflicts

MARTHA BRILL OLCOTT

Introduction

With every passing year the Central Asian states are becoming more distinct from one another. Travelling in the region one now gets a strong sense of moving from country to country. Signs are in different languages and even different alphabets. Skylines in major cities are being transformed in very different ways, and the same old Soviet constructions no longer dominate. Some of these countries are beginning to be part of a global economy while others remain almost as isolated as they were in the Soviet era. Some of the reasons for the emerging differences can be explained by variations in the national culture, but mostly they reflect the different and sometimes conflicting economic and political strategies that are being chosen.

At the same time, the Central Asian states still effectively form a single region, but it is an unstable one that is generally marked by an absence of cooperative spirit. Whether these states like it or not, for the foreseeable future their fates will be tied to one another, by history, culture and geography, but also because of decisions made during the Soviet period.

In a strange way the Central Asian republics were more equal before being granted statehood than afterwards. The Soviet Union established a comprehensive, albeit flawed, social welfare net which provided a system of social guarantees that included comprehensive health care and educational systems, as well as a well-developed pension system. Those republics enjoyed universal literacy and the right to secondary education was on average guaranteed. Health care, on the other hand, was of diminishing quality, and education was skewed to favour graduates of Russian language schools.

During the Soviet days, however, those republics' economic development had largely been designed to maximize their potential as exporters of raw mineral and agricultural materials. In 1986 Central Asia had the lowest per capita industrial output in the country.[1] A large part of the existing industrial production was based on natural resources. As a result, these countries were dependent on the Soviet distribution system for both goods and transfers.[2] They had one of the lowest levels of income per capita and human development index rankings among the Soviet republics.[3]

The old regional transport system showed no respect for borders, nor did energy grids. The latter have created a host of dependences, which will cost tens of millions of dollars and take several decades to untangle. While highways can be recut and electric grids relaid, water resources are harder to reallocate. The region is an arid one, with high water usage by irrigated agriculture in general and cotton-growing in particular. Water for all five states originates in Kyrgyzstan and Tajikistan, is still free to users and is managed by an imperfectly redefined water management system. The big users are downstream—Uzbekistan and Turkmenistan, the latter being tied to the water usage patterns of the former as well as to the other state upstream.

There are human interdependences as well. Soviet administrative boundaries still prevail, and they were designed to create numerous diaspora populations in border areas throughout the region. Although these states are likely to become more mono-national over time, for now the stranded ethnic co-nationals pose a number of real security risks.

Partly this is the result of the kinds of problems that are implicit in the state-building process, particularly in an area like Central Asia, where there is a strong tradition of rivalry between the region's principal ethnic communities. As each of the Central Asian states strives to work out its national identity this competition is exacerbated. The potential consequences are quite deadly. The states of the region are all fragile, and each faces serious economic and political challenges as it tries to consolidate its statehood.

The priority given by all the region's leaders to securing their rule and legacy makes it all the more difficult to manage these challenges. The

Central Asian states have not yet figured out how to manage these relationships. There have been a host of regional initiatives, but they are the products of weak states and do little to address the deeply rooted sense of personal and national competition that still characterizes the relations between the region's leaders.

The failure of these regional initiatives is magnified by the fact that the environment surrounding these states is a potentially dangerous and often hostile one. They are near two potentially aggressive great powers, China and Russia, and border on two other states (Iran and Afghanistan) that are equally capable of disrupting their affairs. Russia's withdrawal is of course the defining event of Central Asian statehood, as it leaves behind five newly independent states which must define their relationships to one another. At the same time, in many ways the collapse of the state in Afghanistan creates an even more immediate threat to the Central Asian states, as it serves as a source of drugs, revolutionary Islamic ideas, weapons and training in their use.

Developments in all five states can play a key role in determining the security climate in the region more generally. The borders of the area are fragile, and trouble easily spreads from one country to another, but for now there are few mechanisms for successfully regulating conflict on the horizon.

A history which both binds and divides

Central Asia has existed as a distinct region since the early Bronze Age. Its boundaries have varied somewhat over time, as has the location of the dominant power centre. At times Central Asia has been more unified than other regions, and it was one of the centres of world civilization during the time of the early Islamic empires, from the 6th to the 10th century CE.[4] For over 300 years, since the fall of the Mongol rulers, there has been no force within the region strong enough to hold it together.

The distinctness of the region has not translated itself into a strong regional, pan-national identity: local forms of loyalty are still potent in the region, which is making it hard for the new national identities to root themselves firmly in popular consciousness as well. History has provided a number of potential binding forces, but none has ever fully succeeded in creating a single community out of the Central Asian peoples.

In many ways the two most powerful binding forces have come from outside the region—the Mongols and the Russians.[5] In the case of some of these conquerors, the Central Asians took from them and made their culture their own. This was certainly the case with the Mongol rulers. All of Central Asia came under Mongol domination, as an army led by Batu, Jengis Khan's grandson, conquered the lands on both sides of the Urals, defeating a huge Kipchak army and eventually invading Rus' in the winter of 1237–1238. While the Mongol empire eventually disintegrated, their rule in Central Asia led to a cultural, political and genetic interweaving of this outside group with the more indigenous elements of Central Asian history. Unlike previous empires that had existed in Eurasia, the Mongol empire gave a 75-year period of relative stability which allowed an unprecedented exchange of ideas, goods and people within Central Asia.[6]

The same cannot be said of the Russians, whose legacy is much more immediate and controversial. Almost a century and a half of Russian and Soviet rule has left a strong imprint on Central Asia. The shared history of colonial rule, including the problems that it created, helps to bond the Central Asian states. The list of ways in which this is true is nearly endless.

While each of these peoples is busy reinterpreting the common history of the pre-colonial past in ways that emphasize their distinctness, the shared experiences of Russian rule are generally bonding ones. For people over a certain age World War II is one such critical element, and is even a source of nostalgia. By contrast there is a shared sense of disappointment about the Gorbachev years, in particular the early years, in which Central Asia and Islam seemed a target of Moscow's displeasure.

Language was a major unifier, and virtually all adults living in the Central Asian states speak, read and write Russian. The elites are all still proficient in Russian, and most continue to use it as their principal professional language. Until recently, all were educated according to a common curriculum and aspired to go to the same elite schools. The administrative structure that was imposed was uniform, especially in the Soviet period, when a highly complex administrative structure created by both party and state organs penetrated to the lowest levels. Yet this shared experience has never formed the basis of a shared national identity.

The shared history of Islam is an even more powerful binding force. Central Asians have always seen themselves as part of the *dar-ul Islam*, the world of Islam, even in periods when they were cut off from easy access to other Muslim populations. Sunni Islam and the Hanafi school of law are dominant throughout the region. Sufism has been a powerful influence through much of the region, and the Naqshabandiya and Yasavi orders both originated in Central Asia.[7] Central Asians are also proud of the accomplishments of a number of prominent scientists and philosophers who lived in the region when it was part of the Islamic empire. These include ibn Sina (Avicenna), al-Farabi, al-Khuwarizmi and al-Biruni, each of whom is claimed by more than one of the present nations as its own.[8] The practice of Islam, however, varied very sharply across the region. A seminarian tradition was strong among the settled populations but almost wholly absent among the nomads. There were also sharp divides between the settled populations in the way they practised Islam, and radical, conservative and reformist elements were present in the region.[9]

There are other deep cultural continuities that are common to these peoples. The Central Asian region is unique in its overlay of Indo-European (proto-Persian in this case), Turkic and Mongol cultures, and the Russian and then Soviet culture that was imprinted on top of this cultural mosaic is another common cultural force. However, the pattern of interplay of these cultures varies across the region. In places the Russian and Kazakh culture have coexisted for over 300 years; Mongol influences are very strong in south-east Kazakhstan and Kyrgyzstan; the Persian culture is strong in Tajikistan and Uzbekistan; and there is an even older Indo-European culture which predated the arrival of the Oguz Turks in Turkmenistan in the ninth century—the founders of the modern Turkmen nation.[10] Turkic languages dominate the region, but not the Turkish culture, at least if we define it as that which we know from Turkey.[11]

While the Turks of Turkey came from, or at least through, Central Asia, Turkey never ruled the region. Nor did Persia, although like Turkey it was ruled by the Seljuks from present-day Turkmenistan. The Mongols, of course, ended the rule of the latter, but under the Timurids the Central Asians again reached out, and Babur (1483–1530) travelled east and established the Moghul dynasty in India.

The imprint which the Mongol conquest set on Central Asian society was more powerful than that of the Russians and Soviets. Although their territories had long been inhabited, today's Uzbek, Kazakh and Kyrgyz nations all effectively date from the period of the decline of Mongol rule. The modern Uzbeks date from the Shaybanid dynasty, and the Kazakhs from the mid-15th century.[12] The Kazakhs and Kyrgyz are not really distinct ethnically, and generally consider themselves to be close kin, with the mountainous geography of the steppe increasing each people's sense of historic uniqueness. The Mongol conquest also ended the political domination of the region's Persian population, although their cultural influence remained strong, especially on the territory of present-day Uzbekistan and Tajikistan. From this time on Turkic or Turko-Mongol princes ruled these formerly Persian-dominated lands.

For almost all of Central Asian history, the region was defined primarily as the lands between the Amu Darya and Syr Darya rivers (which were regularly named and renamed by the region's conquerors), and the rulers of the oasis settlements tried with varying degrees of success to extend their control over the lands of the nomads to the west (the Turkmen) and those to the north and east (the Kazakhs and Kyrgyz). In the century preceding the Russian conquest the Khan of Khiva wielded some power over many of the Turkmen, but the influence of Bukhara and the splinter khanate of Kokand barely extended over the Kazakhs and Kyrgyz. Kazakh unity has been short-lived: for all intents and purposes it was confined to the 17th century; and Kyrgyz unity was even more ephemeral.[13] The power vacuum in the steppe helped entice the Russians to try to conquer Turkestan (as they termed the region), a process which was not fully completed until after the revolution. The conquest of the Turkmen lands proved very difficult, while Khiva and Bukhara were never fully annexed, remaining Russian protectorates until just after the Russian Revolution, albeit both with much-reduced boundaries.[14]

The Russians never governed Central Asia as a single discrete territorial unit, although Russian colonial policies served to stimulate the process of national consolidation in the region. This process had not gone very far when the revolution came. The creation of a State Duma in 1906 and the various reforms that accompanied it created new arenas of political action for Central Asia's nascent nationalists. The Kazakhs had a small but articulate proto-nationalist intelligentsia, which participated in the second Duma and sought to ensure the survival of a distinct Kazakh people, whose existence they believed to be under threat from Russia's agricultural policies.[15] Economic policies also helped shape the agendas of pro-reform groups in Khiva and Bukhara, both of which were still Russian protectorates under the control of local feudal rulers. The development of cotton cultivation was changing economic power relationships. The Russians also seriously limited the economic power of the Islamic establishment, and this had an impact on the development of conservative and radical Islamic movements as well as reformist movements.[16] The modernists were influenced in part by Tatar reformers, with whom they now came into contact on a regular basis, and this helped stimulate national as well as pan-national movements.[17] On the eve of the Russian Revolution, none of these movements posed a serious threat to the state and none of them showed any serious prospect of developing into a movement which would be able to unify the region. Yet their combined influence was sufficient to force the Bolsheviks to spend a decade consolidating their rule over this region. This resistance became known as the Basmachi revolt, and the history of opposition to Soviet rule is another unifying force that binds the Central Asians.

Overall, though, history was a force for the division of the region into discrete parts. The widespread resistance that the Red forces encountered certainly contributed in an important way to Stalin's decision in 1924 to carve up the region into five separate republics, although this process was not completed until the late 1930s. Moreover, he did so in a way that left large diaspora populations scattered throughout the region. While the Tajiks were cut off from their principal cities, large numbers of ethnic Uzbeks were left in the remaining four republics.[18] These large diaspora populations of Uzbeks were still there at the time of independence. According to the 1989 census, 23.5 per cent of the population of Tajikistan was Uzbek, as was 12.9 per cent of the population of Kyrgyzstan, 2 percent of Kazakhstan and 9 per cent of Turkmenistan.[19] The percentage of Uzbeks in Kazakhstan is low, and suggests that many Uzbeks simply opted for Kazakh nationality on their passports.

Moscow wanted to exert strong control over the territories in its domain, and the idea of a unified Turkestan was a potential threat to this. The risk was not simply that of secession, but that the various powerful communist leaders who came up through the years of the civil war might make common cause. Certainly Stalin wanted to take no chances. The populations of Khiva and Bukhara were each distributed between two republics and new capital cities were chosen for each. But Stalin's actions should not lead to the conclusion that a strong Turkestani state was in the offing. Such a state might have developed over time, but the revolution interrupted a process that had as yet no clear outcome.

Pursuing conflicting national strategies

The conditions under which the Central Asian states acquired statehood have made the idea of a single Turkestani state a moot one, at least for the foreseeable future. In ways that vary from practical to symbolic, the five Soviet republics that became independent states are striving hard to distinguish themselves from each other, and with time they are becoming increasingly differentiated.

Statehood is an enormous prize, at least to the Communist Party *nomenklatura* which gained control of these states. These leaders of now independent countries had vast reserves of power under their control, including the responsibility for conveying ownership rights in the formerly state-controlled economy. The strategies of development they chose were not complementary.

In addition, the old Soviet elite system was a highly competitive one, and the atmosphere of competition was sufficient to overwhelm whatever minimal cultural affinity the Central Asian leaders may have felt for one another. The competition has transformed itself into an atmosphere of rivalry among the region's principal rulers. There have been some efforts at regional cooperation, especially in the early years of independence, but they have had limited success.[20] This is true even of the Central Asian Economic Community (CAEC), created in July 1994 by Uzbekistan, Kazakhstan and Kyrgyzstan.[21] By the time Tajikistan joined the organization in July 1998, it was already apparent how little influence it was going to have on the development of the region's economies, which were already developing in mutually non-supportive ways.[22]

Kazakhstan and Kyrgyzstan both opted for macroeconomic reform and relatively free trade regimes. Kyrgyzstan was the first country of the Commonwealth of Independent States (CIS) to be admitted to the WTO (World Trade Organization), and the currencies of both countries are at least partially convertible. By contrast, the Uzbeks and Turkmen have been extremely reluctant to engage in macroeconomic reforms. Both maintain price support regimes and have currencies which are unstable and of limited convertibility. These policies are one major reason why the governments of both countries have introduced tight border controls and trade restrictions with their neighbours.

The only formal military integration effort in the region is the Central Asian Battalion (Centrasbat), which involves only Kazakhstan, Uzbekistan and Kyrgyzstan. The presidents of these countries agreed to form the battalion on 15 December 1995 at a meeting in Jambyl, Kazakhstan. The battalion was to operate under the auspices of the United Nations, with the purpose of preventing conflicts in volatile areas of Central Asia.[23] Kazakhstan, Kyrgyzstan, Tajikistan and Uzbekistan are also members of the

CIS air-defence pact and hold exercises; the most recent was in October–November 1999. Its goal was to coordinate efforts to counteract transnational terrorism. During the March–April Southern Shield 2000 exercise the four Central Asian states and Russia practised techniques of elimination of major terrorist formations.

Over the past two years, such military exercises have become a vehicle for cooperation between Central Asia and Western countries: it has been the focus of two major exercises sponsored by NATO's Partnership for Peace (PfP) programme. The danger stemming from a lack of regional military cooperation is twofold. First, if these states pursue relatively isolated military development, their mutual distrust will not be alleviated and might even be exacerbated, which would increase the risk of conflict in the region. Second, these states are militarily weak, and in most cases it is unlikely that any one of them will be able to provide for its own security needs.[24]

The cases in point are the events of summer and autumn 1999 in Batken, Kyrgyzstan. Uzbek opposition groups that had been pushed out of Tajikistan as part of the reconciliation process were effective in permeating the porous borders in that mountainous region and destabilizing the situation in neighbouring Kyrgyzstan. The countries of the region attempted to make a concerted effort in the face of the threat. In late August 1999 the foreign ministers of Kyrgyzstan, Tajikistan, Uzbekistan and Kazakhstan attempted to devise a joint strategy to fight the terrorists. However, not much came of this action. Tensions between the Central Asian states even increased after Uzbekistan failed to receive clearance from the Kyrgyz Government and its Su-24 planes bombed a village in Kyrgyzstan, killing four Kyrgyz civilians and injuring 17. Uzbek jets had earlier 'inadvertently' bombed Tajik territory. Uzbekistan believed that it was entitled to carry out those operations and justified its actions by claiming that they were aimed at Islamic terrorists who threatened the country's security.

Central Asian states also attempt to provide discussion of regional issues and stimulate broader regional cooperation through a Conference on Interaction and Confidence-Building Measures in Asia (CICA), proposed by President Nursultan Nazarbayev of Kazakhstan at the United Nations in October 1992.[25] However, over the past seven years of its existence it has generated only preparatory meetings and working groups that resulted in a declaration of the basic principles of guaranteed international security—non-interference in each other's internal affairs, respect for sovereignty and territorial integrity, the peaceful settlement of disputes, the non-use of force, economic, social and cultural cooperation, disarmament, arms control and humanitarian issues. The basic design of this forum is still unclear and so far the declaration has been approved at the foreign ministry level only.[26]

Turkmenistan opted out of the Central Asian Economic Community entirely. In fact, Turkmenistan does not really define itself as a part of Central Asia. Maps in government offices depict 'Turkmenistan and its neighbours' and Turkmenistan's foreign policy is to try to give no special favour to either the CIS states or other Central Asian neighbours. The country adopted a policy of 'positive neutrality', which was formally recognized by the United Nations in 1995.[27] It has not had peacekeepers in Tajikistan, claming that the civil war there was not of direct concern to itself. It has also been against adopting a regional initiative in Afghanistan, preferring the '6 plus 2' formula, and being the only state in the region that has de facto recognized the Taliban government.

By contrast, both Uzbekistan and Kazakhstan pay special attention to their relationships with their Central Asian neighbours, although each of their leaders believes that his nation's rightful position is that of the dominant regional force. Historically that role has been played by the power that controls the lands between the region's two rivers—Uzbekistan. This has always been the geographic heart of the region. Our understandings of geography, however, are not fixed, and in the current conditions of the post-industrial world economics may count for more than geography in determining the relative importance of new nations.

Uzbekistan is hoping to capitalize on its geographic advantage and expects that its central place in the region will make it a dominant regional force once international assistance through the TRACECA (Transport Corridor Europe Caucasus Asia) programme helps put a 'new Silk Road' in place from China to Europe through Central Asia and the Caucasus. The TRACECA project is a highly ambitious one that hopes to attract large investments from international financial institutions, including the European Bank for Reconstruction and Development (EBRD), which has already committed over US$250 million to the project. The World Bank has committed an additional $40 million.[28] However, international assistance projects are notoriously slower to get funded and finished than recipient nations generally expect. Moreover, this is a classic 'chicken and egg' situation. The TRACECA link will only take firm hold if the economies in the region begin to take off and the transit route becomes secure. Neither of these necessary preconditions is as yet assured.

Uzbekistan seeks to expand its influence beyond Central Asia in other ways. The expansion of GUAM (Georgia, Ukraine, Azerbaijan and Moldova) into GUUAM, including Uzbekistan, in April 1999 was designed to integrate Uzbekistan into another new Eurasian construct. Like TRACECA, GUUAM was designed to reduce Russia's influence in the affairs of its newly independent neighbours. Formed in 1997, GUAM was intended to tackle issue areas where coordination would be of mutual benefit, such as regional conflict resolution and peacekeeping, making energy supplies reliable, the creation of an Asia–Europe transit corridor, cooperation in international organizations, and the promotion of closer relations with the West.[29] GUUAM's purpose and function lie in its ability to act as a counterbalance to Russia in the CIS. However, a collection of weak states can be little more than a weak organization itself, and with time Uzbekistan seems to become more fearful of distancing itself from Russia.[30] Russia, the Uzbek leaders seem to appreciate, may be the only foreign power willing to engage directly to help the government of President Islam Karimov secure itself in power.

Since the bombings of 16 February 1999, when several explosions were set off in the Uzbek capital simultaneously, allegedly by Islamic terrorists, all of Uzbek domestic and foreign policy has been subordinated to the goal of securing domestic stability. The country's new international borders have been fortified and new internal security check-points are being established to root out alleged Islamic groups.

However, Uzbekistan's strategy is a very risky one, for itself and for its neighbours. Radical Islamic groups feed on deteriorating social and economic conditions. Uzbekistan's choice of a self-contained economic development strategy may have cushioned the population against sharp declines in the standard of living, but it has also led to economic stagnation. This is partly concealed by official statistics, as Uzbekistan claims to have had the smallest decline of all the CIS states in gross domestic product (GDP) since independence: its GDP in 1999 was only 9 per cent less than that of 1991. This remarkable situation is the result of extensive government control over the economy. It is one of the few countries in the region still to have exchange rate controls and severe currency restrictions, including a ban on foreign currency operations within the country. Uzbekistan is largely isolated from the global financial system. The International Monetary Fund (IMF) created a $185 million stand-by facility for it in December 1995, but this was suspended in November 1996 when the Uzbek Government failed to support the flagging som.

As Uzbekistan's leadership begins to hunker down against outside forces, the sense of rivalry with its neighbours increases as well. At the very least, the Uzbek closed border policy is making it harder for neighbouring states to recover economically themselves. The closed border with Tajikistan, which is designed to keep seditious Uzbek elements from re-entering the country, is crippling the economy of Khujand *oblast* (Tajikistan's piece of the Ferghana Valley). There is also talk of Uzbekistan cutting off all trade between southern Kyrgyzstan (Osh *oblast*) and Andijan, and Kyrgyzstan is preparing for this option by building a new highway to connect its two main southern cities (Osh and Dzhalal-Abad).

Further alienating Uzbekistan's neighbours is the country's evolving security agenda, which includes the right of intervention in neighbouring states if its own interests are perceived as threatened. Thus Uzbekistan pressed the Rakhmonov Government to expel armed Uzbek bands trained in Afghanistan from their safe havens in Tajikistan, threatening to wipe them out itself otherwise. When this strategy partly backfired, and the forces of Djuma Namangani took refuge (complete with foreign hostages) in Kyrgyzstan in August 1999, the Uzbeks bombed some Kyrgyz villages, mistaking them for those that were actually hosting the Uzbek fighters.[31] Thus it is hard to see that Uzbekistan will be able to exert any sort of easy natural leadership over its Central Asian neighbours.

The other claimant to natural leadership in the region is Kazakhstan, and in the end natural wealth may count for more than a better strategic location. This is certainly Kazakhstan's hope, and its development strategy has been to maximize its economic potential as quickly as possible in order to help it became a medium-sized power of some global consequence.

Kazakhstan hopes to use foreign economic relations to stimulate economic growth, and has allowed the international financial institutions to shape its policies of economic reform in order to maximize its chances of attracting foreign direct investment (FDI). This could only be done as a result of a complete overhaul of the existing economic structure. The introduction of private property was an important first step. Privatization was done in several stages: privatization of housing using flat coupons (1991–92), mass privatization using investment privatization coupons (1993–95), and privatization on the basis of individual projects (1996–98). As a result, by 1999 the private sector employed around 60 per cent of the labour force.[32] As of July 1999, 75.6 per cent of the economy was privatized, including 80.2 per cent of small enterprises, 40.8 per cent of medium-sized enterprises, and 52 per cent of large enterprises.[33]

Although the process has not been particularly equitable it has worked to Kazakhstan's benefit. Between 1992 and 1998 Kazakhstan received $1.65 billion in World Bank loans, and between 1993 and 1998 $500 million in IMF loans.[34] It has attracted the highest per capita FDI in the CIS—more than $8.2 billion by 2000.[35] Much of the FDI has come in the oil and gas sectors. In 1998 Kazakhstan was in fourth place for FDI per capita in the CIS and Central and East European (CEE) countries. Its per capita GDP is second only to that of Russia, at $1340 in 1997, and if its major energy projects move forward Kazakhstan's GDP could overtake Russia's.[36]

Kazakhstan would also like to maintain close economic ties with Russia and other CIS partner states, but, as in its dealings with its Central Asian neighbours, it views these states as having less to offer it just now than do the developed industrial societies. As already noted, Kyrgyzstan has pursued a similar strategy and makes a natural ally for Kazakhstan.

Kyrgyzstan initially achieved considerable international support for its economic reforms by being the first former Soviet republic to leave the rouble zone (in May 1993) and the first to introduce its own internationally supported currency. It embarked on an ambitious privatization programme, divided into three stages. During the first stage (1991–93), 97.2 per cent of small companies in retail and food production/primary processing, 86.7 per cent of companies in catering, and 100 per cent of service companies were privatized. During the second stage (1994–95) 6269 companies in core sectors, such as industry, transport and construction, were privatized.[37] By April 1997, 62.9 per cent of the economy had been privatized, including 80.4 per cent of industry, 56.8 per cent of construction and 51.2 per cent of transport.[38] The current and third stage aims to privatize large companies in the major sectors of the national economy, subject to certain restrictions.

These policies did little to compensate for Kyrgyzstan's disadvantages —its isolation, tiny domestic market, and limited resources. The country does have the Kumtor gold mine, which is considered the world's 10th largest gold deposit and is being developed by Cameco of Canada.[39] However, investors' confidence began to decline in 1998, in part because of an increasing atmosphere of corruption in Kyrgyzstan, but probably most importantly because the absence of regional cooperation made it impossible for the foreign investor to parlay an investment in Kyrgyzstan into an enhanced regional position. Kyrgyzstan's economy was dealt a further blow by the Russian economic meltdown of 17 August 1998. Dependent on exports to Russia, it saw them collapse as a result of the Russian financial crisis. As a result, its GDP growth slowed from 10 per cent in 1997 to barely 2 per cent in 1998.

Hard times, growing rivalries and increasing security risks

To date none of the development models chosen by the Central Asian states has been particularly successful. Although there is strong reason for believing that those states that have opted for macroeconomic reforms are laying the foundation for economic recovery, especially if they strive to eliminate official and other forms of corruption, the standard of living in the region is dropping and inequalities are increasing.

In Kazakhstan income distribution is becoming more uneven between urban and rural areas. In 1996 a little over one-third of the population lived below the official poverty line. In 1997 the proportion was 43 per cent (39.8 per cent of the urban and 46 per cent of the rural population). The rural population makes up 45.2 per cent of the total population. The incomes of the urban population are 2–2.5 times higher than those of the rural population. At the end of 1998, the number of unemployed receiving unemployment benefits was 149,200 (59.2 per cent), of whom 53,400 lived in rural areas. In addition more than 1500 villages and *auls* do not have any medical personnel.

The Kyrgyz have also been stretching hard and unsuccessfully to maintain a social welfare net. In June 1997, by a decree of President Akayev, 8 per cent of state holdings in several telecommunications and power supply companies and in Air Kyrgyzstan were transferred to benefit war veterans and pensioners.[40] However, the funds raised by this transfer of shares are not sufficient to meet the government's social welfare needs. As recently as December 1999 the government announced that it owed 112 million soms (about $2.5 million) in pension arrears, 54 million soms to the health care system and a similar amount to educational establishments.[41] As a result, public demonstrations by the poorer sectors of society have become a way of life. Since 37 per cent of the population is below 15 years of age, Kyrgyzstan's social problems are sure to grow worse before they get better. In addition, the country is estimated to have about 50,000 refugees—approximately 1 per cent of the population.

The population of Uzbekistan is even more skewed in the proportion of young people. The share of employed people in the total working-age population dropped from 76.4 per cent in 1994 to 72.5 per cent in 1998.[42]

According to official statistics, more than 107,000 people were looking for jobs during the second quarter of 1999, a 22.8 per cent increase over the same period in 1998. This is in spite of the fact that the official unemployment rate in the country is reported to be about 0.7 per cent. Independent observers place it at 5.3 per cent and claim that some 80 per cent of the population lives below the poverty line.[43]

Statistics from Turkmenistan are even more unreliable. However, unemployment is increasing there too. In 1979, 1000 employed persons had to support 1187 unemployed; by 1995 the latter number had risen to 1287. Income distribution was more equal than in other countries. For example, in 1997 the ratio between the richest and poorest deciles in Turkmenistan was 5, as compared to 13 in Russia. However, it has been estimated that 48 per cent of the population lives in poverty.[44] The social safety net is experiencing problems but still functioning. Although the government cut expenditure on wages, pensions, stipends and medicines in order to keep the budget deficit under control, housing and utilities are provided by the state free of charge and key consumer goods remain heavily subsidized. Turkmenistan has abolished the 10-year secondary education and introduced nine-year secondary education. The health care system has received government funding and the number of physicians increased from 2.9 per 1000 people in 1980 to 3.2 in 1994. The number of hospital beds also increased from 10.6 per 1000 people in 1980 to 11.5 in 1994.[45] At the same time the country is witnessing a severe shortage of medicines and equipment. In 1998 it sought to reduce its expenditures on pensions by raising the retirement age for women from 55 to 57 and for men from 60 to 62.

In real terms the economy of Tajikistan has shrunk by approximately 65 per cent since 1991, and over 600,000 Tajiks were displaced by the civil war. An estimated 85 per cent of the population live below the poverty line—something which is fuelling the narcotics trade from Afghanistan, through Tajikistan and then on to the other Central Asian states, Russia and Europe.

The deteriorating social conditions serve to heighten the atmosphere of rivalry and increase the prospects of ethnic tension. Some of this rivalry is implicit in the state-building process. The leaders of each Central Asian nation are looking to the past to write national histories which affirm their claims to statehood. These efforts pose a potential security risk in themselves, because contemporary boundaries and reinterpreted historical ones in no way coincide.

The Uzbeks have made Timur the central figure in their emerging model of national consolidation. His philosophy of state-building is enshrined in a new Tashkent museum, and a gigantic statue of him dominates a main downtown square. By contrast the Tajiks offer a very different history for these same lands. As the region's only Persian state, Tajikistan can lay claim to all of historic Bukhara, the greater part of which lies in Uzbekistan. Recent studies suggest that typical Tajiks still identify strongly with these lands.[46] But Tajikistan is by far the weaker of the two, and the threat of Uzbekistan's Tajik population rising up is far from that country's most immediate security problems. Nonetheless the Uzbeks remain very fearful of what small Tajik terrorist cells might do on Uzbek territory. To date, though, the meddling has all been from the Uzbek side, although the Uzbeks have been relatively unsuccessful in their efforts to influence political developments in Tajikistan's Khujand *oblast*. Informed Tajik sources strongly believe that the Uzbeks aided Colonel Mahmud Khudoberdiev, who sought to seize power in Khujand *oblast* in November 1998, and it is alleged that they provided him with safe passage or asylum when his coup attempt failed.

Turkmenistan and Kazakhstan also have claims on Uzbekistan. Khiva, the post-Mongol successor to Khorezm, is on Uzbek territory, and part of historic north-western Turkmenistan is in Kazakhstan. There are always rumours about the strength of secessionist groups in Khorezm *oblast*, but for now at least any threats that they might pose are still quite distant. For their part the Kazakhs can make claim to Tashkent, Uzbekistan's capital. It was long part of the territory of the Kazakh Great Horde. Uzbekistan, of course, has claims on all these three countries, as well as on Kyrgyzstan's Osh *oblast*. The city of Osh has a large Uzbek population, and evolved historically and culturally in tandem with the other main cities of the Ferghana Valley (including Khujand in Tajikistan). The situation in Osh *oblast* exploded in 1990 when local Uzbeks and Kyrgyz clashed violently.[47] Since independence the situation has been stable, but this stability is created by the de facto granting of limited extra-territorial rights to Uzbekistan. The Uzbeks have arrested human rights activists on Kyrgyz territory. The Kyrgyz also practise self-censorship in the Uzbek-language media broadcast in the region.

Over time the existing irredentist populations may relocate or re-identify. For now, though, the situation is an unnatural and potentially flammable one. Countries can restrict trade across their borders, but such actions are slow to eliminate the interconnections that already exist. The

Soviet road builders laid highways and railways to facilitate integration of the country's principal economic enterprises, and the boundaries between the republics were of little importance in the process. Roads cross national borders throughout the region. The main road between Tashkent and Samarkand cuts through Kazakhstan, while that between Tashkent and Andijan goes through Tajikistan, and the fastest way to go between Osh and Dzhalal-Abad (both in Kyrgyzstan) is via the Andijan highway. Uzbeks living near the border of Turkmenistan must cross over to get the train in Chardzhou, and the railway which crosses northern Kazakhstan crosses Russian territory between each major Kazakh city.

To address these problems highways are being re-cut and railways relaid, and all these projects are causing major expense for the resource-strapped states involved. These transport projects help to legitimate the existing boundaries between the Central Asian states, but these boundaries are not uncontested. The current regimes are not yet ready to engage in systematic demarcation of the national boundaries, although this is de facto being done as the highways are relaid. Boundary questions will have to be addressed at some future date, especially since there are small enclaves of Uzbekistan in Kyrgyzstan and Kazakhstan, and vice versa. The boundary between Tajikistan and Kyrgyzstan is particularly problematic, although for the time being the two have agreed to disagree. When the old Soviet-era rulers make way for a new generation all these questions are likely to be revisited, with even less of a spirit of cooperation.

In April 1996, leaders of Kazakhstan, China, Russia, Kyrgyzstan and Tajikistan formed the 'Shanghai Five', a group aimed at addressing these issues and discussing a series of confidence-building measures along the borders. The five countries committed themselves to cooperation on border issues through the Shanghai Agreement on April 1996 and the Moscow Agreement of April 1997.

Recent efforts by the Uzbeks to fortify part of their border with Kazakhstan are a likely prelude to more serious problems that lie ahead. In January 2000 Kazakhstan lodged an official protest with the Uzbek Government over unilateral moves by the latter to demarcate sections of the two countries' 230 km common border without prior consultation with the Kazakh Government.[48] Such actions even prompted Ghani Kasymov, former head of the Kazakh customs service and former presidential candidate, to call for the creation of a military bloc of Central Asian states aligned against Uzbekistan.[49] Coming on top of incidents of Uzbek border guards opening fire on Kazakhs in the vicinity of the border,[50] the

Kazakh complaint further complicates existing tension over the Kazakh–Uzbek border.

Turkmenistan's borders with Uzbekistan and Kazakhstan remain fluid as well. The stakes are high in this game because of the resources that lie in the sands under the border region. In March 2000 the presidents of Turkmenistan and Uzbekistan signed an agreement to bring the border between those two states in line with international standards.

The region's water system must still be addressed. Much attention has been focused on the fate of the Aral Sea. The two major rivers in the region, the Amu Darya and the Syr Darya, feed this inland sea, which is bisected by the Kazakhstan–Uzbekistan border. Both Kazakhstan and Uzbekistan draw great volumes of water from the rivers, and Soviet planners diverted water from the rivers to various irrigation canals in an attempt to increase the region's cotton production.[51] As a result, the level of the Aral has gone down 15 metres since the 1960s, and its surface area has decreased by half.[52] The sea is now in danger of dying, and the Aral Sea basin has received international attention as an area in extreme ecological distress. In March 2000, however, Turkmenistan's President Saparmurad Niyazov warned the West about the dangers of politicization of this issue, for it may complicate relations among the Central Asian states. He believes the sea can be saved and that efforts should be made to set up an efficient regional water distribution system that Central Asia desperately needs.

In the Soviet era water was shared out between the Central Asian republics according to strict quotas. Kyrgyzstan and Tajikistan were the source of all the region's water, which was provided free to the downstream users. The artificial seas and pumping stations built during this time in Kyrgyzstan alone led to the flooding of 47,000 hectares of arable land.[53] The Soviet authorities put emphasis on agricultural production in the region and as a result the cotton harvest in Uzbekistan increased by 50 per cent, and the rice harvest in Kazakhstan grew from 23,000 to 654,000 metric tonnes. Kyrgyzstan provided much of the water used for irrigation and as a result kept less than a quarter of all the water its lakes and reservoirs collected each year.[54]

This situation has created a host of problems and tensions, including between the two biggest downstream users, the Turkmen and the Uzbeks. The Kyrgyz now have to maintain the expensive Soviet-era reservoir system on their own, and receive no compensation for its costs or for the loss of the profit from the agricultural lands which the country lost.[55]

The Central Asians are working to fashion a new, permanent inter-state committee to regulate water issues, and there have been numerous meetings to address these questions. To date all solutions are still tentative. In August 1997, Kyrgyzstan's Parliament demanded that Uzbekistan, Kazakhstan and Tajikistan pay for water from the Kyrgyzstani-run facilities. In late December 1997, Kyrgyzstan threatened to cut off its water supply to Kazakhstan because Kazakhstan had not supplied the agreed amount of coal in return.

Energy grids are problematic as well, and the Kazakhs and Kyrgyz are both dependent on Uzbek gas. Uzbekistan is in a position to get concessions from the neighbouring countries by threatening to stop or actually stopping gas deliveries, as it did in 1998 to Kazakhstan and Kyrgyzstan, which have run up substantial debts. Since most foreign investments to the region have gone into the oil and gas sectors, countries like Kyrgyzstan, which lack both and are dependent on imports, have found themselves in an economic bind. This too will only slowly change with time. The Kyrgyz would like to see all the water, electric and energy systems linked together in a single interstate energy committee, but there is still little support for this. In the absence of such a system, access to water, gas and electricity will continue to be used as a bargaining chip in inter-state relations.

More problematic than drawing the borders is the issue of controlling the border regions. This has proved to be an increasing problem for both Uzbekistan and Kyrgyzstan, both of whom border on Tajikistan. The Kyrgyz–Tajik border is particularly difficult to control, as it cuts across the Pamir mountains—as does the Tajik–Afghan border. The porousness of the latter has allowed arms, drugs and Islamic insurgents to cross into the region, and the absence of an international boundary along the former allows this conduit to be extended into Kyrgyzstan and Uzbekistan. The transit of drugs has put all the states of the region at some risk. The amounts of drugs seized across the region have increased dramatically in recent years. In 1993–99 law enforcement agencies in Central Asia alone seized at least 260 tons of drugs. The increased traffic in heroin is of particular concern to the authorities. In 1998 law enforcement agents in Central Asia seized over 1 ton of heroin, up from 113 kg in 1996.[56] If it is assumed that enforcement officers seize no more than 5 per cent of the drugs that pass through the region, the scale of the problem is even more disturbing.

The cash that this trade generates has added to the atmosphere of corruption in Central Asia and in Russia. It has already been reported that several million Kyrgyz are involved in the production, refining, sale and trafficking of drugs with an annual turnover of $14 billion.[57] The UN Drugs Control Programme (UNDCP) estimates that in 1999 opium poppy prices in Afghanistan ranged from $27 to $72 per kilo and the total value of the crop at farm gate prices at harvest time was c. $183 million.[58] The street value of the 1999 crop could be as high as $100 billion.[59] Most of the money earned in the drug trade does not go to local producers and traders. Those running drugs within Central Asia easily generate enough income to buy off many of the local security people. In the depressed conditions of Central Asia there are still strong incentives for the producers and traders. Similarly it is quite easy to bribe the local customs officials, especially in Kyrgyzstan, given their depressed incomes.

As already noted, the human traffic is particularly alarming to Uzbekistan, as the mountains have begun to serve as a safe haven for Islamic groups opposed to President Islam Karimov. Members of these groups have had training in Afghanistan and Pakistan and are now returning to the territory of the former Soviet Union; in the past year they have increasingly made their presence known in Chechnya and Dagestan, and now in Central Asia as well.

In April 2000 the presidents of the members of the Central Asian Economic Community signed a treaty on shared efforts to combat terrorism, political and religious extremism, transnational organized crime and other threats to stability and security. It remains to be seen how this will be translated into a common, workable strategy.

Will cooperation work? Prospects for the future

There is very little in the past several years of efforts at regional cooperation to suggest that an effective multilateral strategy to combat any of the region's problems will emerge at any time soon. Yet the threat they pose points to the fragility of the current political situation. It also points up the difficulty of keeping a dangerous situation in one state from affecting the stability of neighbouring countries. At the time of the civil war in Tajikistan most leaders said that this was a risk. The situation did not immediately bear these warnings out, but developments over the past two years show that all it required was time for these conditions to fester.

The future could be fraught with even greater risks, especially when many of today's leaders pass from the political scene. While the five states of the region are going their own way economically and politically, each of them maintains relatively good relations with the other four. Some of these, however, especially those between Uzbekistan and Tajikistan, are already beginning to erode. What if in the future one or more of these states is headed by a regime that is ideologically opposed to the government of its immediate neighbour? In this region a 'cold war' could easily become a 'hot' one. At the same time, none of the states is yet able to fully defend its borders, especially the undemarcated and largely unpatrollable former 'internal' ones. What would any of these states do if its water supply were indefinitely cut off by the upstream providers, or gas and electricity supplies permanently disrupted?

The risk that Central Asia will turn into a highly unstable region is a real one. This is not inevitable. The current leaders are very sensitive to the risks that are implicit in the region, and while they are in power at least there is good reason to believe that the region will continue to keep the goal of cooperation alive. Yet it is not enough for the Central Asian leaders to wish for cooperation. For regional efforts to succeed, states have to be willing to subordinate their national interests in the service of common goals.

In fact, the opposite has been the case: each of the states has rather been determined to go its own way with relatively little concern for what this means for neighbouring countries. As long as this is not a priority, there will be a serious risk that the underlying tensions and competitions that prevail in the region will predominate. Weak states make bad neighbours, and all the Central Asian states are still weak to varying degrees. Moreover, they are becoming stronger at very different rates, and in ways that seem to be driving them further apart rather than bringing them closer together. Some of them are being successfully drawn into the global community; others are becoming increasingly isolated pockets of criminal activity and disorder. Over time the stronger states of the region will have less and less interest in cooperating with the weaker ones, and the whole notion of Central Asia as a distinct region may come into question.

Notes

1. For an excellent overview of the economic and social conditions prior to the collapse of the Soviet Union, see US Congress, Joint Economic Committee, *The Former Soviet Union in Transition*, Study papers submitted to the Joint Economic Committee, 103rd Congress, 1st session, May 1993, S. Print 103-11 (Washington, DC: US Government Printing Office, 1993), vol. 2.

2. For example, official transfers from Moscow averaged 10% of the Kyrgyz GDP in 1989–91. World Bank, *Kyrgyzstan: The Transition to a Market Economy*, Country report, 1993, p. xv.

3. *The Former Soviet Union in Transition*, vol. 2, p. 1121.

4. For a more detailed history of the various classical kingdoms and empires of Central Asia, see Janos Harmatto, *History of Civilizations of Central Asia, Volume II* (Paris: UNESCO, 1994); and David Christian, *A History of Russia, Central Asia, and Mongolia. Volume I: Inner Eurasia from Prehistory to the Mongol Empire* (Oxford: Blackwell, 1998).

5. Christian, *op. cit.*, pp. 385–429.

6. Christian, *op. cit.*, p. 426.

7. The Naqshabandiya, one of the most widespread of the Sufi orders, originated in the late 14th century in Bukhara and spread throughout the Muslim world within 100 years. New impetus was given to its expansion by the rise of the Mujaddidi branch, which by the end of the 18th century was synonymous with the order as a whole throughout Central Asia. The main characteristics of Naqshabandiya are strict adherence to the shariah, sobriety in devotional practice, the shunning of music and dance, a preference for silent *dhikr*, and a tendency to political involvement. John L. Esposito, ed., *The Oxford Encyclopedia of the Islamic World, Volume 3* (New York: Oxford University Press, 1995), p. 226. Ahmad Yasavi was a Central Asian Turkic Sufi and poet, born in the second half of the 11th century near the city of Sayram in Turkestan. His poems created a new genre of religious folk poetry in Central Asian Turkic literature and influenced many religious poets in the following centuries. John L. Esposito, ed., *The Oxford Encyclopedia of the Islamic World, Volume 1* (New York: Oxford University Press, 1995), p. 271.

8. Abu Ali ibn Sina (980–1035), known to the West as Avicenna, was an Islamic philosopher and mystic who also wrote on many other disciplines, including mathematics, music, linguistics, medicine and theology. ibn Sina wrote about 250 works, the most influential being on metaphysics. St Thomas Aquinas used many of his central themes and quoted him hundreds of times. John L. Esposito, ed., *The Oxford Encyclopedia of the Islamic World, Volume 4* (New York: Oxford University Press, 1995), p. 220. The great thinker al-Farabi (870–950) may be called the founder of Islamic political philosophy. He wrote commentaries on Aristotle and several other works on various aspects of philosophy. His most famous work is the *Principles of the Opinions of the People of the Virtuous City*, a vast work that covers the relationship between human nature and politics. John L. Esposito, ed., *The Oxford Encyclopedia of the Islamic World, Volume 3*, p. 12. The mathematician al-Khuwarizmi (d. 933) wrote *Kitab mukhtasar fi al-hisab al-jabr wa-al-muqabalah*, a ground-breaking treatise devoted to algebra. He also invented the algorithm. John L. Esposito, ed., *The Oxford Encyclopedia of the Islamic World, Volume 3*, p. 67. The scholar al-Biruni (973–c. 1050) from Kwarazm wrote on such topics as natural science, mathematics, astronomy and chronology. His best-known work is a deep, expansive text on India. For most of his life he was a subject of the Ghaznavid sultan. P. M. Holt, Ann K. S. Lamb-

ton and Bernard Lewis, eds., *The Cambridge History of Islam, Volume I* (London: Cambridge University Press, 1970), p. 148.

9. For an introduction, see Beatrice F. Manz, 'Varieties of Religious Authority and Practice in Central Asia', *NCEER Report*, November 1999.

10. On the influence of Persian culture in Tajikistan, see Richard N. Frye, *Bukhara, the Medieval Achievement* (Norman: University of Oklahoma Press, 1965); and Richard N. Frye, *The Heritage of Central Asia: from Antiquity to the Turkish Expansion* (Princeton, N.J.: Markus Wiener Publishers, 1996).

11. For more a detailed description of the Turkmen culture, see V. V. Bartol'd, *Turkestan down to the Mongol Invasion* (London: Luzac, 1968).

12. In the 15th and 16th centuries, Muhammad Shaybani Khan, founder of the Shaybanid dynasty, was the leader of the Uzbeks, who during this period formed a decentralized polity based in several conquered cities, including Bukhara, Samarkand, Tashkent and Balkh. John L. Esposito, ed., *The Oxford Encyclopedia of the Islamic World, Volume 1*, p. 33.

13. Martha Brill Olcott, *The Kazakhs*, 2nd edn (Stanford: Hoover Institution Press, 1995), p. 16.

14. Hélène Carrère d'Encausse, 'The National Republics Lose Their Independence' in Edward Allworth, ed., *Central Asia: 130 Years of Russian Dominance, A Historical Overview* (Durham: Duke University Press, 1994), pp. 232–235.

15. See A. I. Kastelianskii, ed., *Formy natsional'nogo dvizheniya* (St. Petersburg: 1910) for a survey of these nationalist agendas, written by the nationalists themselves.

16. Ian Murray Matley, 'Agricultural Development 1865–1963' in Allworth, *op. cit.*, pp. 266–309.

17. For more information on the impact of Russian expansionism on Islamic movements, see Adeeb Khalid, *The Politics of Muslim Cultural Reform: Jadidism in Central Asia* (Berkeley: University of California Press, 1998).

18. For a more detailed discussion on national demarcation, see Stephen Blank, *The Sorcerer as Apprentice: Stalin as Commissar of Nationalities, 1917–1924* (Westport, Conn.: Greenwood Press, 1994).

19. Ian Bremmer and Ray Taras, eds, *New States, New Politics: Building the Post Soviet Nations* (Cambridge: Cambridge University Press, 1997), pp. 609, 660, 549, 638.

20. Martha Brill Olcott, Anders Åslund and Sherman W. Garnett, *Getting It Wrong: Regional Cooperation and the Commonwealth of Independent States* (Washington, DC: Carnegie Endowment for International Peace, 1999), pp. 157–178.

21. *Ibid.*, p. 160.

22. Sergei Gretsky, 'Regional Integration in Central Asia', *Analysis of Current Events*, vol. 10, no. 9–10 (September/October 1998).

23. Vladimir Akimov, 'Central Asian, US Peacekeepers to Hold Joint Exercise', ITAR-TASS, 11 March 1997.

24. Of course, if promises of vast energy wealth materialize, these countries could choose to invest in defence, but such promises remain decidedly hypothetical.

25. 'Kazakhstan Initiates Idea of Collective Security in Asia', Xinhua, 5 October 1992.

26. The Conference on Interaction and Confidence-Building Measures in Asia comprises Azerbaijan, Afghanistan, Egypt, India, Iran, Israel, Kazakhstan, China, Kyrgyzstan, Palestine, Pakistan, Russia, Tajikistan, Turkey and Uzbekistan. Taking part in the process as observers are the US, Australia, Thailand, Indonesia, Viet Nam, Lebanon, Japan, Korea, Malaysia, Mongolia and Ukraine and four international organizations—the UN, the OSCE, the Arab League, and the Inter-state Council of Kazakhstan, Kyrgyzstan, Tajikistan and Uzbekistan. Interfax, 13 April 2000.

27. Olcott, Åslund and Garnett, op. cit., p. 22.

28. 'What Is TRACECA?' as published on the Internet website of TRACECA, URL <http://www.traceca.org/whatis.htm>.

29. Olcott, Åslund and Garnett, op. cit., p. 167.

30. The GUUAM defence ministers' meeting originally scheduled for January was cancelled, allegedly because of increasing cooperation between Russia and Uzbekistan. Radio Free Europe/Radio Liberty, RFE/RL Newsline, vol. 4, no. 16, Pt I (24 January 2000).

31. RFE/RL Newsline, 29 August 1999. Such mistakes occurred on more than one occasion. For example, in August 1999, Uzbek combat jets on a mission against guerrillas in southern Kyrgyzstan 'inadvertently' dropped bombs on the Tajik territory. RFE/RL Newsline, 19 August 1999. According to a statement released by the Tajik Government and the United Tajik Opposition (UTO), the Uzbek Air Force dropped two bombs on Tandikul on 2 October 1999, three bombs on Darai-Choi on 3 October, and six bombs on Sultag and 13 on Gushagba on 4 October. Furthermore, the statement says, on 3 October the Uzbek air force raided Nushor and Nushori-Bolo in Tajikabad District and several communities in Garm District, causing loss of life.

32. European Commission, Economic Trends: Kazakhstan, April–June 1999, p. 31.

33. European Commission, Economic Trends: Kazakhstan, April–June 1999, p. 164.

34. ITAR-TASS, 26 June 1998 in Jamestown Monitor, 3 June 1998.

35. Embassy of Kazakhstan in the United States, Kazakhstan Embassy Bulletin, vol. 1 (Washington, DC, 31 March 2000).

36. World Bank, World Development Report: Knowledge for Development (New York: Oxford University Press, 1999).

37. Kazkommerts Securities, Kyrgyzstan General Economic Guide, September 1998, URL <http://www.emgmkts.com/kazkommerts/research/econ_guide_98sep/privatisations.htm>.

38. As published on the Internet website of the CIS Inter-State Economic Committee, URL <http://www.mek.ru/archive/issues/economic/1/p6.htm>.

39. The International Finance Corporation (IFC) will provide a loan of US$30 million of its own funds and US$10 million in quasi-equity. Loans will also be provided by the EBRD (US$30 million), the Export Development Corporation of Canada (US$50 million) and commercial banks (US$140 million). In addition,

the EBRD will provide US$10 million in quasi-equity. Cameco will invest US$90 million in loans and equity. IFC press release, 11 July 1995.

40. *PlanEcon Review and Outlook for the Former Soviet Republics*, November 1998, p. 143.

41. *RFE/RL*, 9 December 1999.

42. European Commission, *Economic Trends: Uzbekistan*, January–March 1999, p. 114.

43. UNDP, *Human Development Report 1998*.

44. Report by the Turkmen National Institute for Statistics and Forecasting.

45. World Bank, *World Development Indicators 1998*.

46. Saodat Olimova, 'Nation-States and Ethnic Territories', Paper presented at an international seminar on Multidimensional Borders in Central Asia, 19–20 October 1999, Cholpon-Ata, Kyrgyzstan.

47. Valerii Tishkov, 'Don't Kill Me, I'm a Kyrgyz!: An Anthropological Analysis of Violence in the Osh Ethnic Conflict', *Journal of Peace Research*, vol. 32, no. 2 (1995), pp. 133–149; and Olcott, Åslund and Garnett, *op. cit.*, p. 121.

48. ITAR-TASS, 26 January 2000.

49. *RFE/RL Newsline*, 23 March 2000.

50. *RFE/RL Newsline*, 14 January 2000.

51. By the late 1970s, no water from the Syr Darya was reaching the Aral. The estimated amount of water diverted from the Amu Darya to the Karakum Canal (now the Niyazov Canal) is *c.* 15–20 billion cubic metres per year. Michael H. Glantz, 'Creeping Environmental Problems in the Aral Sea Basin' in Iwao Kobori and Michael H. Glantz, eds, *Central Eurasian Water Crisis: Caspian, Aral, and Dead Seas* (Tokyo: United Nations University Press, 1998), p. 45.

52. Michael H. Glantz, *op. cit.*, p. 25.

53. Vladimir Berezovskiy, '"Water Bomb" over Central Asia', *Rossiiskaia Gazeta*, 2 August 1997 in Foreign Broadcast Information Service, *Daily Report–Central Eurasia*, FBIS-SOV-97-218, 6 August 1997.

54. *RFE/RL*, 14 October 1997.

55. Although 51 billion cubic metres of water per year originate in Kyrgyzstan, it only uses one-fifth of that. Vladimir Berezovskiy, *Rossiyskaya Gazeta*, 2 August 1997 in FBIS-SOV-97-218, 7 August 1997. ITAR-TASS, 26 December 1997 in *Summary of World Broadcasts* (British Broadcasting Corporation), 3 December 1997.

56. Information from the UNDCP Tashkent office.

57. Gennadii Voskresenskii, 'Free Market for Drugs', *Vechernii Bishkek*, 1998.

58. UNDCP, *Afghanistan: Annual Opium Poppy Survey 1999* (Islamabad: UNDCP Regional Office, 1999), p. iii.

59. For more information, see Martha Brill Olcott and Natalia Udalova, *Drug Trafficking on the Great Silk Road: the Security Environment in Central Asia*, Working Paper 11 (Washington, DC: Carnegie Endowment for International Peace, March 2000).

CHAPTER THREE

Islam in Central Asia

ALEXEI MALASHENKO

Islam in Central Asian society

The purpose of this chapter is to discuss Islam as a factor both for consolidating and for dividing the Central Asian states.

In spite of their differences, all the former Soviet Central Asian republics are Muslim societies. Kazakhstan is the most secularized: 34 per cent of its population is made up of Russian speaking people. Even so, the native populations, who are Muslims, are in a dominant position. Moreover, in Kazakhstan as everywhere in Central Asia a revival of traditions is taking place in society. Specialists use the terms 'archaization' and 'indigenization' for this phenomenon. The Islamization of society is a part of this process and it is noticeable in the southern regions of Kazakhstan.

At the beginning of the 1990s there was intense discussion of how to categorize the countries of Central Asia—as post-Soviet or Muslim. Gradually these discussions have declined, and former Soviet Central Asia is now considered a legitimate part of the Muslim world. The overwhelming majority of the native populations here identify themselves with Islam, and the processes characteristic of most Muslim countries are developing within these societies—among them the spread of political Islam and fundamentalism.

It is noticeable that the current leaders of the Central Asian states openly declare that their countries are not fully-fledged Muslim societies. According to the Uzbek President, Islam Karimov, his country should not be ranked among those conforming to Islamic standards.[1] The ruling elites relate cautiously to Islam, especially to its manifestation in politics. They remember that they themselves carry considerable responsibility for religious persecution under Soviet power. For example, in Uzbekistan in June 1991, at the height of *perestroika*, the leaders of the Andijan, Bukhara and Kashkadaryinskii regions were criticized for slackening in their atheistic work, and the Communist Party of the Republic of Uzbekistan issued a special decree which Karimov (at that time Secretary of the Central Committee of the republic's Communist Party) helped to prepare.[2] On the other hand, the ruling circles fear, not without reason, competition from Islamists in the struggle for people's minds.

Certainly, there is a considerable difference between Tajikistan and Kazakhstan: in the former, since 1998 one-third of the seats in the ruling coalition have been assigned to the United Tajik Opposition (UTO), which is influenced by fundamentalist ideology, whereas in the latter political Islam is only taking its first, if active, steps in the south of the country. Nevertheless, the dynamics of political development during the last decade show that the authority and the influence of the Islamists keep growing in society, if as yet in circuitous ways.

Under these conditions of the 're-traditionalizing' of society, the present elites are less confident in the 'Islamic field' and feel forced to adopt more and more severe measures to suppress their real and potential fundamentalist opponents. The leadership itself is not alien to Islam. The Muslim religion is being incorporated into the official ideology. The presidents, who demonstrate a greater or lesser adherence to Islam, never forget the growing influence in their states of forces which are more dedicated to Islam and more ready to use religion in politics.

In relations between the Central Asian states Islam plays no significant role. Of course, while the concept of these relations is being formed, the common culture and traditions are often referred to. However, emphasis tends to be put on the openness of Central Asian culture and the aspects which the peoples have in common. The religious dimension—that is, Islamic solidarity—is of secondary importance, and often seems to be more for show.

In this connection it is significant that on the eve of the break-up of the USSR, when the question was raised whether or not to maintain the Central Asian Religious Board of Muslims (SADUM), which was common to all the Central Asian republics, the secular political leaders unanimously came out in favour of breaking it up into republican *kasiats* and creating independent national *muftiats*. The growing influence of the fundamentalists was used as a pretext for destroying the SADUM. Thus, even in the sphere of the coordination of religious activity Islam did not become an integrating factor among the Central Asian states. National interests clearly prevailed over Islamic solidarity. It should also be noted that relations between the national *muftiats* remain mainly formal.

Islam may not influence interstate relations in Central Asia, but its effect is felt on the mutual perceptions of people living there. Although sociological studies in Central Asia do not provide information on the attitudes to Islam of neighbouring ethnic groups, there is still a notional 'ranking' of people from the point of view of their adherence to Islam. The Tajiks come first, the Uzbeks next, followed by the Kyrgyz, the Kazakhs and the Turkmen. Many local intellectuals see the Kazakhs and Kyrgyz as inconsistent in their relation to Islam. One of them is Chokan Valikhanov, who thought that 'Islam has not yet penetrated our [the Kazakhs'] flesh and blood'.[3] The Russian geographer V. Streletskii writes: 'The Kyrgyz assimilated Islam in a more perfunctory way than the Tajiks and Uzbeks'.[4] A sociologist shares this opinion: 'the Kyrgyz occupy the last place in the hierarchy of the native peoples of the region with regard to religiosity'.[5] The negative aspects of inter-ethnic relations, which are not established by scientific research and are connected with different degrees of Islamization, sometimes find their reflection in local folklore.

It would be futile to try to differentiate between 'bad' and 'good' Muslims today. However, it is significant that political Islam and fundamentalist tendencies increased in states where the native population identified themselves as 'good' Muslims and were perceived in that way by their neighbours. In Tajikistan the Islamists entered the government; in Uzbekistan they became a large and influential opposition and have the potential to exercise a powerful influence on society. Against the background of the archaization of society this may bring a gradual incorporation of the Islamists into the ruling elites, resulting in a more active use of traditional norms for organizing state and society.

So far Islamic radicalism, more often called Wahhabism, has furthered the unity of the ruling elites in Central Asian states. The domestic threat to the secular regimes by Islamic radicals was revealed in Tajikistan at the end of the 1980s, but many thought that this threat was the exception rather than the rule, was specific to Tajikistan, and would not spread to neighbouring states. Statements expressing fear of the spread of Islam in the region were exaggerated and were a pretext for intimidating the population in order to consolidate the incumbents' hold on power. In fact, the actions of the Tajik Islamists and their opposition to the secular rulers contributed to the outbreak of a bloody civil war from which the presidents of all the Central Asian states drew lessons. They blamed Tajikistan and pointed to the consequences of a weakening of state power and indecisive behaviour when dealing with Islamists.

At the beginning of the 1990s Islamic political organizations and movements appeared in all the Central Asian countries except in Turkmenistan, which at an early stage decisively took the path of strict authoritarianism. In Uzbekistan the Islamic Party of Revival, Adolat, and the Islamic Party of Turkestan were formed; in Kazakhstan the Alash Party of National Salvation; in Kyrgyzstan the Islamic Centre. Needless to say, in Tajikistan the local party of Islamic Revival became one of the most powerful political forces.

The process of involving the Muslim clergy in politics continued. It goes without saying that the Islamic opposition was not interested in the great majority of the former Soviet mullahs. When the Central Asian states became independent the mullahs remained obedient, but this obedience was transferred to the new national state power. However, among the post-Soviet institutional clergy a kind of non-conformism appeared which expressed opinions that differed from official views. The most notable representatives of this non-conformism were Akbar Turajonzoda, and the head of the Spiritual Board of Muslims of Uzbekistan (the former SADUM), mufti Mukhammad-Sodik Mukhammad-Usef. In the early 1990s the Uzbek authorities accused the latter of an inclination towards the Islamic fundamentalists (although he was deeply opposed to the creation of an Islamic party in Uzbekistan) and for supporting the Tajik Islamic opposition. Mukhammad-Sodik Mukhammad-Usef wrote a number of theological books and pamphlets in which he expressed views which did not correspond to the secular principles of state ideology, and he was forced to leave Uzbekistan. However, as a result he became—without being an apologist for Islam Karimov's regime—a strong critic of the local Islamic opposition and condemned the activity of the Islamic Movement of Uzbekistan.[6]

Representatives of the younger generation of ecclesiastics played and still play a large part in the Islamic movements in Central Asia. Among them are hundreds of graduates from Islamic universities and institutes abroad. They have acquired their knowledge of Islam from Arabic and Persian literature, which it was forbidden to import during Soviet times but which poured into Central Asia after the break-up of the Soviet Union. This category of ecclesiastics as well as foreign missionaries spread the fundamentalists' ideas in a simple form among the local populations.

That was the first wave of Islamic revival, or 're-Islamization', in which political interests and ambitions were expressed, often in a simple and populist form. At first, there was no coordination between these parties and groups at a regional level. Each of them acted according to its interpretation of national interests.

During the first half of the 1990s national Islamic opposition movements had no adequate social base, except in Tajikistan, and they lacked political experience (the Adolat movement, active in the city of Namangan in the Ferghana Valley, was an exception). People in general were indifferent to religious views and were often even hostile to radicalism. At that time the majority believed in the promises of the ruling elites about solving the social and economic crisis in the region. The 'Islamic alternative' offered by the fundamentalists was not in demand. The bloody civil war in Tajikistan demonstrated to people the danger of a destabilization of society if the Islamic political movement were to grow, and the security services of the local ruling regimes kept an eye on the opposition, arrested its members, and sentenced many of them to long terms of imprisonment.

All these factors deprived the Islamic opposition of the opportunity to work actively to enrol large numbers of people and to set up a corresponding organizational structure. In 1993–94 the Islamic opposition found itself in a peculiar vacuum: people feared making contact with it lest they be persecuted by the special services; and its call for the introduction of shariah law and the formation of an Islamic state found no real response.

Under such conditions it was futile to speak of creating a united Islamic opposition for the whole of Central Asia. This was clearly the main reason why up to the mid-1990s the ruling elites did not consider political Islam to be a challenge that was common to the states in the region.

Radical Islam and the Central Asian states

In 1996 the situation suddenly changed when the Taliban movement established a radical Islamic regime in neighbouring Afghanistan. It seems that the Central Asian elites did not believe in the possibility of the Taliban expanding to the north and invading Uzbekistan and Tajikistan, but feared rather that the success of radical Islam would produce euphoria among like-minded people in Central Asia, in particular in the Ferghana Valley, where an Islamic opposition by that time had already appeared (although it was not yet organized) and among the radicals of the UTO.[7]

The victory of the Taliban facilitated if not coordination at least an increase in contacts between different Islamic groups. The impulse it gave did not pass without leaving any trace. Without doubt the authority of political Islam grew. Some people accepted this with fear, others with hope. In any case, the threat of 'radical Islam' became a common regional concern. As a result cooperation began between the ruling elites in response to the coordination of Islamist efforts. At first, however, except for 'anti-fundamentalist' invective, no practical steps were taken.

In contrast to his colleagues, Turkmen President Saparmurat Niyazov tried all possible ways to avoid criticism of Islamic radicalism and to avoid making a common cause against it in Central Asia. In autumn 1996 he declared that: 'The situation in Afghanistan cannot be considered from any common platform. Each of the countries bordering Afghanistan has its own peculiarities in relations with that country.'[8]

The next summit meeting of the Commonwealth of Independent States (CIS) was devoted to the Afghan problem and, although very different opinions were put forward, anxiety prevailed. The delegations of Uzbekistan and Tajikistan were particularly concerned; Kazakh and Kyrgyz politicians were less disturbed. On the eve of the summit, for instance, the Secretary of the Security Council of Kazakhstan, Baltash Tursumbayev, declared in an interview that the Taliban should not be viewed as representing a danger to Uzbekistan and Kazakhstan as they had 'only six captured helicopters and five or six tanks'.[9] However, other sources spoke of the Taliban army as consisting of up to 50,000 well-trained fighters, several dozen tanks and 16 old but quite combat-ready aircraft of Soviet vintage. But the optimism of the Kazakh representative contrasted with statements by the presidents of Kazakhstan and Kyrgyzstan, Nursultan Nazarbayev and Askar Akayev, who from autumn 1996 began to mention Islamic fundamentalism in their speeches as a destabilizing factor in the region. The mass media more often spoke of the 'serious fears' caused by the import of Wahhabist ideas which were characterized as 'a most uncompromising branch of Islam'.[10]

Attitudes towards the Taliban were not always negative. Every time a dialogue with them became possible, criticism of Islamic radicalism became more cautious, especially in Uzbekistan, which feared the Islamists more than other countries did. In 1998 it became acceptable in Tashkent to speak of the Taliban in an objective and restrained tone. Yet the Taliban regime remained a potential threat in the eyes of the Central Asian leaders as it was a constant source of ideological and financial nourishment for local Islamists.

In 1999 a shift took place from only talking about regional cooperation to taking real measures against the Islamists. It was precipitated by two events. The first was the series of explosions in Tashkent in February 1999, the aim of which, according to the official view, was not just the destabilization of the republic but the murder of President Karimov; the second was the Islamist invasion in August 1999 of the Batken region in Kyrgyzstan, close to Tajikistan. Without specifying the different interpretations of these events,[11] it can be noted that the terrorist acts prompted all the presidents of the Central Asian countries to recognize the threat from the Islamists.

After the explosions and the capture by Islamic fighters of dozens of hostages, including four Japanese geologists, the coordination of efforts by the central Asian regimes against the Islamists became more urgent. Moreover, the Islamist opposition also emerged at the regional, or more precisely subregional, level. In summer 1999 there was reliable information that there had been cases of armed groups of the United Tajik Opposition (UTO) and the Islamic Movement of Uzbekistan (IMU) merging locally—for example, in the Dzhigirtal region in Tajikistan where the head of the IMU, Djuma Namangani, an ethnic Uzbek and the organizer of the Batken action, took command of the united group. Foreign Muslim organizations, among them state organizations, assisted in reinforcing contacts between different national Islamic formations.

In the second half of 1999 several regional meetings were held, the most notable being a meeting of four of the Central Asian presidents (President Niyazov of Turkmenistan did not take part) in August 1999 in Osh in Kyrgyzstan. The military response that followed was not always successful,[12] and as a consequence there were misunderstandings between the politicians and the military command of Uzbekistan, Kyrgyzstan and Tajikistan. Even so, this was the first experience of joint opposition in the Central Asian government to the Islamic radicals and an important precedent for further practical joint efforts. At the time both the Central Asian and the Russian mass media expressed the hope that 'the leaders of the Central Asian republics that found themselves involved in the conflict voluntarily or involuntarily will set their offences against each other aside and pool their efforts against the extremists'.[13]

After the events of 1999 it became obvious that the military activity of the Islamists was not an isolated episode and would continue. Exactly one year later, in August 2000, fighters of the IMU and the Uzbek branch of the international Islamic organization Hizb al-Takhrir al-Islamy (the Party of Islamic Liberation, which has a subsidiary in Uzbekistan) invaded the territory of Uzbekistan in the Surkhan-Darya region.[14] According to the Chairman of the Uzbekistan National Security Council, Mirakbar Pakhmonkulov, 'it was not an invasion that took place, but rather fighters in small groups gradually infiltrated the Saraasiisk district of the Surkhan-Darya region'.[15] The Islamists were penetrating into Uzbekistan from Tajikistan (which gave Uzbekistan grounds to blame the Tajik authorities for all but assisting the Islamists) and from Kyrgyzstan. Compared with 1999 their actions were more organized: while one group occupied several Uzbek *kishlaks*, another group, captured a part of the road through the Kamchik pass, and cut off part of the Ferghana Valley from Uzbekistan. The battles were protracted and gradually spread to Kyrgyzstan.

The IMU is supported by extremist Islamic organizations and is alleged to receive money from the major financier of religious extremism, Osama bin-Laden. During the military skirmishes in 2000 there was far more interaction between the IMU and Hizb al-Takhrir than was the case in 1999. In essence, the two groups appeared as a united front, although formally their goals are not the same: the IMU views its principal task as deposing the Karimov regime and the declaration of an Islamic state in Uzbekistan, while Hizb-al-Takhrir's strategic aim is to found such a state for the whole Central Asian region and even to restore the Islamic caliphate throughout the Muslim world.

Even taking into consideration the superior organization and combat-readiness of the IMU groups and their allies, there is no real likelihood of such a regime being established. However, Islamist activity has been growing for the past four years, across a potentially wide social base, as there is no noticeable improvement in material and social living standards in the region, and the Uzbek and especially the Kyrgyz troops[16] are far from capable of repulsing the attacks of the Islamists, many of whom have been well prepared in special training centres in Afghanistan.

The events of the second half of 2000 confirmed that the threat from the Islamists is a regional one. Since then, the coordination of efforts in the struggle against the Islamists has been a condition of the internal stability of the Central Asian states and in a sense of their survival. It is

2001

1 60   53-57

53

possible that the claims of the states against each other in the economic and financial spheres will be downplayed for a while. In Tashkent in April 2000 the heads of state of Kazakhstan, Kyrgyzstan and Uzbekistan signed an agreement committing them jointly to struggle against international terrorism, religious extremism and organized crime. A meeting of four Central Asian presidents in August 2000 in Bishkek reinforced this effort.[17]

The 'Islamic factor' and the role of Russia

There was an understanding in the capitals of the Central Asian states that the efficacy of the struggle against the Islamists was largely determined by the support Russia was prepared to offer. Islamic radicalism, especially in the North Caucasus, represented a serious problem for Russia as well. The situation developed in such a way that the 'Islamic factor' encouraged the rise of common strategic tasks for Russia and Central Asia. Thus the struggle of the Central Asian regimes against the Islamists became an important element of their foreign policy.

Relations between Russia and the former Soviet republics of Central Asia have been established on a pragmatic basis: each party is guided by its own national economic and political interests. However, the religious factor has its own indirect effect on them. Here we have relations between states where the bulk of the population belongs to different faiths and cultures. This fact alone has an influence on how each society and its political and cultural elite perceive the neighbouring people, and this consequently affects each state's foreign policy orientation.

Russia and Central Asia, of course, do not only exist and interact as civilizational systems. 'In addition to the tentative embrace of Muslim identity . . . the Central Asian leaders also variously characterized their states as part of a Turkic continuum, and as part of Asian civilization.'[18] To these influences on the Central Asian identity can be added Eurasianism, the Silk Road, and Russia's idea of 'an enlarged Europe', which to some extent reduce the importance of religious factors. Yet, as has been noted before, it would be short-sighted to overlook completely the effect of these factors on the geopolitical or merely political predilections of Russia and Central Asia.

In the 1990s the number of mosques, Islamic schools and universities increased greatly in Central Asia. This reflected the active process of penetration of radical Islamic ideology. Above all, the sense of transition from the Soviet or post-Soviet political identity to a Muslim one was growing. The former 'Soviet way of life' of the Central Asian republics and their perception of themselves as part of the Muslim world were beginning to conflict. This inevitably influenced relations between Russia and its southern neighbours—even more so as it became politically correct in Russia to refer to its religion, Orthodox Christianity, as a principal component of a specific Russian identity. President Islam Karimov in a mosque and President Boris Yeltsin in a church holding a candle, appeared to be more like heads resepectively of a Muslim and a Christian state than like former secretaries of the Communist Party. The presidents and their entourages cannot help taking this into account. It was also impossible not to notice that the presidents of the Central Asian states were sworn in on the Koran and that the Patriarch of the Russian Orthodox Church was present at the ceremony when Boris Yeltsin handed over his duties as President of the Russian Federation to Vladimir Putin.

It is no wonder that allegiance to different faiths became a factor in distancing Russia from Central Asia. For generations the populations of the Central Asian republics were weaned away from Islam; attempts were made to instil hostility to their own religion and to separate people's secular traditions from the religious one. There were official and implicit prohibitions on religious ceremonies, and this irritated the population. Thus, to the native population of Central Asia, embracing Islam is a kind of guarantee both that they can overcome the 'younger brother' complex formed during the Soviet period and that the status of 'Russian satellite' cannot be revived. This is one of the religious and ideological bases of national independence.

However, differences in the cultural and religious identities of the Russian and Central Asian societies are theoretically not a barrier to mutual understanding, nor do they exclude a common view of the growing danger from the 'Islamic radicals'. 'Uzbekistan [in its struggle against the Islamic radicals] is expecting help from Russia,'[19] writes Sergei Karelin, an analyst from Tashkent, referring to the Uzbek ruling elite.

In Central Asia Uzbekistan and Kyrgyzstan are the countries that are most worried about this danger. In Tajikistan the situation is more complicated: on the one hand President Emomali Rakhmonov and his supporters are wary of radical Islam; on the other hand the UTO, which is part of the government coalition, itself follows the fundamentalist ideology. It seems that for the secular part of the Tajik leaders Russian support against religious extremism is a kind of guarantee against pressure from the 'Islamists within'. The UTO itself and its allies regard the Russian presence as a protection against excessive pressure on it from the Afghan Taliban.

In 1998, as a result of negotiations between Yeltsin and Karimov, the idea arose of creating a triple coalition of Russia, Uzbekistan and Tajikistan, the 'troika'. The Ambassador of Uzbekistan in Russia, Shakhmansur Shakhamilov, declared at the time that 'Uzbekistan was ready to develop bilateral relations with Russia in the field of defence policy, including military–technical cooperation, with the aim of protecting its national security from possible military threats'.[20] For different reasons, however, such cooperation has only developed hesitantly. Moreover, in 1998 the hope arose in Tashkent that relations with the Taliban could be improved, and this reduced Uzbekistan's interest in joining forces with Russia in the struggle against Islamic extremism in Afghanistan. Nevertheless, there is still support for the idea of turning to Russia for assistance in order to repulse Islamic radicalism within Central Asia.

Without doubt, Russia is also interested in this. Russia interprets the current operations in the North Caucasus both as a struggle against separatism and at the same time as a war with international terrorism. The mass media of Central Asia and Russia in 1999 gave many examples of connections between the fighters in the North Caucasus, the Ferghana Valley and Tajikistan. The Russian authorities claim that there were Tajiks and Uzbeks among the fighters killed in Chechnya. In the words of one of the most authoritative Russian journalists, 'there is a rotation of fighters between the Caucasus and Central Asia'.[21] The Central Asian press has reported on the influences of Chechnya on the local Islamists.[22] Local newspapers freely quoted the assertion of the Russian Prime Minister and acting President, Vladimir Putin, that 'the terrorists shamelessly declared the area of their aggressive interests, from the North Caucasus up to the Pamir'.[23]

In autumn 1999 in Russia and Central Asia 'Caucasophobia' became more noticeable than usual. It was especially notable in Kazakhstan, where several thousand Chechens have been living since the Stalin deportations in 1944. At the end of 1999 Vainakh, the association of Kazakhstan Chechens, was even forced to send an appeal to President Nazarbayev expressing 'serious concern' and 'a sense of bitterness' at the propagation of the 'Chechen syndrome'.[24]

In May 2000 Russia, through Sergei Yastrzhembskii, the President's representative, made a statement about the possibility of striking preventive blows against the camps in Afghanistan where Islamic fighters were being trained. While the majority of Russian and foreign experts agreed that this statement was a bluff and an expression of wishful thinking, it was a step in the direction of a new military–political self-assertiveness on the part of Russia in Central Asia.

No strikes took place against Afghanistan. Nevertheless, Russian leaders stated repeatedly that their intentions were serious and that they were ready to assist their southern neighbours if the Islamists attacked. In May 2000, two months before the situation in the Ferghana Valley and around it deteriorated again, Vladimir Putin, now Russian President, declared that 'the threat to Uzbekistan means a threat to Russia'.[25] In the capitals of Central Asia this démarche was received with understanding and in certain quarters even with hope. However, some local politicians were worried about the possibility of a strengthening of Russian influence here and the consequences for the foreign policy orientation of the Central Asian states.

The option of Russia assisting its southern neighbours became even more topical in August 2000, when Uzbekistan and Kyrgyzstan appeared to be involved in protracted military operations. Shots were being fired 100 km from Tashkent (in the Bostanlyk region). The roads to Tashkent were fortified with concrete blocks,[26] and in Kyrgyzstan military action spread to the Osh region where support for local Islamic radicals has traditionally been strong. Military units were placed on alert in the south of Kazakhstan (similar measures had not been taken in Kazakhstan during the campaign in 1999). In these conditions, without waiting for official requests for assistance, the first deputy Chief of the Russian General Staff, General Valerii Manilov, declared that 'Russia was ready to render any assistance to Uzbekistan and Kyrgyzstan in order to destroy the "bandit formations"', adding that 'the resolute joint efforts of Russia, Uzbekistan and Kyrgyzstan would make it possible to rapidly stabilize the situation'.[27]

On the whole, it can be concluded that in the second half of the 1990s the Islamic factor promoted a rapprochement between Russia and the states of Central Asia. The military–political threat posed by the Islamic radicals is forcing the Central Asian regimes if not to ask for direct military help at least to agree on a strengthening of the system of regional collective security.[28] In May 2000 at a session of the CIS Collective Security Council a special 'Memorandum to improve the efficiency of the Collective Security Treaty and to adapt it to the present geopolitical situation' was adopted. This indicated the intention of Russia, as well as Kazakhstan, Kyrgyzstan and some other CIS countries, to use collective means if necessary to repulse an external threat from the Islamic radicals.

It seems that this situation will continue, as Islamism is now a permanent political feature of Central Asia. Its steady rise has been conditioned (a) by the general 're-traditionalizing' of society and public consciousness in the countries of the region, which inevitably affects both their domestic and to a lesser degree their foreign policy, and (b) by the strengthening of the Islamist opposition. Its activity in the North Caucasus (and possibly some other Russian regions) will continue to disturb the Russian authorities as well. For this reason the role of the Islamic factor in the relationships between Russia and Central Asia will grow. It will not be a linear process, but will fluctuate. Islamic influence on society and policy in Central Asia has its limitations.[29]

The phenomenon of re-traditionalizing in Central Asian society will inevitably involve the future ethnic elites. The main contradiction among those elites may prove to be that between tradition and technocracy. If under favourable conditions the technocrats can become the most mobile and effective force in the economic and scientific–technical spheres, their progressive ambitions will be checked by the more inactive but also more numerous 'traditionalists'. Russia, where a profound transformation of the political elite is also probable, will have to take this into consideration.

Central Asia and the wider Muslim world

How important is the Islamic factor for the relations of Central Asia with the rest of the Islamic world, in particular with the countries of Saudi Arabia, Turkey, Iran and Pakistan?

At first sight the influence of the Islamic factor should be most evident here. However, the role of Islam in this regard is far from simple, and at times it turns out to be contradictory.

In the early 1990s, immediately after the former Soviet republics became independent states, they initiated a search for new guiding lights in foreign policy. And these new guiding lights were the Muslim countries, which in their turn were caught unprepared by the disappearance of the USSR and the unexpected simultaneous entry of several new states into the Muslim world.

In Central Asia there was genuine hope that cooperation with Arab countries—Turkey, Iran and Pakistan—would be the way to overcome the economic crisis and reach out to the Muslim community. Naturally, Central Asian politicians put pragmatic considerations first. It cannot be denied, however, that some of them in their own way were fascinated with romantic ideas of Islamic solidarity and felt tempted to believe in its force. Some really came to believe that a prosperous state could be established with the advice of Turkish technocrats, Saudi *ulem* or Iranian ayatollahs. At the end of 1991 the Tajik semi-official *Narodnaya gazeta* noted in an editorial that, according to President Karimov of Uzbekistan, 'Turkey would be a model of the state structure for Uzbekistan' and 'Tajikistan is obviously attracted to Iran—a fact that Europe will have to take into account'.[30]

However, it soon became obvious that in interstate relations ideologies were of minor importance compared to a sober pragmatic approach to the economic and political advantages of cooperation. Moreover, this cooperation was originally unbalanced, as the economically weak Central Asian countries were often in the position of begging. By the mid-1990s the partners began to express dissatisfaction with the cooperation which had been seen as a panacea for all economic difficulties, while the Muslim world regarded the former Soviet republics as an economic and political 'wilderness' to be developed and used to large extent for its own purposes.

Together with the mutual suspicion, the myth of religious fraternity and Islamic solidarity was wearing off.

Appealing to spiritual union makes sense while trying to formulate common political and strategic directions as well as ideological grounds for cooperation. This adds to and in a sense is able to radicalize the ideology of Pan-Turkism, Pan-Turanism and other theories of inter-Muslim cooperation. This synthesis is probably most characteristic of Pan-Turkic ideology, which was very popular among certain parts of the Turkic-speaking population at the beginning of the 1990s, and in Kazakhstan the small Party of National Liberation, Alash, was organized with a programme based on the triad 'Turkism–Islam–Democracy'. The Islamic Party of Turkestan was established in Uzbekistan. However, 'unionist' ideologies were not widespread and were even less used by the ruling elites, which saw national interests as the highest priority, taking precedence over all other ideas, including that of spiritual solidarity.

The influence of Iran in Central Asia has always been local and in fact was limited to Persian-speaking Tajikistan. In spite of the rapprochement between Iran and Tajikistan, the local politicians in Tajikistan have never missed the chance to restate that, regardless of cultural and religious similarity and of Iran's desire to play a more active role in internal Tajik affairs, in particular as a mediator in the military and political conflict, they regard themselves as 'younger brothers' and put their national interests above any solidarity with Iran.

As regards other countries, including Saudi Arabia and Pakistan, one can agree with the opinion of Turkish expert Yilmaz Bingol that 'they are not major players in Central Asia', even taking into consideration that Pakistan 'with its experience in banking, insurance and knowledge of English appears to be a possible rival for Turkey'.[31] Moreover, in Central Asia Pakistan is regarded as one of the initiators (if not the organizer) of the Taliban movement which it now cannot fully control.

International Islamic solidarity remains and most likely will remain a symbol that can be used under certain circumstances as an instrument to achieve certain political goals or to serve certain national ambitions. It is hardly more than that.

The moderate position of the Central Asian countries towards Russian policy in Chechnya was unexpectedly similar to that of the Organization of the Islamic Conference (OIC), whose delegation, headed by the Iranian Speaker and Minister for Foreign Affairs Kamal Kharrazi, visited both Moscow and the North Caucasus in December 1999. In the course of his visit and in view of Russia's friendly relations with Iran since the 1990s, Kharrazi actually only 'mildly reprimanded' Moscow for excessively violent military operations, having recognized the Chechnya conflict as an internal Russian affair.

It would be too simple to say that the Islamic factor is something entirely positive seen from the perspective of relations between the Central Asian countries and the Near and Middle East. Its influence can also be negative. This is true of the attempts of some Muslim countries to export to Central Asia their own interpretation of Islam, which is alien to local societies. It should be remembered that the overwhelming majority of the Muslim ethnic groups of the region belong to the more liberal *khanafit mazkhab* (theological law school) of Sunni Islam. (Only ten per cent of the native population in Tajikistan are Shi'ites, and to be more exact they are Ismaelis). Those proselytes who are most active in Central Asia are the representatives of other, 'stricter' *mazkhabs* of the khanbalit school, which is particularly widespread in Saudi Arabia, or followers of *salafy*, the doctrine of pure Islam, associated with fundamentalism. There is evidence that the religious renaissance taking place in the region is being partly activated by the followers of these schools and interpretations of

Islam, different from and sometimes even contradictory to those that are observed locally. In fact the issue is one of religious indoctrination and even a confrontation between national (Uzbek, Kyrgyz and so on) Islam and its Middle Eastern, Pakistani or Iranian versions.

Islamic foreign organizations are financing the construction of mosques, setting up madrassas and institutes, and sending out teachers and preachers. Several thousand young people are studying abroad and upon coming home start the work of propagating an 'alien' Islam. In this respect, one can mention such organizations as the World Muslim League, the International Relief Organization and the World Assembly of Muslim Youth, and among the Islamic universities the Saudi King Abdul Aziz University, the famous Al-Azkhar University in Cairo and others.

This growing influence of Islamic views from abroad is causing concern both to the local elites and to the clergy in Central Asia. The clergy is cooperating with the elites as it is fearful of losing its authority. Furthermore, the professional level of the foreign missionaries who graduated from Middle Eastern, Pakistani and Iranian universities is higher than that of the local Central Asian mullahs.

The secular authorities supported by the national clergy are attempting to restrict the activities of foreign preachers and to control the curricula and teaching in Islamic schools and institutes. In some cases they use extreme measures and deport preachers who confuse local Muslims by forcing on them 'alien' interpretations of Islam. In the mid-1990s preachers from Saudi Arabia and Iran were deported from Uzbekistan and Turkmenistan—some 300 from Turkmenistan alone.[32]

Finally, the international fundamentalist organizations provide regular assistance, including financial assistance, to local radicals. Particularly active are Hizb al-Takhrir, Hizbollah and the Muslim Brotherhood.

All this is placing relations between the countries of Central Asia and other Muslim states under strain. Certainly, the latter officially declare their non-interference in the internal matters of their fellow believers, but in fact such interference does occur. Moreover support to local radicals is offered not by the state structures but by social, religious or private organizations. The supporting countries such as Saudi Arabia, Pakistan, Sudan and Jordan are well aware of these activities.

Obviously, such foreign interference in the Central Asian region is inevitable and the local elites will always have to accept it, despite their discontent and attempts to oppose it. Furthermore, their efforts to restrict the activity of the foreign preachers and to put their educational work under control are normally met with understanding in the Muslim world. The Iranian, Saudi and Pakistani authorities, trying to take into consideration the specific character of the Central Asian countries, do sometimes abstain from the most objectionable forms of propaganda. For example, Iranians had to abandon the thesis of an 'Islamic revolution' in Tajikistan, a culturally similar country, first, because it is associated with radicalism and, second, because it is reminiscent of the Bolshevik Revolution of 1917.

As can be seen, economic cooperation between Central Asia and the Muslim countries occurs independently of the Islamic factor. Turkish and to lesser degree Iranian, Pakistani and Arab companies are not willing to let their presence in the region be interpreted as evidence of extended Islamic solidarity. Declarations of such intentions are made in the Central Asian press, but they are just a form of lip-service.

An echo of the Islamic factor can be identified in the relations between the Central Asian countries and the rest of world. Thus, aspiring to prove their adherence to common values, the leaders of the local countries, and especially Kyrgyzstan, Kazakhstan and Uzbekistan, often stress that their states are a kind of 'stronghold' able to contain the expansion of religious radicalism.[33]

The Islamic factor is also relevant in the context of relations between Central Asian countries, primarily Kazakhstan and Kyrgyzstan, and China. Two issues should be mentioned in this respect. First, none of these states has ever stressed its Muslim character, either from an ideological or from a practical perspective. Nor does China regard its relations with Kazakhstan and Kyrgyzstan from the Muslim perspective. But both sides express their interest in opposing Islamic radicalism, which is regarded as a threat to stability in China. China is concerned about Islamist activities in the Xinjiang Uighur Autonomous Region (XUAR), which borders on Kazakhstan (see Chapter 7). Kazakhstan in its turn expresses solidarity with the position of China, as the Islamists, the majority of them Uighurs in the border area, trouble the Kazakh authorities as well. Thus, the Islamic factor in fact promotes mutual understanding between the Central Asian states and their powerful neighbour to the East.

Prospects for the future

There are certain obvious general conclusions about the influence of the Islamic factor on the external relations of the Central Asian countries.

Islam is not a principal factor but it retains a certain influence: it has a role first in the domestic politics of the Central Asian states and second in the immediate neighbourhood.

The current elites may maintain that they support their secular positions regarding the form of government and foreign policies, but the possibility cannot be excluded that their successors, to use the words of Uzbek President Islam Karimov quoted above, would like to return to 'Islamic standards', and this would probably affect the external relations of the five Central Asian countries. Islamic radicals might search more intensively for allies abroad.

Such a trend would inevitably be welcomed by the Muslim world, in particular by such countries as Pakistan and Saudi Arabia. However, new elite groups as well as more traditional ones would probably oppose foreign Islamic influence in Central Asia, and in order to strengthen their positions they would conform to 'national Islam'. As a result, a situation may arise in which the difference between the ethnic perception of Islam and its theological and legal interpretations slows down the development of contacts between Central Asia and the broader Muslim world. It is well known that the idea of the preservation of local national versions of Islam has deep roots in Central Asia and in the consciousness of its people.

The future participation of moderate Islamists in the governing coalitions of some Central Asian countries is a scenario which concerns Western countries, but this will most likely not be an insurmountable obstacle for relations between Central Asia and the Western world.

As for Russia, its position can evolve. In the last decade of the 20th century Russia, prompted by its internal problem with radical Islam, opposed Islamic radicalism and allied itself with secular regimes. Eventually, however, Moscow might find itself in a situation in which the Central Asian regimes grow more tolerant of the Islamists and cooperate or are forced to cooperate with them. In this case Russia will be guided by pragmatic considerations, will maintain friendly relations with these regimes, and is likely to abandon its political and ideological stereotypes of the 1990s.

Notes

1. Islam Karimov, 'Uzbekistan ne Aisberg, chtoby Dreifovat' [Uzbekistan is not a drifting iceberg], *Narodnoye Slovo* (Tashkent), 12 November 1997, p. 1.

2. A. V. Malashenko, *Musulmanskii mir SNG* [The Muslim world of the CIS] (Moscow, 1996), p. 71.

3. Ch. Ch. Valikhanov, 'Pro Islame na Stepe' [About Islam in the Steppe] *Collected Works, vol 4* (Almaty, 1985), p. 71.

4. *Nezavisimaya gazeta*, 5 March 1993.

5. N. Kosmarskaya, 'Sotsialno-Psikhologicheskie Aspekty Mezhnatsionalnykh Otnoshenii v Severnom Priyssykkule' [Social–psychological aspects of relations between nations in northern Pri-Issyk-Kul], *Etnosotsialnye protsessy v Kirgizstane* (Moscow, 1994), p. 52.

6. The former Mufti of Uzbekistan is of the opinion that the official authorities are responsible for the rise of the Islamic opposition since they forced Mukhammad–Sodik and his allies to leave the Uzbekistan *muftiat* and replaced his people with people from Namangan, some of whom later became opponents to President Karimov while others joined the UTO. Mufti Mukhammad-Sodik, 'S Shariatom Speshit Nelzya' [It not possible to hurry on Shariah], *Vremya Novostei*, 15 May 2000, p. 6.

7. According to the Kyrgyz press the Taliban leaders met with the deputy leader of the Islamic Revival Movement of Tajikistan, Davlat Usmon, soon after seizing power to discuss the problems of cooperation between the Tajik and Afghan Islamic radicals. 'Pozdravleniya Talibam' [Congratulations to the Taliban], *Slovo Kirgizstana* (Bishkek), 11–12 October 1996, p. 3.

8. *Neytralnyi Turkmenistan* (Ashgabat), 30 October 1996, p. 1. The statement by Niyazov was made in the context of the prospects of constructing a gas pipeline on the territory of Afghanistan with the help of the US company UNOCAL in order to export Turkmen gas to Pakistan.

9. 'Almatinskoe Ekho Kabula' [The echo of Almaty from Kabul]', *Kazakhstanskaya Pravda* (Almaty), 5 October 1996.

10. Akhmet Makhmutov and Magbat Spanov, 'Predely Natsionalnoi Bezopasnosti' [The limits of national security], *Delovaya Nedelya* (Almaty), 18 December 1998, p. 13.

11. There are several explanations of the explosions in Tashkent, one of which is that they were organized by the local special services in order to give the authorities a pretext to suppress any opposition. This argument is not acceptable, because the Uzbek President has so many opponents anyway, especially among the Islamists.

12. Uzbek aircraft bombed regions of Tajikistan and Kyrgyzstan by mistake.

13. Natalia Pulina and Ekaterina Tesemnikova, 'Lokalnaya Voina na Yuge Kirgizii Prodolzhaetsya' [Local war in the south of Kyrgyzstan continues], *Nezavisimaya Gazeta*, 24 August 1999.

14. According to different sources, the number of IMU fighters varies between 1500 and 2000, and the number of members of the Uzbek section of Hizb al-Takhrir al-Islamy is 15,000.

15. 'Novosti iz Ferganskoi Doliny' [News from the Ferghana Valley], p. 5, URL <www.ferghana.ru>.

16. In 1999 volunteers—including officers and soldiers from the reserve—took part in combat on the Kyrgyz side. They were promised double pay and some other privileges. After the operation was finished, the military command refused to pay them the agreed sum and deducted from it the cost of the uniforms

worn during combat. Justice was only done after a protest demonstration organized by the participants in the operation. According to the Kyrgyz military, during the operation the command advised them to economize on cartridges as the state was short of money to buy them. Information supplied to the author by participants in the operation.

17. Anvar Bakeev, 'Peregovory pod Grokhot Boev' [Talks under the roar of combat], *Vremya MN*, 22 August 2000.

18. Martha Brill Olcott, Anders Åslund and Sherman W. Garnett, *Getting It Wrong: Regional Cooperation and the Commonwealth of Independent States* (Washington, DC: Carnegie Endowment for International Peace, 1999), pp. 193–94.

19. Sergei Karelin, 'Uzbekistan Zhdet Pomoshchi ot Rossii' [Uzbekistan is waiting for help from Russia], *Nezavisimaya Gazeta*, 3 July 1998.

20. Togzhan Kasenova, 'Moskva i Tashkent Stanovyatsya Soyuznikami' [Moscow and Tashkent are becoming allies], *Delovaya Nedelya* (Almaty), 15 May 1998.

21. Murat Nuriev, 'Krugovorot Boevikov mezhdu Kavkazom i Srednei Aziei' [Rotation of fighters between the Caucasus and Central Asia], *Profil* (Moscow), no. 11 (1999), pp. 36–40.

22. 'O Situatsii na Yuge Kyrgyzstana' [On the situation in the south of Kyrgyzstan], *Narodnoe Slovo*, 21 September 1999, p. 1.

23. 'Terroristy v Tupike' [Terrorists are at a loss], *Narodnoe Slovo*, 1 September 1999, p. 1.

24. *Panorama* (Almaty), 16 December 1999, p. 4.

25. *Narodnoe Slovo*, 20 May 2000.

26. Nikolai Plotnikov, 'Ochag Napryazhennosti v Srednoi Azii' [Centre of tension in Central Asia], *Nezavisimaya Gazeta*, 25 August 2000, p. 5.

27. Military News Agency, 25 August 2000, p. 1 of 1.

28. In summer 2000 in the Russian press it was again rumoured that Uzbekistan might join the 1992 Tashkent Treaty of Collective Security. The parties to the treaty at the time were Armenia, Belarus, Kazakhstan, Kyrgyzstan, Russia and Tajikistan. Uzbekistan did not join.

29. Alexei Malashenko, 'Musul'mane i Gosudarstva ot Kaspiya do Issyk-Kulya' [Muslims and the states from the Caspian to Issyk-Kul], *NG Sodruzhestvo* [supplement to *Nezavisimaya Gazeta*], 2 June 1998.

30. Vladomir Vorobev, 'Vozvrashchenie v Semyu' [The return to the family] *Narodnaya Gazeta* (Dushanbe), 24 December 1991.

31. Yilmaz Bingol, 'Turkey's Policy toward Post-Soviet Central Asia: Opportunities and Challenges', *Eurasian Studies*, no. 14 (summer/autumn 1998), p. 12.

32. Vitaly Ponomaryov, 'Turkmenskie Vlasti i Islam: Protivostoyanie Prodolzhaetsya' [The Turkmen authorities and Islam: confrontation continues] Keston Institute, 14 August 2000.

33. President Geidar Aliyev of Azerbaijan takes the same position in the South Caucasus.

CHAPTER FOUR

Water in Central Asia: Regional Cooperation or Conflict?

STUART HORSMAN

Introduction

As a region, Central Asia is subject to a number of major environmental concerns, including the desiccation of the Aral Sea, the depletion and degradation of river and irrigation waters, and the consequences of Soviet and Chinese nuclear weapon testing at Semipalatinsk (now known as Semey) and Lop Nor, respectively. However, riverine water, particularly when linked with irrigated land, is perhaps the only regional environmental issue that demonstrates a 'probable linkage between environmental degradation and the outbreak of violent civil or interstate conflict'.[1]

This 'narrow' definition of environmental security, which will guide this chapter, is also advocated by Libiszewski. He defines an environmental conflict as 'a conflict caused by a human-sourced disturbance of the normal regeneration rate of a renewable resource'.[2] Both of the above definitions emphasize the distinct character and source of an environmental threat while maintaining the core foci of security—competition and violence. These definitions are applicable to the dynamics of Central Asia's water security. The depletion and degradation of and competition over the renewable resource is the result of mismanagement and over-utilization. While irrigation has made water an economic asset, it has retained an ecological as well as cultural and political role beyond its direct economic value. Other environmental issues, while they have serious ecological, economic, political and social implications, are unlikely to cause conflict. Consequently, these can be incorporated within a broader environmental security concept, with either an indirect causal relationship with physical violence, or entirely distinct from the traditional security focus.[3]

It is also expedient to recognize the distinction between the environment and natural resources. The former should be applied to phenomena in which there are 'ecological feedbacks and equilibria' while the latter is 'characterized by a fixed stock steadily depleted over time, or systems in which the feedbacks are *strictly* economic and not ecological, [and] ought not to be considered environmental'.[4]

This definition places the region's waters within an environmental framework distinct from resource security. The latter relates to the region's oil and gas reserves, for example, while natural resources have traditionally been a component of mainstream security discourse; environmental issues are still not accorded a significant role in this discourse.[5]

Water insecurity in Central Asia

Water, via the Aral Sea and more importantly the Amu Darya and Syr Darya rivers, acts as a cultural, economic, geographical and political core for Central Asia.[6] The Aral Sea Basin encompasses nearly all of Kyrgyzstan, Tajikistan, Turkmenistan and Uzbekistan, the Kazakhstani *oblasti* of Qyzylorda and Shymkent, and parts of Afghanistan and Iran.[7] It supports 75 per cent of Central Asia's population, and contains 90 per cent of its surface water.[8]

The present water crisis can be attributed to a large extent to two Soviet policies—the establishment and demarcation of the five Soviet Socialist Republics (SSRs) and the rapid expansion of irrigation agriculture since the 1950s. These two processes created a regional economic complex, but also led to associated problems and tensions.

The mis- and over-allocation of water, its economic significance and competing demands which are expected to increase in the near future are the key sources of friction between the riparian states. Each of the four main rivers—the Amu Darya, Syr Darya, Kashkadarya and Zeravshan— is shared between at least two states. Over 50 per cent of water supplies for Turkmenistan, Uzbekistan and the two southern Kazakhstani provinces are extra-republican in source. The figure for Turkmenistan reaches 98 per cent.[9] While this in itself does not indicate a source of tension, these supplies are over-utilized and matters are further complicated by charges of inequitable allocations of water. Under the existing water agreements the three downstream states (Kazakhstan, Turkmenistan and Uzbekistan) receive 73 per cent of total withdrawals from the Aral Sea Basin.[10] This contrasts with upstream Kyrgyzstan and Tajikistan. These two countries are the source of 90 per cent of all available waters, but are allocated only 0.4 per cent and 11 per cent, respectively.[11] Sub-state water requirements are even more acute. Two-thirds of the Central Asian provinces derive at least 50 per cent of their supply from sources outside the province.[12] Although some provinces are supplied from within the same republic, the evidence of past communal conflict, related to irrigated land and water supplies, does not suggest that intra-state water competition will be easily managed.[13]

These allocation problems are significant because of the economic significance of riverine water. Levy argues that 'for any environmental threat to be a security threat, there must be some demonstrable connection to some vital national interest'.[14] Given its economic value, water fits this criterion for the Aral Sea Basin republics, and in particular Turkmenistan and Uzbekistan.[15] Irrigated land produces 90 per cent of the region's crops.[16] Cotton, the single most important irrigation crop, is the leading source of income and employment for Turkmenistan and Uzbekistan. It employs 44 per cent of Turkmenistan's work-force and is responsible for 76 per cent of Uzbekistan's hard currency revenue.[17] Similarly, over 50 per cent of both Kyrgyzstan's and Tajikistan's electricity production is generated using hydroelectric power.[18] This percentage would be larger but for the continuation of cotton-led water allocations. The removal of the integrated Soviet economic system has complicated the water-based economic structure. This has meant the promotion of national economic interests and mutually incompatible demands for water.

Demographic pressures add to the problem. Between 1959 and 1989, the population of the Basin states grew by 140 per cent and it is predicted to grow by one-third again by 2020.[19] Individual provinces, mostly in the Ferghana Valley, are witnessing phenomenal increases.[20] Fifty per cent of the region's population lives in 20 per cent of its area—the Ferghana Valley, Lower Zeravshan and the Tashkent–Khujand Corridor.[21] These are prime irrigated areas, emphasizing the relationship between population pressures and competition for limited access to water and fertile land, as was evident in the Kyrgyz–Tajik violence during the 1980s.[22]

Regional initiatives in the water crisis

With this range of interlinked structural problems in a period of economic and political transition, it is understandable that regional politicians and numerous external commentators have cited a relationship between Central Asia's water crisis and regional stability.[23] Water-related conflict is dependent upon political considerations as much as quantitative factors. Although most water disputes are resolved through negotiations, in regions (including Central Asia) where scarcity and competition are acute, water has become part of 'high politics' and 'the probability of water-related violence is increasing'.[24] A fraught and distrustful regional political environment will not be conducive to the settlement of water issues.[25] Cooperation on water issues is attainable as long as other more deep-seated political differences can be managed.

With the collapse of the USSR, '[a]ll of a sudden, a very complex water management problem became a very complex *transboundary* water management problem'.[26] Previously, water and the irrigation systems were managed by a central agency, the Ministry of Land Reclamation and Water Resources, based in Moscow.[27] While disagreements existed, there was a single and final arbiter—Moscow.[28] Independence replaced this with five sovereign states. In most other regions where states share water systems, agreements and management structures between littoral states have gradually evolved over time. This has not been the case for Central Asia. Here the states were forced to rapidly develop management strategies and assume responsibility.

The newly independent republics quickly acknowledged, in the 1992 Almaty Agreement, that 'only [through] unification and joint coordination of action' could the region's water crisis be managed effectively. Under the agreement, the states retained their Soviet-period water allocations, refrained from projects infringing on other states and promised an open exchange of information.[29] The republics established a number of institutional structures—the Interstate Coordinating Water Commission (ICWC), the subordinate Amu Darya and Syr Darya Basin Management Authorities (BVOs), the Interstate Council on Problems of the Aral Sea Basin (ICAS) and the International Fund for the Aral Sea (IFAS). Institutional reforms resulted in the ICWC being subsumed in the ICAS, it-self subsequently integrated into the IFAS. It was hoped that the merger, in 1997, would simplify administrative procedures and reduce duplication of effort and bureaucratic inertia.[30] This was an indication of the states' awareness of the serious nature of the crisis and the need to coordinate their response more effectively. As early as 1994, over 300 agreements concerning the Aral Sea region had been signed. The region's elites continue to stress their commitment to cooperative water management, as was evident in a joint presidential proposal for further intergovernmental agreements on water use at the Central Asian Economic Community's June 2000 meeting.[31]

Collectively, the institutions' responsibilities include deciding water allocations among the republics (and the Aral Sea), overseeing the 'regulation, use and the protection of water courses', acting as a conduit for the riparian states to give notification of intentions to act, and, most significantly for this study, the avoidance of 'disputes before they arise'.[32]

As Bedford and Micklin independently state, institutional arrangements could play a significant role on water management but they have been hamstrung by weak political commitment and cooperation, and financial and legal constraints.[33] Consequently inter-republican cooperation is limited and water related tensions are evident.

The agreements signed have not been accorded the status of international law, as is the norm for other treaty-based river basin commissions. Similarly, the BVOs are not recognized by national legislatures and therefore lack authority.[34] They need to be transformed from inter-republican to treaty-based international organizations and complemented with the establishment of further BVOs for all the region's other international rivers. Financial problems have also impeded cooperative action. Initially, it was proposed that the IFAS would rely on contributions from the member states of 1 per cent of their individual gross national products (GNPs), with additional international donations.[35] The IFAS reduced the level of contributions to 0.3 per cent for Kazakhstan, Turkmenistan and Uzbekistan, and 0.1 per cent for Kyrgyzstan and Tajikistan. Despite this, the states have been slow in paying.[36]

To a great extent the regional water situation is symbolic and indicative of the broader political context. Newly found independence and sovereignty have impeded integrative and cooperative objectives. This is most evident in the responses of Turkmenistan and Uzbekistan to multilateral initiatives. When invited by the Organization for Security and

Cooperation in Europe (OSCE) to participate in collective negotiations, Ashgabat and Tashkent both declared that they favoured bilateral approaches.[37] The presidents of both republics had previously been absent from a trans-boundary water resources seminar in Almaty.[38] Their response perhaps demonstrates the division between pro-status quo Turkmenistan and Uzbekistan and 'revisionist' Kyrgyzstan and Tajikistan. The former two have the most to lose if allocations are renegotiated, while multilateral negotiations provide the best option for the latter to reverse what they perceive as inequitable quotas.[39]

Regional policy makers at times have applied nationalist, protectionist and 'zero-sum' attitudes to the problem. The oft-cited mantra 'we have our own path to development' is resonant in the environmental debate.[40] One Kazakhstani environmental policy maker urged international cooperation for the 'ecologically vulnerable Central Asian states' while simultaneously declaring that 'we [Kazakhstanis] don't count on other specialists' points of view'.[41] Similarly the refusal of President Islam Karimov of Uzbekistan to participate in proposed multilateral discussions in London within the OSCE framework was accompanied by the retort that Uzbekistan had 1000 years of managing its own water problems.[42]

The present relations between downstream and upstream states where water is concerned are poor. The key source of tension between Kyrgyzstan and Tajikistan, and Kazakhstan, Turkmenistan and Uzbekistan, is allocation. The states have found it difficult to adhere to the relevant agreements. The upstream states require water for hydroelectric power production and irrigation, and the downstream states principally for irrigation use. Water from the two upstream states' reservoirs is, however, released primarily during the cotton-growing season rather than reserved for indigenous hydroelectric power production. Agreements between Kyrgyzstan and Tajikistan on the one hand and between Kazakhstan and Uzbekistan on the other stipulate energy transfers, including deliveries of coal and gas, from the latter in return for water supplies. During the Soviet period the region's integrated agricultural, industrial and power policy, although favouring the cotton producers, was to some extent mutually beneficial. The energy needs of Kyrgyzstan and Tajikistan were compensated by electricity produced by the Kazakh and Uzbek SSRs. The present allocations are based on these historical patterns, which Kyrgyzstan and Tajikistan wish to see revised in order to allow them to expand their irrigation agriculture and winter hydroelectric power production—their main requirement. During talks on water allocation in January 1996, Kyrgyzstan and Tajikistan proposed an expansion of their irrigated lands. Uzbekistan was able to force the former to retract its proposal, but not to change Tajikistan's plan for a 200,000-hectares expansion. Previously, Tajikistan had also expressed an interest in withdrawing an additional 600 million m³ per annum from the upper reaches of the Zeravshan.[43]

Kyrgyzstan has repeatedly flouted the ICWC's water release agreements, although there are some legitimate reasons for its actions.[44] Kyrgyzstan threatened to cut off electricity and water supplies to Kazakhstan in late 1997 after the latter failed to honour agreed energy transfers and pay outstanding debts.[45] After similar problems, water supplies to Kazakhstan were terminated for 10 days in May 1998.[46]

Similar disputes exist between Kyrgyzstan and Uzbekistan, between Tajikistan and Uzbekistan, and between Uzbekistan and Kazakhstan.[47] In 1995, after Kyrgyzstan used water allocated for cotton for domestic energy production, an agreement was reached between Bishkek and Tashkent. Under this, Kyrgyzstan would maintain a 'cotton optimal' policy, even though its winter water reserves were low. In return, Uzbekistan would provide electricity to its neighbour. Kyrgyzstan stated it would have preferred hard currency transactions for the reciprocal trade of water and electricity but had to accept a barter arrangement.[48] During summer 1998 and winter 1999–2000 Tashkent cut gas deliveries to Kyrgyzstan because of Bishkek's mounting debts.[49] In June 1997, Kyrgyzstan stated that it was planning to charge Kazakhstan and Uzbekistan for water.[50] Kyrgyzstan, which spends $4 billion per annum to maintain its reservoirs, does not believe that it has received equitable economic benefits from this framework.[51] In July 1997, localized Kazakh protests against Uzbekistani border guards resulted when Uzbekistan reduced by 70 per cent the flow of the Druzhba Canal, which supplies 100,000 hectares in southern Kazakhstan.[52] Tashkent, mindful of previous inter-ethnic violence in the area during the 1980s, restored supplies, indicating an awareness of the security implications of the issue and a clear wish not to escalate the situation.[53]

A tripartite dispute between Kazakhstan, Kyrgyzstan and Uzbekistan emerged in July 2000. Southern Kazakhstan faced a serious water shortage after Bishkek cut supplies because of Kazakhstan's failure to meet agreed energy supplies, and Uzbekistan reportedly extracted more water than it was entitled to. Kazakh TeleCom's temporary suspension of international relays from Uzbekistan was perceived as an act of retaliation.[54]

The likelihood of these disputes escalating to physical violence is limited, although bellicose rhetoric has accompanied each of these incidents.

Uzbekistan has been willing to exercise its political strength in this dispute. One report claimed that it threatened to use military force to seize the Toktogul dam on the Kyrgyzstani section of the Syr Darya if Kyrgyzstan attempted to alter the existing distribution policy.[55] Previously elements in Tajikistan had discussed the idea of using the Syr Darya as 'an offensive weapon in any territorial dispute with Uzbekistan'.[56] It is not clear whether either of these threats had any substance. The constraints on the upstream states have been apparent to Kyrgyzstan's politicians. Opposition politician Doonbek Sadyrbayev stated that 'if the Uzbeks want to play rough there are a hundred ways they can make sure life is difficult including the cutting of winter electricity supplies or raising export tariffs'.[57] The assessment of Kyrgyzstan's former Deputy Prime Minister, Karimsher Abdimunov, that the republic's water dispute with Uzbekistan 'will be resolved in a civilized way' is probably correct and applicable to other water tensions in the region.[58] The bellicose and threatening rhetoric does, however, illustrate the political milieu in which confidence and cooperation are weak.

Water disputes also pervade relations between Turkmenistan and Uzbekistan. For a number of qualitative and quantitative reasons—the tense personal relationship between presidents Karimov and Niyazov, the economic significance of irrigation agriculture and the two states' near-total dependence on the Amu Darya—water has been elevated from a political dispute to a potential cause of conflict.[59] This re-emphasizes Gleick's view that the political context in which water disputes are discussed determines whether they can be settled in a negotiated manner or by force.[60] The political rivalry between two leaders, both of whom have authoritarian leadership styles and have promoted their states as self-reliant and regionally significant actors, has restricted the potential for compromise. The two presidents did not met each other until January 1996, five years after the collapse of the USSR, in response to border tensions of the previous year. At this meeting water management was discussed and a border protection agreement signed.[61] Niyazov's antipathy to Karimov's appointment as head of the IFAS marred the organization's February 1997 summit meeting.[62]

Turkmenistan has followed a unilateral, isolationist regional policy: multilateral organizations 'shall not infringe upon [Turkmenistan's] sovereignty'.[63] This approach has been evident in the republic's water politics and policies, which include plans to increase land under irrigation and extend the Kara Kum and Tuyamauvun canals.[64] Turkmenistan claims that because these waterways are entirely on its territory interstate consultation is not required, thus going counter to the spirit if not the word of the ICWC's and International Water Law principles on the Prevention of Significant Harm to Other States and Obligation to Notify and Inform to which the republic is a signatory.[65]

The Turkmenistan–Uzbekistan situation 'may be the single most serious regional resource-related dispute'.[66] Border and water disputes have raised stress levels between the capitals.[67] Military tensions along the Bukhara–Lebap border were recorded in late 1995. Water may have been the source of this incident.[68] A Russian newspaper reported that Uzbekistan has contingency plans for the occupation of north-eastern Turkmenistan.[69] Rumours of these alleged plans do little to establish confidence between the two states.

The intra-state situation has greater potential for environment-related conflict. The regions that faced water-related conflicts in the late Soviet period—Batken–Isfara, Osh, the lower Zeravshan and the lower Amu Darya—remain potential flash-points. However, the only significant environmental-related conflict so far has been the 'kolkhozes war' in the Kurgan Teppa, in 1992.[70] Low-level tensions including water poaching, rerouting of irrigation canals and tensions between private and *kolkhoz* farms have been recorded but it is unlikely that such incidents will escalate into interstate conflict.[71]

The role and impact of external actors on the water management crisis

This potentially volatile water security environment has attracted considerable extra-regional interest. The types and influences of external actors can be divided into contiguous states, on the one hand, and non-contiguous states and regional and international organizations, on the other. The former have a more direct, usually bilateral and frequently negative influence on the security dynamic. The latter have more positive roles and objectives, seeking dispute management via institutional structures.

Because of the difference between hydrological and political boundaries, three neighbouring states outside the Commonwealth of Independent States (CIS)—Afghanistan, China and Iran—have a direct impact on the region's water security milieu. Two other states with regional influence and interests—Pakistan and Turkey—may further complicate allocation disputes.

Afghanistan and Iran on the Amu Darya have markedly different influences on this dynamic. As only 2 per cent of Iran's territory and less than 1 per cent of its population are within the Aral Sea Basin, its related water concerns are limited.[72] Consequently, Iran does not and will not play a significant role in the region's water security debate.

The influence of Afghanistan is more complex and potentially detrimental. Forty per cent of its territory and 33 per cent of its population are within the Aral Sea Basin.[73] It shares the Amu Darya with the three southern CIS Central Asian republics. It also shares the Tejen river with Iran and Turkmenistan, and is the source of the Atrek and Murgab, both of which terminate in Turkmenistan. Peace and stability in Afghanistan, while they will probably reduce regional insecurity, for example in terms of arms proliferation, narcotics smuggling and guerrilla training, may have negative repercussions for water-related security.[74] According to figures from 1985, Afghanistan withdrew only 1.5 km^3 per annum from the Amu Darya—2.2 per cent of the river's annual flow.[75] The river could, however, provide approximately half of Afghanistan's hydroelectric power potential and significant irrigation supplies.[76] This would require consultation and possibly joint ventures with neighbouring riparian states. Potential post-conflict increase in water extraction will have inevitable consequences for downstream states. Given that total withdrawals from the Amu Darya already outstrip the inflow, any water-related economic expansion in northern Afghanistan would place further pressure on the system.[77]

The security and diplomatic implications of water disputes between an alienated and militarized Afghanistan and its apprehensive co-riparian states are liable to be tense. The absence of Afghanistan from the Amu Darya BVO and the ICWC seriously weakens any long-term and regional institutional solution—a concern the World Bank has voiced.[78] Externally encouraged diplomatic initiatives may be a means of addressing this problem. The Economic Cooperation Organisation (ECO) has been cited as a possible vehicle for dialogue between Afghanistan and its co-riparian states. With the exception of Azerbaijan, all its members are either Amu Darya riparian states or interested in Afghanistan.[79] However, previous incidents suggest that Afghanistan's approach to water disputes may not encourage cooperative management. In theory the ECO could have a positive role, reducing interstate competition and rivalry, and encouraging integration through economic and cultural ties,[80] but its lack of a security policy profile, its financial constraints and the limited ability of all its members to place regional and cooperative objectives above national interests reduce its efficiency in this specific case and in other intra-membership disputes.[81] The Iranian newspaper *Emrooz* accused the Taliban of blocking the Helmand River in order to exert pressure on Tehran during the Afghanistan Peace Conference in Saudi Arabia in spring 2000. This 'political blackmail [was cited as an] indication of the [Taliban's] shameful position in the international scene'.[82] The statement emphasizes that water disputes are conditioned by the broader political context. Similarly, the World Bank's attempt to involve Kabul in water management institutions was declined.

China's water demands and policies are also liable to have negative development and security implications for at least one Central Asian state—Kazakhstan. China plans to extract water from the Ili and Irtysh rivers for Urumchi and oilfield developments in the Xinjiang Uighur Autonomous Region.[83] Both rivers rise in China. The Ili then flows through Kazakhstan approximately 100 km north of Almaty before terminating in Lake Balkhash. The Irtysh passes Öskemen, Semey and Pavlodar before crossing the Russian border near Omsk and eventually joining the Ob river.[84]

The proposal has both economic and political objectives—to stimulate the economy of Xinjiang, to raise living standards and to erode support for Uighur irredentism. If it succeeds in the last of these it will reduce one source of trans-border insecurity.[85] However, it is unlikely that it will resolve the irredentist challenge in Xinjiang. The irrigation scheme, while providing water for urban and industrial use, is likely to have environmental, developmental and political consequences similar to those found in Central Asia. It may in fact reinforce the linkage between environmental degradation and political activism, erosion of regime legitimacy and instability.[86] An environmental audit of China has suggested that the greatest pressure from environmental degradation will be experienced in north-west China, including Xinjiang.[87] One study even suggests a possible linkage between environmental degradation in China and the weakening of its political structures and the possible escalation of tensions between core and periphery.[88] Insecurity in Xinjiang, with a possible environmental dimension, is likely to have a negative impact on Central Asia's stability in general and Kazakhstan's in particular.[89]

As well as probably failing to satisfy its own domestic security concerns, with indirect security consequences for Kazakhstan, China's unilateral and aggressive water policies will be directly detrimental to its weaker downstream neighbour.[90] Eighty per cent of Kazakhstan's Ili Valley water originates in China, while the Irtysh supplies the industrial regions of eastern Kazakhstan and Pavlodar, and Karaganda via a canal.[91] The Irtysh has also been proposed as a possible additional source of water for the new Kazakh capital, Astana.[92] Kazakhstan expects that demographic and economic growth will take place in the north-east as a result of the relocation of the capital. This will place additional pressure on water supplies in the region, which China's proposals will only exacerbate.[93] As well as the constraints on economic growth and living standards, other negative consequences may include the shallowing of the rivers and the Balkhash and Zaisan lakes, increased salinization and micro-climate change, including reduced humidity—problems which are already evident around the Aral Sea. These have 'broader environmental security' implications related to ecological, development, health and migration concerns. The 'narrower' security implications (i.e., the potential for violence) of these developments are uncertain. However, a violent outcome is more probable in the Irtysh–Ili region than in the Aral Sea littoral region because of the former's relatively more developed civil society, political activism and greater economic significance.

The Kazakhstan–China scenario echoes Homer-Dixon's findings that upstream–downstream disputes are liable to remain stable when the upstream state is politically dominant. Competition and revision of allocations are more likely if the 'downstream riparian [state] is highly dependent on river water and is strong in comparison to the upstream riparian [state] . . . This is particularly dangerous if the downstream country also believes it has the military power to rectify the situation'.[94]

On its own Kazakhstan is unable to mount such a challenge. However, the other downstream state liable to be affected by China's Irtysh extraction plans is Russia. The two downstream states, if closely aligned, could present China with a united and more equal negotiating partner. Russia seems reluctant to damage its relatively good relations with China over this 'minor' environmental concern.[95] The 'Shanghai Five'—China, Kazakhstan, Kyrgyzstan, Russia and Tajikistan—may prove useful for dialogue and confidence building between China and its neighbours of the former Soviet Union on this sensitive trans-border issue.[96] This forum has already succeeded in producing a multilateral agreement on military reductions along the joint border—a more traditional security concern.[97] However, the Shanghai Five may not be able to resolve the water dispute.

Hitherto negotiations on the states' water resources have been bilateral in nature. It is unclear whether China has refused to expand water negotiations from bilateral (Kazakhstan and China) to multilateral discussions (to include Russia), or whether the latter has declined the invitation.[98] The negotiations have also failed to incorporate principles of international law or to make provision for multilateral water supplies.[99] China has contravened both international law and bilateral agreements: in particular it has failed to notify and consult Kazakhstan on its intentions or provide environmental impact assessments.[100] It is evident that China is unwilling to engage in meaningful cooperation or compromise in the pursuit of its water demands.

Henning places the Irtysh scenario within Asia's broader and bleak environmental security dynamic. China's assertive water policy is indicative of a trend in some Asian states which are keen to ensure their national water supplies, often to the detriment of the stability of other states and the region. Acute water scarcity in Asia, competitive demands for water, exclusive perceptions of water rights and complex diplomatic relations make cooperative water management 'increasingly improbable'. In essence this security dynamic will be determined by the culture of regional diplomacy, traditional interstate alliances and geopolitical concerns as much as by the core water dispute.[101]

Kazakhstan's concerns over China's proposals feed into wider populist and elite anti-Chinese sentiments in the Central Asian republic, which have an environmental dimension.[102] This environmental–nationalist linkage was noted earlier in the Kazakh and Kyrgyz protests against Chinese nuclear testing at Lop Nor.[103] It alarmed Beijing, which feared that this externally-located environmental protest could act as a catalyst for Muslim nationalist irredentism in Xinjiang.[104] Depletion of Uighur and Kazakh water resources may reinvigorate this form of political activism.

Pakistan's search for energy supplies may impinge, albeit in a minor way, negatively on Central Asian water security. Before the Tajik civil war, Pakistan had offered Tajikistan a $500 million agreement to develop a hydroelectric power project to supply energy-poor northern Pakistan.[105] The project has not been realized. Obstacles to the proposal include poor communications, high development costs and instability in Afghanistan and Tajikistan.[106] If it is implemented, however, the security implications would be uncertain. Potentially the project could provide employment and hard currency for Tajikistan, the poorest state in the CIS. However, if the hydroelectric power generated is for winter use, which is highly probable, it would further exacerbate the divisions between upstream and downstream, winter and summer, and hydroelectric power and irrigation allocations on the Amu Darya. It is also unclear what the broader regional security implications would be. As an alternative to Iranian–Central Asian energy links, the Pakistani proposal would be welcomed by the USA.

Turkey, while not directly involved in the region's water security situation, has set a disturbing precedent for its near neighbours through its plans to dam the Euphrates. Turkey has refused to consult downstream Iraq and Syria, which is it is obliged to do under international law.[107] These two states have voiced concerns about the proposal and warned about the potential for conflict.[108]

The role of other extra-state actors is best illustrated by examining interested international (donor) organizations. Unlike the neighbouring states, whose impact has been ambiguous, international organizations and (most) non-contiguous states have had a positive influence. The organizations involved include the Asian Development Bank, the World Bank (through the International Bank for Reconstruction and Development), the European Union's Technical Assistance to the Commonwealth of Independent States programme (TACIS), NATO and the OSCE. These bodies have to varying degrees focused on technical and financial assistance and support for effective regional legislation, institutions and negotiations.

In general security concerns have been an indirect and subordinate feature in the international organizations' involvement. Despite this caveat, extra-regional involvement has had a positive influence on the broader political context in which regional water security is debated and at times has a direct impact on the core security dynamic. Some international bodies and their projects also have an implicit or explicit environmental security dimension. The objectives of the Sustainable Development programme of the UN Development Programme (UNDP) in the region are the elimination of poverty, job creation, gender empowerment and environmental regeneration.[109] These initiatives, whether intentionally or not, can be regarded as positive contributions to the broader security milieu. If they are successful in remedying economic decline, social instability and migration-related tensions, they will help break the relationship between environmental degradation and physical violence.

Two 'explicitly' security-oriented organizations have been active in the region. NATO, through its Cooperation Partners Programme, has promoted scientific collaboration with the CIS states in priority areas, including the environment. In Central Asia technical scientific aid has included a collaborative Geographic Information System (GIS) project in Karakalpakstan.[110] The OSCE's inclusive Eurasian membership, comprehensive concept of the term *security* (which includes an environmental dimension) and cooperative approach to resolving security problems are positive attributes for its participation in the region.[111] It is not surprising, therefore, that the 'Central Asian republics have called upon the OSCE to assist in addressing the environmental issues of security in the region, particularly the question of water resources'.[112] The OSCE's role in the region has focused on the promotion of consensus building and support for negotiated and institutional approaches to water management.[113] However, its cooperative security objectives, founded on 'true partnership based on mutual accountability, transparency and confidence at both the domestic and the foreign policy level', have not prospered in Central Asia.

Two states, the USA and Israel, have specifically used environmental assistance for security objectives. US efforts on regional environmental issues via the Agency for International Development (USAID) have been used to encourage confidence and cooperation within the region, with the ultimate strategic objective of creating a stable regional environment for US economic interests, notably in the oil and gas sector.[114] Israel has used environmental aid in a similar manner with considerable success. In addition to normal diplomatic and security contacts with the republics, Israel has used irrigation-related technical assistance as a cost-effective component of its regional policy.[115] A principal objective of this policy has been to counter Iranian influence in the region.[116] The example emphasizes that interest in water resources is often a minor component of broader political and security considerations. In this case, water is being used as an instrument rather than cause or objective of state policy.

International involvement has acted neither as a catalyst of nor as a panacea for regional water disputes. External actors have been unable to significantly influence the basic attitudes and approaches of individual riparian states or to alter the direction of particular scenarios. Despite the involvement of the US Environmental Policy and Technology Project (EPT) and the EU, Kazakhstan, Kyrgyzstan and Uzbekistan have found it difficult to resolve the Toktogul reservoir dispute.[117] Similarly the World Bank's overtures to Afghanistan have been unsuccessful.

The international community's limited influence on the region's water security milieu is understandable. Some of the difficulties and impediments faced are common throughout the international system, others specific to the region or associated with the dynamics of the donor community.

One major impediment is the level of global and in particular Western interest in the region. 'The provision of assistance to Central Asia is closely related to the value that the outside world attaches [to the region and] the degree to which assistance can be expected to build long-term relationships that are valuable to the donor.'[118] For a large number of states this is, unfortunately, limited. The exception to this rule—interest in the region's oil and gas reserves—has not translated into more comprehensive involvement. Regional problems, even the most acute ones such as the Afghan and Tajik civil wars, have failed to elicit commensurate international responses. International assistance to and interest in the immediate Aral Sea region has been more forthcoming. This interest may be misplaced, diverting international attention, energy and funding from the fundamental causes—water mismanagement and irrigation-based cotton agriculture—to what is essentially a symptom of the basic factors.[119]

The international donor community needs to be aware of and capable of working with local political sensitivities.[120] A key interest of a number of international organizations, including the World Bank, USAID and the EU through TACIS, has been the promotion of water pricing as means of improving water efficiency and therefore reducing the potential for scarcity-related competition.[121] Except in Kyrgyzstan and to a lesser extent Kazakhstan, antipathy has dominated Central Asian elite and grassroots responses to this objective. This resistance is related to cultural attitudes towards land and water ownership, concerns about corrupt and unfair distribution, financial and technical difficulties in implementation, and the inability of many water users to pay anything more than a negligible price for supplies.[122] This debate is indicative of the divergence between regional and extra-regional attitudes and assumptions.

Prospects for the future

Water is a contested and strategic asset for the countries of the Aral Sea Basin and likely to become so between China and Kazakhstan in the near future. How far water-related conflict is likely in the future is difficult to gauge. International evidence, particularly from the Middle East, suggests that interstate water-related conflict is the exception rather than the norm.[123] It is fortunate that water rarely results in interstate violence. Demand for water is, however, intense and predicted to increase in the near future, and is accompanied by a number of negative political factors— poor collective management, proposals for further water extraction, tension in interstate relations, bellicose diplomatic rhetoric and sporadic but low-level violence at the communal level.

The countries of the Aral Sea Basin do not appear to have acknowledged either individually or collectively the seriousness of the situation or the expediency of cooperative political action and an integrated management system in resolving this issue. As Micklin notes:

> Looking at the future, the only rational avenue for the Aral Sea Basin states to follow is cooperation and compromise in managing and sharing their trans-national water resources. This is not only necessary to avoid interstate conflict, perhaps even military confrontation but to develop an integrated basin-wide strategy to optimize water use efficiency and maximize efforts to restore and protect key water related ecosystems.[124]

The republics have taken tentative steps towards collective water management, although 'progress is slow and uneven, and the most critical problems remain formidable and largely unresolved'.[125] Further pressures, the deterioration of the existing irrigation infrastructure, the continued economic reliance on irrigation agriculture, demographic growth, and the water demands of Afghanistan and China, as well as non-water-related disputes (for example, on border demarcation), suggest the region's water security milieu will continue to be tense, although not openly hostile.[126]

The role of external actors in this tense and confused security environment is on the whole positive but limited. The possible exceptions to this rule are the roles of China and to a lesser extent Afghanistan. Their assertive pursuit of their own water requirements and apparent disregard for multilateral and at times negotiated settlements suggest the potential for exacerbating Central Asia's water competition further.

Other extra-regional states and in particular the donor organizations can play a useful but essentially supportive role. Encouragement and incentives for more efficient water provision, cooperative water management and conflict prevention have not necessarily found a receptive audience in Central Asia. Although the Central Asian republics have been resistant to some initiatives, the international community is also to blame for this failure. International organizations and individual states have failed to maintain clear and consistent objectives. Economic and strategic objectives have often run counter to policies encouraging collective regional behaviour. Confusion and competition between initiatives of different states and international organizations have also hindered the goal of cooperative water management.

The focus of future international attention with respect to Central Asia's water resources should be: increased and simplified cooperation within the donor community and with regional bodies in order to produce a more coherent, efficient and less conflictual management structure; the provision of 'a know-how transfer concerning the legal basis of international river basins [and] the organization of water management'; a shift from alleviation of the symptom (the drying up of the Aral Sea) to reform of the fundamental cause, irrigation agriculture; increased support for civil society activities in general, and those related to the agricultural and environmental sectors in particular; and, according to the Central Asian states' response to the World Bank's 1996 *ASBP Review*, financial support.[127]

Ultimately, however, both the international donor community and the Central Asian leaderships should recognize the limitations of extra-regional parties in this dynamic. The key role for 'the international donor community [is] to remind the Aral Basin governments that whereas the international community is committed to assisting the region in resolving the Aral Crises, fundamental responsibility for this rests with the Aral Sea Basin countries'.[128]

Notes

1. L. Sarty, 'Environmental Security after Communism: The Debate' in J. DeBardeleben and J. Hannigan, eds, *Environmental Security and Quality after Communism: Eastern Europe and the Soviet Successor States* (Boulder, Colo.: Westview Press, 1995), p. 19.

Environmental security, a highly contested concept, is usually applied to at least one of five spheres: (*a*) the environment as a cause and/or object of conflict; (*b*) the environment used as an instrument of war; (*c*) environmental degradation resulting from military action; (*d*) the indirect influence of environmental degradation on security via development and welfare issues; and (*e*) environmental degradation and protection, distinct from its political and security implications.

For a critical review of the environmental security debate, see N. Gleditsch, 'Armed Conflict and the Environment: A Critique of the Literature', *Journal of Peace Research*, vol. 35, no 3 (1998), pp. 381–400.

2. M. Levy, 'Is the Environment a National Security Issue?', *International Security*, vol. 20, no. 2 (1995), p. 39; and S. Libiszewski, *What Is an Environmental Conflict?*, ENCOP Occasional Paper no. 1 (Zurich/Berne: Center for Security Policy and Conflict Research/Swiss Peace Foundation, 1992), p. 6.

3. This distinction is examined in S. Horsman, 'The Environmental Security Agenda in Central Asia', *Non-Military Security Threats in Central Asia and the Caucasus* (University of Manchester, 1 June 2000).

4. Libiszewski, *op. cit.*, p. 3.

5. J. Vogler, 'Introduction', in J. Vogler and M. Imber, eds, *The Environment and International Relations* (London: Routledge, 1996), p. 3.

6. In the khanates, irrigation was 'one of the principal functions of state power'. H. Carrère d'Encausse, *Islam and the Russian Empire: Reform and Revolution in Central Asia* (London: I. B. Tauris, 1988), p. 8. The political and security significance of irrigated land was also evident in the Bolsheviks' attempt to pacify the Ferghana Valley and in the national delimitation process of 1924–36. M. Rywkin, *Moscow's Muslim Challenge: Soviet Central Asia* (Armonk: M. E. Sharpe, 1982), p. 42.

7. For detailed agricultural and hydrological information, see P. Micklin, 'Water Management in Soviet Central Asia', *Carl Beck Papers in Russian and East European Studies*, no. 905 (University of Pittsburgh, 1991); P. Micklin, *Managing Water in Central Asia* (London: Royal Institute of International Affairs, 2000); S. O'Hara, 'Managing Central Asia's Water Resources: Prospects for the 21st Century', ICREES Seminar on Environmental Issues in Central Asia, University of Nottingham, 9 December 1998; and D. R. Smith, 'Environmental Security and Shared Water Resources in Post-Soviet Central Asia', *Post-Soviet Geography*, vol. 36, no. 6 (1995), pp. 387–98.

8. P. Micklin, 'Water Management in Soviet Central Asia' (note 7), p. 99, Table 2: Central Asia: Drainage Basin Characteristics.

9. Smith, *op. cit.*, pp. 361–62.

10. Uzbekistan receives 38% and Turkmenistan 26% of the basin's total withdrawals. Kazakhstan receives 30% of Syr Darya withdrawals. (The Aral Sea has been allocated 16% of total withdrawals.) Micklin, *Managing Water in Central Asia* (note 7), pp. 43–48 and table 2 (p. 44).

11. Micklin, *Managing Water in Central Asia* (note 7), pp. 43–48 and table 2 (p. 44).

12. The provinces with the most acute water problems are Andizhan, Bukhara, Karakalpakstan, Khorazm, Namangan, Samarkand, Sukhandarya and Sirdarya (all in Uzbekistan), Khatlon (Tajikistan) and Ahal (Turkmenistan). Smith, *op. cit.*, pp. 361–62.

13. Y. Roi, 'Central Asia Riots and Disturbances, 1989–90: Causes and Context', *Central Asian Survey*, vol. 10, no. 3 (1991), p. 24; and V. Tishkov, *Ethnicity, Nationalism and Conflicts In and After the Soviet Union* (London: Peace Research Institute, Oslo (PRIO) and Sage, 1997), pp. 74, 76.

14. Levy, *op. cit.*, p. 45.

15. Kazakhstan is excluded as less than 17% of its exports profits are cotton-related. *Kazakhstan Economic Trends* (Almaty: Government of Kazakhstan/TACIS), 1st quarter 1997, p. 136. There are, however, concerns about the impact on Kazakhstan's north-eastern industrial heartland from proposed Chinese water extraction on the Ili and Irtysh rivers.

16. N. F. Vasil'yev, 'Land Reclamation in the Front Line of *Perestroika*', *Gidrotekhnika i melioratsiya*, no. 11 (no date), quoted in P. Micklin, 'The Water Crisis in Soviet Central Asia' in P. Pryde, *Environmental Management in the Soviet Union* (Cambridge: Cambridge University Press, 1991), p. 217.

17. These are 1991 figures. UN Development Programme, *Turkmenistan: Human Development Report* (UNDP: Ashgabat, 1997); and H. Carlisle, 'Forced Student Labor in Central Asia's Cotton Fields', *Surviving Together*, vol. 14, no. 4 (1996), p. 31.

18. S. Klötzli, *The Water and Soil Crisis in Central Asia: A Source for Future Conflicts?*, ENCOP Occasional Paper, no. 11 (Zurich/Bern: Center for Security Policy and Conflict Research/Swiss Peace Foundation, May 1994), Table 3, Importance of Hydropower in Aral Sea Basin (number of power plants for differing categories of electricity production per year).

19. G. Gleason, 'The Struggle for Control over Water in Central Asia: Republican Sovereignty and Collective Action', Radio Free Europe/Radio Liberty (hereafter RFE/RL), *RFE/RL Report on the USSR*, 21 June 1991, p. 12 (i); and Tashkent Institute of Engineers of Irrigation and Agricultural Mechanization and the Aral Sea International Committee, *Mirzaev Report* (May 1998), table 1, cited in Micklin, *Managing Water in Central Asia* (note 7), p. 68.

20. Smith, *op. cit.*, pp. 361–62.

21. P. Micklin, 'The Aral Sea Crisis: An Introduction to the Special Edition', *Post-Soviet Geography*, vol. 33, no. 5 (1992), p. 89.

22. Tishkov, *op. cit.*, p. 74.

23. See, e.g., Gleason, 'The Struggle for Control over Water in Central Asia' (note 19), pp. 11–19; D. J. Petersen, *Troubled Lands: The Legacy of Soviet Environmental Destruction* (Boulder, Colo.: Westview Press, 1993); and Smith, *op. cit.*, pp. 351–70. In February 2000, Nursultan Nazarbayev, President of Kazakhstan, raised concerns about the possibility of water-inspired insecurity in Central Asia. *Turkistan Economy Bulletin*, vol. 101, no. 16 (28 February 2000).

24. P. H. Gleick, 'Water and Conflict: Fresh Water Resources and International Security' in S. Lynn-Jones and S. Miller, eds, *Global Dangers: Changing Dimensions of International Security* (Cambridge, Mass.: MIT Press, 1995), p. 85.

25. For a review of the literature on water politics and the peace process in the Middle East, see A. Garfinkle, 'Hung Out to Dry or All Wet? Water in the Jordan Valley', *Orbis*, vol. 39, no. 1 (1990), pp. 129–38.

26. L. Veiga da Cunha, 'The Aral Sea Crisis: A Great Challenge in Transboundary Water Resources Management', NATO Advanced Research Workshop on Transboundary Water Resources Management: Technical and Institutional Issues, Skopelos, Greece, May 1994, p. 6.

27. It was renamed the Ministry of Water Management Construction (Min-VodKhoz) and then restructured as a scientific research institute in 1990. Gleason, 'The Struggle for Control over Water in Central Asia' (note 19), p. 17.

28. *Inside Central Asia*, 25–31 March 1996, p. 4.

29. O'Hara, 'Managing Central Asia's Water Resources: Prospects for the 21st Century' (note 7), pp. 13–14.

30. Micklin, *Managing Water in Central Asia* (note 7), pp. 50–51.

31. *RFE/RL Newsline*, vol. 4, no. 112, Pt I (9 June 2000).

32. Micklin, *Managing Water in Central Asia* (note 7), pp. 43–48; O'Hara, 'Managing Central Asia's Water Resources: Prospects for the 21st Century' (note 7), pp. 13–14; and Smith, *op. cit.*, p. 366.

33. D. Bedford, 'International Water Management in the Aral Sea', *Water International*, no. 21 (1996), quoted in O'Hara, 'Managing Central Asia's Water Resources: Prospects for the 21st Century' (note 7), p. 15; and Micklin, *Managing Water in Central Asia* (note 7), p. 52.

34. O'Hara, 'Managing Central Asia's Water Resources: Prospects for the 21st Century' (note 7), p. 15.

35. Veiga da Cunha, *op. cit.*, p. 13.

36. P. Micklin, 'Regional and International Responses to the Aral Crisis', *Post-Soviet Geography and Economics*, 1998 (draft version), p. 15.

37. R. Eggleston, 'OSCE Seeks Agreement on Central Asian Water', *RFE/RL Newsline*, vol. 4, no. 110, Pt 1 (7 June 2000).

38. *Ibid.*

39. *Ibid.*

40. This phrase is most closely associated with President Karimov's book, *Uzbekistan: The Road of Independence and Progress* (Tashkent, 1992).

41. Author's interview, Almaty, 2 October 1996.

42. Eggleston, *op. cit.*

43. Y. Fomina, 'It Is Not Safe to Drink the Water in the Republic: A Lot of Money Will Be Needed to Set Things Right', *Nezavisimaya gazeta*, 23 November 1994, p. 3 in Foreign Broadcast Information Service, *Environmental Issues*, FBIS-JPRS-TEN-94-030, 30 December 1994, pp. 94–55, quoted in Smith, *op. cit.*, p. 358.

44. Micklin, *Managing Water in Central Asia* (note 7), p. 46.

45. ITAR-TASS, Moscow, 23 December 1997, 1549 GMT in *Summary of World Broadcasts* (British Broadcasting Corporation), SUW/0518, WE/4, 2 January 1998.

46. *RFE/RL Newsline*, vol. 3, no. 104, Pt 1 (28 May 1999).

47. On water relations between Tajikistan and Uzbekistan, see S. Aioubov, 'Relations Warming between Tajikistan and Uzbekistan', *RFE News Briefs*, 20 February 1997.

48. J. Branslen, 'Kyrgyzstan/Uzbekistan: The Politics of Water', *RFE/RL Newsline*, 14 October 1997.

49. *RFE/RL Newsline*, vol. 2, no. 149, Pt 1 (5 August /1998); BBC World Service, 13 December 1999, 1506 GMT; and *RFE/RL Newsline*, vol. 4, no. 11, Pt 1 (17 January 2000).

50. *RFE/RL Newsline*, vol. 1, no. 53, Pt 1 (16 June 1997).

51. *Ibid.*

52. *RFE/RL Newsline*, vol. 1, no. 78, Pt 1 (22 July 1997).

53. *Oxford Analytica, East European Daily Brief*, 22 July 1997.

54. *RFE/RL Newsline*, vol. 4, no. 137, Pt I (19 July 2000); and vol. 4, no. 138, Pt I (20 July 2000).

55. B. Roberts, 'More on Water in Central Asia', Cenasia E-mail Discussion Group, 14 April 1996.

56. S. Akiner, 'Conflict, Stability and Development in Central Asia' in C. J. Dick, ed., *Instabilities in Post-Communist Europe* (Portsmouth: Carmichael & Sweet, 1996), p. 14.

57. Doonbek Sadyrbayev, quoted in Branslen, *op. cit.*

58. *Ibid.*

59. Smith, *op. cit.*, p. 361.

60. Gleick, *op. cit.*, p. 85.

61. R. Kangas, 'Taking the Lead in Central Asian Security', *Transitions*, vol. 2, no. 9 (3 May 1996), p. 54.

62. Open Media Research Institute (OMRI), *OMRI Daily Digest*, no. 45, Pt I (5 March 1997). The position rotates between the two presidents every two years. Karimov was eventually appointed head of the Fund in 1997. *OMRI Daily Digest*, no. 43, Pt 1 (3 March 1997).

63. S. Niyazov, *Komsomol'skaya pravda*, 27 October 1994, quoted in K. Nourzhanov, 'Turkmenistan: Halfway Through to the Golden Age?', *Central Asian Monitor*, no. 1 (1995), p. 12.

64. S. O'Hara, 'Irrigation and Land Degradation: Implications for Agriculture in Turkmenistan, Central Asia', *Journal of Arid Environments*, no. 3 (1997), pp. 165–179: and S. O'Hara, 'Agriculture and Land Reform in Turkmenistan since Independence', *Post Soviet Geography and Economics*, no. 38 (1997) (draft version). For a discussion of the principles of international law on shared water resources, see Gleick, *op. cit.*, pp. 111–14; and Smith, *op. cit.*, pp. 364–66.

65. O'Hara, 'Managing Central Asia's Water Resources: Prospects for the 21st Century' (note 7), p. 21.

66. Smith, *op. cit.*, p. 358.

67. G. Gleason, 'Uzbekistan: From Statehood to Nationhood' in I. Bremmer and R. Taras, eds, *Nations and Politics in the Soviet Successor States* (Cambridge: Cambridge University Press, 1993), pp. 351–53.

68. *OMRI Daily Digest*, no. 13, Pt 1 (18 January 1996).

69. Nourzhanov, *op. cit.*, p. 13.

70. O. Roy, *Islam in Tajikistan*, Project on Open Society in Central Eurasia Occasional Paper no. 1 ([New York]: Open Society Institute, 1996), p. 7.

71. P. Goble and B. Pannier, 'A Watershed in Central Asia', *RFE/RL Newsline*, vol. 1, no. 82, Pt 1 (1997); P. Micklin, *Water and Environmental Management Policy in Uzbekistan: Final Project Report to the Government of Uzbekistan* (Almaty: Environmental Policy and Technology Project for the New Independent States of

the former Soviet Union/USAID, 1997); and private correspondence. Water has also been evident in more traditional security scenarios. During the November 1998 insurrection, the rebel Tajik commander, Makhmud Khudoberdiyev, threatened to destroy a dam on the Kairakkhum channel. 'Tajik Rebels: "We Will Blow up Dam"', BBC News Online, 6 November 1998, 00.02.37 GMT.

72. Iran is also the source of the Tedjen, which is shared with Afghanistan and Turkmenistan, where it feeds the Kara Kum Canal. Micklin, *Managing Water in Central Asia* (note 7), p. 4.

73. Micklin, *Managing Water in Central Asia* (note 7), p. 3.

74. D. Loyn, 'The Taliban's One-Eyed Strongman Hides in His Lair and Laughs at the Rest of the World', *The Observer*, 9 March 1997, p. 11.

75. Smith, *op. cit.*, pp. 355, 358, Table 1, Water Balances for the Syr Darya, Amu Darya, and Zeravshan River Basins, 1985 (km³/year).

76. Smith, *op. cit.*, pp. 355, 358, 366, Table 1, Water Balances for the Syr Darya, Amu Darya, and Zeravshan River Basins, 1985 (km³/year). During the Soviet occupation, Afghanistan's hydroelectric power and irrigation schemes were restricted in order to favour downstream Soviet users. Projects established in this period were integrated into the Soviet Central Asian infrastructure. E. Girardet, *Afghanistan: The Soviet War* (London: Croom Helm, 1985).

77. Smith, *op. cit.*, p. 355. Total withdrawals can exceed total supply because of the use of return flow waters and non-surface supplies. Micklin, 'Water Management in Soviet Central Asia' (note 7), pp. 5–6.

78. Roberts, *op. cit.*

79. The members of the ECO are Afghanistan, Azerbaijan, Iran, Pakistan, Turkey and the five Central Asian republics.

80. T. Amin, 'Pakistan, Afghanistan and the Central Asian States' in A. Banuazizi and M. Weiner, eds, *The New Geopolitics of Central Asia and Its Borderlands* (London: I. B. Tauris, 1994), pp. 223–24.

81. R. Allison, 'Central Asia: A Region in the Making', paper presented at the conference on Central Asia in a New Security Context, Swedish Institute of International Affairs, Stockholm, 2–3 September 1999, p. 9; and A. Hyman, 'Central Asia's Relations with Afghanistan and South Asia' in P. Ferdinand, ed., *The New Central Asia and its Neighbours* (London: Royal Institute of International Affairs and Pinter, 1994), p. 92.

82. N. Karimjuni, 'Taleban: A Dangerous Game', *Emrooz*, 23 April 2000, quoted in 'Iranian Paper Criticises Afghan Taleban for Blocking Helmand River', *BBC Monitoring International Report*, 12 May 2000.

83. For detailed discussion of the proposals, see E. Sievers, 'China Set to Divert the World's Fifth Largest River', *Ecostan*, vol. 7, no. 7 (July 2000).

84. B. Pannier and E. Magauin, 'Kazakhstan: China Discusses Future of Irtysh Rivers', *RFE/RL Weekday Magazine*, 28 May 1999.

85. Astana and Bishkek, under lobbying from China, have declared that they are opposed to 'certain forces pushing for the right of people of northwest China to self-determination'. Daulet Sembaev, Foreign Minister of Kazakhstan, April 1996, quoted in L. Bezanis, 'Uighurs Casualty of "Confidence Building" in Asia',

RFE Analytical Brief, vol. 1, no. 75 (2 April 1996). See also B. Dave, 'Kazakhstan Staggers under Its Nuclear Burden', *Transitions*, vol. 1, no. 21 (17 November 1995), p. 13; and *Jamestown Monitor*, vol. 6, no. 93 (11 May 2000).

86. Z. Goldman, 'Environmentalism and Nationalism: An Unlikely Twist in an Unlikely Direction' in J. Massey Stewart, ed., *The Soviet Environment: Problems, Policies and Politics* (Cambridge: Cambridge University Press, 1992); T. Homer-Dixon, 'Environmental Scarcities and Violent Conflict: Evidence from Cases' in S. Lynn-Jones and S. Miller, eds, *Global Dangers: Changing Dimensions of International Security* (Cambridge, Mass.: MIT Press, 1995), p. 164; and S. Horsman, 'The Environment, Identity and Politics in Central Asia: An Unhealthy Relationship?' in A. Dobson and J. Stanyer, eds, *Contemporary Political Studies 1998* (Nottingham: Political Studies Association, 1998), pp. 182–93.

87. V. Smil, *Environmental Change as a Source of Conflict and Economic Loss in China*, Project on Environmental Change and Acute Conflict, Occasional Paper no. 2 (December 1992), quoted in Homer-Dixon, *op. cit.*, pp. 163, 177. Only two other developing states, Bangladesh and Egypt, have less arable land per capita than China.

88. J. Goldstone, *Imminent Political Conflict Arising from China's Environmental Crisis*, Project on Environmental Change and Acute Conflict, Occasional Paper no. two (December 1992), quoted in Homer-Dixon, *op. cit.*, p. 178.

89. On the situation in Xinjiang, see Bezanis, *op. cit.*; and *OMRI Daily Digest*, no. 33, Pt 1 (17 February 1997).

90. J. Henning, 'Water: Potential Spark of Asian Regional Conflict', *The Analyst*, 24 May 2000, URL <http://www.cacianalyst.org>.

91. G. Gleason, *The Central Asian States: Discovering Independence* (Boulder, Colo.: Westview Press, 1997), p. 146; and T. Bakhytjan, 'Water Dispute Threatens Central Asian Stability: Astana is Seriously Concerned over Plans by China to Divert Several Cross-Border Rivers' in *Turkistan Newsletter*, vol. 4, no. 111 (29 May 2000). See also Pannier and Magauin, *op. cit.*

92. Astana receives most of its water from the Ishim River and previously the Nura–Ishim Canal, but because of mercury pollution the canal is no longer used. Pannier and Magauin, *op. cit.*

93. *Ibid.*

94. Homer-Dixon, *op. cit.*, pp. 158–59.

95. For differing accounts, see Henning, *op. cit.*; and Sievers, *op. cit.*

96. For further discussion on the Shanghai Five, see R. Allison, *op. cit.*, p. 9. See also Bakhytjan, *op. cit.*

97. Allison, *op. cit.*, p. 9.

98. Bakhytjan, *op. cit.*; and Sievers, *op. cit.*

99. Sievers, *op. cit.*

100. *Ibid.*

101. Asia's water shortages are predicted to increase during the next 25 years. Henning, *op. cit.*

102. K. Khafizova, 'Transboarding [*sic*] Relations: Sinkian–Kazakhstan', paper presented at the conference on Central Asia in a New Security Context, Swedish Institute of International Affairs, Stockholm, 2–3 September 1999.

103. Eric Sievers, quoted in J. Critchlow, 'Central Asia: How to Pick Up the Pieces?' in J. DeBardeleben, and J. Hannigan, eds, *Environmental Security and Quality after Communism: Eastern Europe and the Soviet Successor States* (Boulder, Colo.: Westview Press, 1995), p. 145. See also Dave, *op. cit.*; and Horsman, 'The Environment, Identity and Politics in Central Asia: An Unhealthy Relationship?' (note 86), p. 191.

104. M. B. Olcott, *Central Asia's New States: Independence, Foreign Policy, and Regional Security* (Washington, DC: US Institute for Peace, 1996), p. 17.

105. Amin, *op. cit.*, p. 221.

106. The power lines would have to cross Afghanistan through the Wakham Corridor.

107. These include the UN Charter, the International Court of Justice and the Convention on the Protection of Transboundary Watercourses. P. Brown, 'Aid for Turkey Dam May Face Court Challenge', *The Guardian*, 25 April 2000, p. 5.

108. *Ibid.*

109. Micklin, 'Regional and International Responses to the Aral Crisis' (note 36), p. 12.

110. *Ibid.*, p. 13.

111. *OSCE Handbook* (Vienna: OSCE, 1999), pp. 1, 133. See also 'Seventh Economic Forum Focuses on "Security Aspects in the Field of the Environment"', *OSCE Newsletter*, vol. 6, no. 5 (May 1999), pp. 2–3.

112. *OSCE Newsletter*, vol. 6, no. 11/12 (November–December 1999), p. 14.

113. *OSCE Newsletter*, vol. 6, no. 5 (May 1999), p. 3.

114. E. Weinthal, 'In Focus: Central Asia: Aral Sea Problem', *Foreign Policy in Focus*, vol. 5, no. 6 (March 2000), URL <http://www.foreignpolicyinfocus. org/briefs/vol5/v5n6aral.html>.

115. As a result of good practice and technological innovation, cotton production in Israel uses only one-third of the water required in Turkmenistan. O'Hara, 'Agriculture and Land Reform in Turkmenistan since Independence' (note 64), p. 13.

116. C. Boucek, 'Iranian Spy Trail Highlights Israeli–Central Asian Security Relations', *The Analyst*, 7 June 2000, URL <http://www.cacianalyst.org>.

117. Micklin, 'Regional and International Responses to the Aral Crisis' (note 36), p. 11.

118. Gleason, 'Uzbekistan: From Statehood to Nationhood' (note 67), p. 154.

119. Weinthal, *op. cit.*

120. N. Lubin, 'New Threats in Central Asia and the Caucasus: An Old Story with a New Twist' in R. Menon, Yu. Fedorov and G. Nodia, eds, *Russia, The Caucasus and Central Asia: The 21st Security Environment* (Armonk, N.Y.: M. E. Sharpe, 1999), p. 223.

121. O'Hara, 'Managing Central Asia's Water Resources: Prospects for the 21st Century' (note 7), p. 24.

122. Micklin, *Managing Water in Central Asia* (note 7), pp. 65–66; and *RFE/RL Newsline,* vol 4, no. 127, Pt I (30 June 2000).

123. T. Naff and R. Matson, eds, *Water in the Middle East: Conflict or Cooperation?* (Boulder, Colo.: Westview Press, 1984), quoted in Smith, *op. cit.*, p. 357.

124. Micklin, 'Regional and International Responses to the Aral Crisis' (note 36), p. 80.

125. *Ibid.*

126. R. Dion, 'The Decline of Central Asian Integration', *The Analyst*, 29 March 2000, URL <http://www.cacianalyst.org>.

127. Micklin, *Managing Water in Central Asia* (note 7), p. 49; and Weinthal, *op. cit.*

128. Micklin, 'Regional and International Responses to the Aral Crisis' (note 36), p. 17.

CHAPTER FIVE

Russia and Central Asia

LENA JONSON

Introduction

Towards the mid-1990s many observers believed that Russia was winning back the role and influence it had lost after the Soviet Union broke up and the Central Asian republics became independent states. Yet what appeared to be a trend of Russia returning to the region was followed during the second half of the 1990s by a process of rapid though involuntary disengagement by Russia.[1] Russia was losing influence in the economic, political, cultural and security spheres. While it remained the strongest external power in Central Asia and a core player with regard to security in the region, its position as a 'security guarantor' in Central Asia was undermined as other external actors became more engaged.

Western engagement in the Caucasus and in Central Asia—in plans and projects for constructing pipelines to Turkey across the Caucasus and the Caspian Sea and in security cooperation with states of the region—reflected a drastic change of the strategic scene, with direct consequences for Russia. Frustrated at losing influence over what it regards as its own 'backyard', Russia struggled to find a policy to counter its disengagement from the region. This chapter aims, first, to analyse Russian policy and the changing security relations between Russia and Central Asia; and, second, to discuss the prospects for these relations in the future.

It is often questioned whether there exists a Russian policy towards Central Asia. In this chapter 'policy' is understood as the pattern (however inconsistent) of Russian official behaviour towards Central Asia derived from the words and deeds of the Russian official actors.

After the dissolution of the Soviet Union Russian analysts exaggerated the importance of factors which would induce Central Asia to maintain close cooperation with Russia. Most commentators believed that geographic location, shared history, common production systems, infrastructure and institutions, and old dependences on Russian financial subsidies and on the Russian market would guarantee a continued interest in extensive cooperation with Russia. They also believed that a shared identity and common values, derived from a long history of cohabitation, had survived the break-up of the Soviet Union. These assumptions proved to be overstated.

The Central Asian leaders had been reluctant to leave the USSR. However, Russia had no part in their search for national identity and values. Its contradictory and inconsistent behaviour during the early 1990s also contributed to distance the Central Asian states from Russia politically. This trend was clearly expressed by Kazakh President Nursultan Nazarbayev, the closest ally of Russia, who in early 1997 spoke out in public about his deep disappointment with Russian policy.[2] Thus, what had once been common values between Soviet republics were replaced by separate identities, suspicions about Russia's intentions, and pragmatic calculations of what Russia could deliver. Instead of a security community including Central Asian states and grouped around Russia, a web of bilateral agreements developed between Russia and the Central Asian states, most of the latter being careful, however, to preserve their sovereignty in these treaties.

Russia watched with concern as along its southern border independently-minded states began to cooperate and shift their orientation away from Russia. Uzbekistan became the most outspoken critic of Russia among the Central Asian states and the most eager to enter cooperation with the USA. Turkmenistan limited its military cooperation with Russia on the grounds of its status, recognized by the UN General Assembly, of 'permanent neutrality'. As Russia saw its influence in Central Asia decline, it feared that it would be supplanted by the engagement of outside powers in the region.

The vision

Russian visions with regard to Central Asia vacillated radically during the 1990s.

The first Russian government under the reformist Yegor Gaidar as acting Prime Minister regarded Central Asia as an economic burden in a situation when Russia had to concentrate on reforming its own economy. In 1992–93 bilateral agreements on friendship and mutual assistance were signed, which also included cooperation in the military field, between Russia and the Central Asian states. When in 1992 civil war broke out in Tajikistan, the Russian military intervened. Yet the Russian Government remained highly ambivalent towards Central Asia. The foreign policy consensus which began to evolve in Russian debate after 1993 initiated a change of attitude towards Central Asia. Relations with member states of the Commonwealth of Independent States (CIS) and among them Central Asian states became far more important when the government declared its intention to recover great-power status for Russia. Still, Russian policy remained ambivalent, especially with regard to economic relations, reflecting the dilemma the country was in—wishing for integration and leadership at the same time as trying to avoid all obligations that might be costly or harmful to Russia's own economic development.[3]

President Boris Yeltsin's decree of September 1995 on a policy to create a CIS economic, political and defence union reflected the new determination to integrate CIS territory, including the Central Asian states.[4] This policy could not be implemented, however, and was set aside. The Central Asian leaders were unwilling, as were the leaders of most CIS states, to set up multilateral integrated structures. When Yevgenii Primakov became Russian Foreign Minister in 1996, the government took on a pragmatic low-profile policy towards the CIS states and modified its ambitions with regard to CIS integration. The emphasis in Russian policy shifted to bilateral agreements and functional cooperation on specific issues. A diversified policy followed which concentrated on developing cooperation with those states that were most willing to enter such agreements. Thus a differentiated policy evolved with regard to Central Asian states.

Economic cooperation was declared to be the basis of future CIS integration, yet military relations with Central Asian states remained the most important. The breakdown of the common Soviet production system and infrastructure had led to a faltering in economic relations. In the field of traditional military security, on the other hand, Russia had more to offer. It assisted in reconstructing the national armies of the Central Asian states, and some of its military units initially remained deployed in the Central Asian states.

Russia's interests in Central Asia since the break-up of the Soviet Union are mainly related to strategic and security concerns.[5] The strategic concerns are two-fold: first, to integrate the Central Asian states in the CIS sphere and make them into close allies of Russia; and, second, to deny external powers strategic access to Central Asia.

Strategic concerns were reflected in 1993 when then Foreign Minister Andrei Kozyrev pointed to a risk that Russian withdrawal would create a vacuum on former Soviet territory, which would rapidly be filled by states unfriendly to Russia. A 1994 report by the Russian Foreign Intelligence Service (SVR), headed at the time by Yevgenii Primakov, warned that the West in general and the USA in particular were undermining Russian efforts to integrate the CIS and to recover a great-power position.[6] The report gave a good deal of attention to the changing situation in Central Asia and to what its authors considered to be foreign involvement in the region by both Western and Muslim states—among the latter Iran and Turkey. At the time the report was published it did not, however, fully reflect government policy.

In his June 1996 address to Parliament on national security President Yeltsin paid attention to the changing strategic scene on CIS territory and described 'actions by states and their alliances . . . to undermine Russia's relations with former Soviet republics' as a threat to Russian national security.[7] The draft of the address, prepared by security adviser Yurii Baturin, pointed more clearly to a general trend of disintegration on former Soviet territory and of Russia losing influence. The draft was also more specific with regard to developments in the Caucasus and Central Asia.[8] The Central Asian states were described as not capable of following an independent policy and therefore increasingly targets for foreign influence. In the ongoing struggle for influence in Central Asia the draft pointed to Turkey, Iran, Pakistan, Saudi Arabia, the USA and NATO (especially Germany) as the main external actors. In a worst-case scenario, it warned, a new buffer zone could be created to the south-east on former Soviet territory by states unfriendly to Russia.

During the years that followed Russia watched with concern as plans and projects developed for the construction of oil and gas pipelines, in cooperation with Western partners, from the Caspian Sea region along routes that avoided Russian territory. It noted the growth of Central Asian trade with Western and Asian partners at the same time as trade with Russia decreased.

Russian and Central Asian threat perceptions clearly diverged as from a Russian perspective the engagement of external powers was viewed as a threat to Russian (as well as Central Asian) national and strategic interests. From a Central Asian perspective, greater involvement by the USA, Turkey, Iran or China offered instead a promise for future economic development, and foreign investors were welcomed. The Central Asian leaders also remained sceptical about Russian proposals for military integration. They developed cooperation with Western countries within the framework of the NATO Partnership for Peace (PfP); joint military manoeuvres were carried out involving NATO soldiers in exercises on Central Asian territory, and Central Asian officers received military training in the USA.

Events outside Central Asia added to Russian concern about developments in the Caucasus and Central Asia. Russia reacted strongly to the 1994 decision to enlarge NATO eastwards. The 1999 enlargement, the 1999 NATO strategic concept, which provided for out-of-area-operations, and the bombing of Kosovo and Serbia in spring of the same year left Russia highly frustrated. The process culminated half a year later with Western criticism of the Russian military offensive in Chechnya.

The new Russian military doctrine, published as a draft in October 1999 and signed by the President in April 2000, and the National Security Concept of February 2000 reflected the Russian reaction to the changing strategic scene. With the new keywords of 'multipolarity' and 'unipolarity', these documents provided a conceptual basis for criticism of US policy and in favour of tactical alliances in order to counter a growing US and Western influence in the Caucasus and Central Asia.[9] The main 'threats in the international sphere' were associated with the West and with the eastward expansion of Western-based military cooperation. The National Security Concept thus stated that Russia's national interests in the international arena are threatened by 'attempts of other states' to prevent it from asserting its national interests 'in Europe, the Middle East, the Caucasus, Central Asia and the Asia–Pacific region'.

In the immediate aftermath of the break-up of the Soviet Union security concerns in official statements had been more pronounced than strategic concerns. The draft of the first military doctrine published in May 1992 pointed to the threat to Russian security posed by local and regional conflicts and wars erupting along Russia's borders.[10] It made it a crucial task for the Russian military to assist actively in localizing 'the source of tension and stopping the hostilities as early as possible'. The draft referred indirectly to an Islamic threat when specifically mentioning local conflicts fanned by 'aggressive nationalism or religious intolerance'. The threat of Islam was also referred to in the declaration signed by Russia and the three Central Asian states in September 1993 to set up a CIS Collective Peacekeeping force in Tajikistan. Then, however, it was characterized as an external threat, from war-ridden Afghanistan.

Russia feared that instability in Central Asia would spill over into Muslim regions of Russia. The threat of 'Muslim fundamentalism' received the attention of then Foreign Minister Kozyrev. Not only did he express a historically rooted fear of Islamic encirclement; he also developed a more ideological and cultural view of the Islamic factor, advocating a thorough and sustained containment policy. In his view, Moscow had to be ready to play its part in the containment of this threat on behalf of the 'civilized world'.[11] In the 1994 report by the Foreign Intelligence Service, 'Islamic extremism' was branded as a serious threat emanating from Central Asia and Afghanistan. Primakov, however, had a more sophisticated understanding of Islam and Muslim countries, making a distinction between fundamentalism and extremism.

The report presented a number of scenarios for the future development of the CIS. According to one scenario, the position of 'Islamic extremists in CIS states with a Muslim population' is expected to become stronger and pose a threat to security to Russia and other CIS states. Fear of Islamic extremism spreading from Tajikistan to the rest of Central Asia was reflected in the Russian strategy of supporting the Tajik Government against the United Tajik Opposition (UTO).

Radical Islam, which so far had been a limited phenomenon in Central Asia, spread during the 1990s as part of the general process of Islamization in these societies. The development of fundamentalist and Islamist movements in Russia and the Central Asian region during the following years led Russia to point more clearly to an Islamist threat. In May 1998 a coalition of Russia, Uzbekistan and Tajikistan was created in a joint effort to fight 'religious extremism'.

The Islamist offensives in August 1999 in southern Kyrgyzstan and Dagestan, followed by the war in Chechnya, contributed to the 'Islamic threat' being redefined as a threat of 'international terrorism' in the National Security Concept published in February 2000 and moved to the forefront of the Russian political agenda. The events in Kyrgyzstan initiated a wave of Russian activity to promote military and security cooperation with Central Asian states.

With no proper border guards or customs control along the more than 6500-km long new state border with Kazakhstan, the Russian border became open to drug trafficking, smuggling and illegal trespassing.[12] This was soon considered a serious security problem and the Russian Government initiated common efforts to prevent these activities across the outer borders of the Central Asian states.

Russian concerns in Central Asia also followed from the presence of large Russian populations in some of the Central Asian countries, in particular Kazakhstan, where 33.9 per cent of the population is Russian, and Kyrgyzstan, with 15.5 per cent.[13] The government assumed the responsibility of helping to improve their situation, but was criticized for passivity. The position of the Russian minorities remained a politically delicate topic in Russian debate.

The Chechnya conflict brought Vladimir Putin to power. Under his leadership the Russian Government adopted a more active and determined policy of reversing the trend and strengthening Russian influence in Central Asia and the Caucasus. In an address to Russia's Federation Council on 22 December, nine days before his appointment as acting President of Russia, Putin gave a new emphasis to relations with the Central Asian region.[14] His first visits abroad after he became Prime Minister, to Tajikistan in November 1999 and to Uzbekistan the following month, indicated this emphasis. As newly inaugurated president he first went to Uzbekistan and Turkmenistan in May 2000. Uzbekistan, which had left the Treaty of Collective Security in April 1999, signed bilateral agreements on military and military–technical cooperation, leading Putin to describe Russian–Uzbek relations as a 'strategic partnership'. The chain of events in Dagestan, Chechnya and Kyrgyzstan had increased a common fear of Islamic extremism and terrorism and provided Putin with a platform to suggest closer cooperation in the military and security fields and the means for a renewed effort to reorient the Central Asian states back towards Russia.

Economic and energy relations

The dissolution of the Soviet Union broke up the old Soviet pattern of production and trade, and the new national customs arrangements and protectionism of the independent states prevented trade from developing. In spite of a certain revival towards the mid-1990s, intra-CIS trade therefore did not recover to the scope and volume of Soviet internal trade. Kazakhstan and Belarus joined Russia in a CIS Customs Union in 1995; Kyrgyzstan did so in 1996, and Tajikistan followed in 1998; still, the volume of intra-CIS trade fell.[15] Russia remained the largest trading partner of Kazakhstan, Kyrgyzstan and Tajikistan but on a lower level than before. Parallel to this, Central Asian trade with Asian and Western countries increased.

A strong card of Russia for maintaining control in the region was its monopoly of the pipeline system for oil and gas exports. If Kazakh oil and gas and Turkmen gas were to reach foreign markets they had to pass through Russian pipeline infrastructure and territory. In spite of this dependence, difficulties in coming to terms with the Russian partners on transport quotas, fees, price levels and forms of payment made export across Russian territory a less attractive option to Turkmenistan and Kazakhstan. In 1997 the export of Turkmen gas to Ukraine across Russia was interrupted and efforts by the Russian Government to create an understanding with Turkmenistan were thwarted by Gazprom, the Russian gas monopoly. Oil exports from Atyrau in Kazakhstan through the Russian export pipeline from Samara were hampered by disputes over quotas and prices. The line via Grozny and Tikhoretsk to Novorossiisk on the Black Sea was restricted and later closed. An extension which would link the Kazakh oilfields in Tengiz with Novorossiisk via Komsomolsk was initiated in 1992, to be built by the Caspian Pipeline Consortium (CPC) in which the Russian company Lukoil and US Chevron are partners, but the project was delayed.

In order to secure alternative outlets to foreign markets, plans for new pipelines were drawn up and discussed—to the east (to China), to the south (via Iran and Afghanistan) and to the west (via the Caucasus). Difficulties in financing such costly international projects, the political risk, and uncertainties over the volume of hydrocarbons to be evacuated from the region resulted, however, in the final decisions being postponed. In the meantime smaller temporary arrangements and new short extensions provided the alternatives to Russian outlets.

In autumn 1999 Russian efforts to ensure the Baku–Novorossiisk pipeline for significant quantities of future Azerbaijani oil were in disarray, and Russia seemed to be losing the race for the main pipeline for south Caspian oil. First, the second Russian military campaign in Chechnya, which started in September 1999, destroyed the prospects for a wide-diameter transit pipeline through Chechnya for years to come. Second, the memorandum of understanding of November 1999, signed by the presidents of Turkmenistan, Azerbaijan, Georgia and Turkey, on constructing an oil pipeline from Baku to the Turkish Mediterranean port of Ceyhan was a distinct blow to Russian interests. Against the background of strong

Western political–strategic interests and Western-financed projects that were part of the broader Eurasian corridor idea supported by the European Union's TRASECA (Transport Corridor Europe Caucasus Asia) and INOGATE (Interstate Oil and Gas Transport to Europe) programmes, the Baku–Ceyhan line seemed to have a good chance of eventually being constructed. The question how it would be financed remained unresolved.

In autumn 1999 the Russian Government initiated a counter-offensive to win back influence in the energy sector. In November 1999 construction work was also finally launched in earnest on the CPC pipeline from Tengiz in Kazakhstan to Novorossiisk, to be completed in 2001.[16] In order to improve the prospects for a major oil pipeline through the North Caucasus, Russia hurried to construct a bypass line crossing Dagestan to Novorossiisk (circumventing Chechnya), which became operational in April 2000.

Parallel to the November 1999 memorandum on the construction of the Baku–Ceyhan oil pipeline, a second memorandum was signed to encourage the construction of a Transcaspian gas pipeline for the export of Turkmen gas to Turkey. This was a challenge to the plans of the Russian company Gazprom to build a gas pipeline across the Black Sea for export of Russian gas to Turkey, the Blue Stream project. As the two large gas pipeline projects were competing for international financial support as well as for the Turkish gas market, which could not absorb the projected volumes of gas from both Russia and Turkmenistan, Russia tried to make the Gazprom proposal more attractive. In December 1999 the Russian Duma therefore hastily adopted a government package of tax breaks and other incentives—at the expense of Russia's hard-pressed budget—for the Blue Stream pipeline project. The Russian Government made no secret of its intention to stop the Transcaspian project in its tracks. Vladimir Putin and other government officials told the Duma that the arrival of Turkmen gas in Turkey and, via Turkey, its trans-shipment to the Balkans and Eastern Europe would mean Russia losing those gas markets. They argued that the Blue Stream project, if carried out, would enable Russia both to continue functioning as the sole transit country for Turkmen gas and to thwart the Caspian–South Caucasus–Turkey oil and gas pipeline route.[17] Despite this belated effort to bolster Blue Stream, this very expensive project has problems in finding financing. As part of its efforts to make Turkmenistan less interested in a Transcaspian gas pipeline, Russia suggested increased Turkmen gas export to Russia on long-term contracts. An agreement on an increase in gas exports was signed in May 2000, but Turkmenistan maintained its interest in alternative outlets, including a Transcaspian gas pipeline.

In April 2000, at the Russian Security Council, Putin stated that Russia should become more active in the Caspian region. He requested greater Russian engagement in the exploitation of Caspian energy resources and the coordination of Russian policy by companies and ministries. The position of representative of the President in the Caspian region was created, with responsibility for coordinating policy and dealing with all foreign policy issues concerning the region, including the legal division of the Caspian Sea.[18] The former Minister for energy, Viktor Kalyuzhnin, was appointed.

In 2000 Russia seemed to be recovering some of the influence it had lost during the late 1990s. The opening of the CPC pipeline for Kazakh oil to Novorossiisk, planned for 2001, will provide Kazakhstan with a main option for its oil. With the by-pass through Dagestan, the Baku–Novorossiisk pipeline was again operational in spite of the Chechnya war. Yet Russia's ability to control Central Asia's export of oil and gas had become drastically reduced.

Military and security relations

In the aftermath of the break-up of the Soviet Union Russia signed bilateral agreements with Central Asian states on military and defence cooperation. In May 1992 the embryo of a joint defence organization was created when the Treaty of Collective Security was signed in Tashkent. To Russia such a treaty was important in order to ensure that close military and security relations would remain with the new states on former Soviet territory and to guarantee Russia a leading position in the future. The treaty was mainly concerned with external threats, but the signatories also committed themselves to refrain from the use of force against one another. Six states signed the treaty, and three more did so a year later. All the Central Asian states except Turkmenistan became signatories.

The Tashkent Treaty did not have the desired effect and military integration did not follow. No joint CIS forces were ever created and no common military policy was agreed upon. Councils for coordinating policy on military and security affairs were created but no legal basis for the use of force in the event of an emergency was elaborated.[19] Most states were unwilling to integrate militarily. Turkmenistan never participated in CIS discussions on military issues and Uzbekistan soon stopped participating in expert meetings on military affairs. When the parties to the

Tashkent Treaty were to decide in April 1999 on whether to prolong it for another five-year period, Uzbekistan did not renew its participation.

The intervention by so-called peacekeeping troops in the Tajik civil war in 1993 had made peacekeeping a central issue for functional cooperation between Russia and the CIS Central Asian states (except Turkmenistan). 'Peacekeeping' thereby became the buzz word for promoting military cooperation during the following years. Joint activity to tackle conflicts could have developed into a field of cooperation, but there was considerable reluctance among the Central Asian states. Kazakhstan, Kyrgyzstan and Uzbekistan agreed in 1993 to provide troops which were of symbolic rather than real value, and Russia itself had to take on the main role as peacekeeper in Tajikistan. Russia's proposals during the following years for permanent structures and mechanisms for conflict resolution and standing troops for peacekeeping were more or less ignored by other CIS states. Instead in 1996 Kazakhstan, Kyrgyzstan and Uzbekistan set up national peacekeeping units of their own and developed cooperation between themselves and with the PfP programme.

Bilateral agreements linked the Central Asian states to Russia, but this web of relations was slowly undermined. Uzbekistan, the most populous and militarily powerful state in the region, which in the early 1990s had seemed to be Russia's closest military ally and which together with Russia had turned the course of events in the Tajik civil war in 1992–93,[20] from 1995–96 reduced its military cooperation with Russia. Today no Russian military forces or military facilities remain on Uzbek territory. When Uzbekistan announced in February 1999 that it would not extend its participation in the Tashkent Treaty, it declared officially that it disagreed with 'Russia's military activity in certain states of the CIS'.[21] This meant first of all Russian policy in Tajikistan and especially its efforts to create a Russian military base there.[22] A member of the GUUAM grouping (composed of Georgia, Ukraine, Azerbaijan and Moldova) since April 1999, Uzbekistan came to be regarded by Russian analysts as a leading state in an evolving anti-Russian military bloc on former Soviet territory.[23]

As Uzbekistan remains a potential power for the future, Russia was encouraged to seek cooperation with it. The framework for cooperation initiated in May 1998 between Russia, Uzbekistan and Tajikistan, with the purpose of preventing the spread of aggressive fundamentalism and extremism in the region, could be viewed, therefore, as an effort to find a new basis for cooperation with Uzbekistan. At the time several Russian analysts considered the agreement a mistake and as offering no benefit in advancing Russian interests. It would rather create a danger if Russia with a large Muslim population of its own becomes involved in problems that are mainly of concern to Uzbekistan.[24] In October 1998 the heads of the three states also signed a declaration on mutual assistance including a clause on military assistance in the event of aggression.[25] In July 1999 further documents on cooperation were signed calling for regular trilateral contacts to counter 'aggressive religious and other extremists, terrorists, criminal border infiltrators and drug and arms traffickers'.[26]

Not much came of these agreements. The Islamist attacks in south Kyrgyzstan in August 1999 changed Russian–Uzbek relations. Prompted by joint fears of Islamic militancy, Russia and Uzbekistan signed agreements on expanded security and military–technical cooperation when Putin visited Tashkent in December 1999 and May 2000. After talks with Uzbekistan's President Islam Karimov, Putin claimed that 'we are coming to a qualitatively new level of relations in security matters' and that 'we are ready through joint efforts to place a barrier against the spread of terrorism and extremism'.[27] At that time some Russian observers played down the treaty and denied that it would mean any strategic turn in Uzbekistan's external relations.[28] Nevertheless, in autumn 1999 Uzbekistan started to participate in military exercises held on Russia's initiative and under Russian command, together with the three Central Asian members of the Treaty of Collective Security.

Turkmenistan received Russian assistance to build up its national army after the break-up of the Soviet Union but avoided all CIS military cooperation. It never joined the Treaty of Collective Security and after the mid-1990s reduced its military cooperation with Russia. There are no Russian military forces or facilities on Turkmen territory. Russian border guards continued to patrol the Turkmen–Afghan border until the end of 1999. In May 1999 the Turkmen side unilaterally announced its decision to end the 1993 Russian–Turkmen treaty on border cooperation on the grounds that the Russians had completed their work, and at the end of the year Russian border troops left Turkmenistan.[29] Like Uzbekistan, Turkmenistan is a member of the PfP programme. It regards cooperation with the PfP as consistent with its neutral status and in May 1999 signed an agreement for a programme of further cooperation with the PfP.[30]

Kazakhstan is of particular strategic importance to Russia as the two states share a border more than 6500 km long which lacks proper demarcation and border control. Both Kazakhstan and Kyrgyzstan are continuing close military cooperation with Russia and stress the importance of this cooperation for their national defence. They participate in the CIS Common Air Defence System and since May 1996 air defence units have been operating jointly.[31] For this purpose small contingents of Russian military personnel are still present in Kazakhstan. However, it is a sign of Kazakhstan's security reorientation that in spite of its fairly close military cooperation with Russia Kazakhstan also stresses the importance of cooperation with the PfP.[32] Kazakhstan, Kyrgyzstan and Uzbekistan have declared that the Central Asian peacekeeping battalion (Centrasbat) can only be used in a conflict if a UN mandate exists. There are still Russian border troops along the Kazakh–Chinese border, but they are gradually being replaced by national Kazakh border troops.

Kyrgyzstan, squeezed geographically between much larger states, continues its military cooperation with Russia and the CIS states. Nevertheless, it gives great importance to cooperation with the PfP. A small contingent of Russian military forces is still present in the country related to Kyrgyzstan's participation in the CIS Common Air Defence System. In January 1999 a Kyrgyz national border service was set up and national border troops gradually replaced Russian border guards until they left Kyrgyzstan in the end of 1999.[33] Russian assistance was limited thereafter to the training of Kyrgyz border guards.[34] However, the 1999 incursion of terrorists onto its territory clearly demonstrated Kyrgyzstan's vulnerability.

In contrast to the general picture in Central Asia, Russian cooperation with Tajikistan strengthened during the late 1990s. The most volatile of all the Central Asian states, torn by civil war and with a regime that would have fallen several years ago without Russian support, Tajikistan became Russia's major ally in the region. Russia intervened in the civil war and in 1993 the Russian 201st Motor Rifle Division, already deployed in Tajikistan, was reorganized into a 'peacekeeping force'. The peace agreement signed in June 1997 by the conflicting parties—the regime of President Emomali Rakhmonov and the UTO—changed the prospects for a future Russian military presence. The withdrawal of Uzbek, Kyrgyz and Kazakh peacekeeping units from Tajikistan in 1998 changed the character of the so-called CIS collective peacekeeping troops, and in June 2000 the CIS mandate formally ended.

To guarantee a future Russian military presence in Tajikistan a treaty was agreed on in April 1999 between the two countries by which the 201st Division will be reorganized into a Russian military base. The treaty, which will last for 10 years, has not yet been ratified by the Russian

Duma. Prime Minister Putin declared in November 1999 that 'Russia's troops and border units will be here as long as circumstances require'.[35] Following Putin's visit an agreement was concluded on setting up Russian military installations in Tajikistan for tracking satellites and aircraft.[36]

There is in general a consensus in Moscow that Tajikistan is important to Russian security and national interests. More Russian troops were concentrated there than in any other conflict on CIS territory. In 1996 a draft proposal for a Russian military withdrawal was discussed in the Duma, but was turned down; instead Russian policy was revised in favour of a political compromise between the parties to the conflict. Reasons given for maintaining troops in Tajikistan have included the need to guarantee stability inside Tajikistan, the danger of 'Islamic fundamentalism' spreading into Central Asia, and the fact that Tajikistan's borders are open for the transit of narcotics and weapons. When the 1999 treaty on a Russian military base was announced, the wider task of contributing to stability in the whole Central Asian region was also assigned to the Russian troops.

Control of the 1400-km long Tajik–Afghan border, along which a large contingent of Russian border troops remains, is a high priority for Russia. Nevertheless, reductions have been made since the peace agreement was signed. In late 1997 the number of troops was reduced from 16,000 to 14,500 and by July 1999 there were only 11,000.[37] Russia transferred the responsibility for protecting some stretches of the border to its Tajik counterparts.[38]

Except in Tajikistan Russia has played no role in guaranteeing the domestic security of the Central Asian states. There was no legal framework for intervention by Russian troops in any Central Asian country unless specifically invited in by the government concerned. The May 1998 agreement between Russia, Uzbekistan and Tajikistan on 'preventing the spread of aggressive fundamentalism and extremism in the region' therefore indicated something new.

The incursion by Uzbek Islamists in August 1999 into Kyrgyzstan stimulated Russian efforts to build security and military cooperation with these three Central Asian states.[39] Under the banner of the struggle against 'international terrorism', Russia introduced a new basis for cooperation. At the emergency session of the CIS Council of Defence Ministers in Moscow on 15 September 1999, with ministers from Russia, Uzbekistan, Kyrgyzstan, Tajikistan, Kazakhstan, Armenia and Belarus participating, Putin announced the establishment of an 'anti-criminal coalition' to deal with extremists 'everywhere from the Caucasus to the Pamirs'.[40] The CIS summit in January 2000 agreed on the need to work out an interstate programme on joint measures to combat extremism, terrorism and organized crime.[41] The CIS summit in June 2000 adopted such a programme and agreed to create an anti-terrorist centre.

The Central Asian states remained reluctant to commit themselves to the creation of permanent structures under Russian leadership or 'joint rapid-deployment anti-terrorist forces' under the Treaty of Collective Security as was suggested by the Russian government in November 1999.[42] Yet they participated in operational training. In late October and early November 1999 a joint command-and-staff exercise, Commonwealth Southern Shield-99, was conducted with troops from the same four states —Russia, Kyrgyzstan, Tajikistan and Uzbekistan. The scenario envisaged a resolution by CIS heads of state as the 'legal basis' for a collective decision by defence ministers to launch a joint military operation. Its mission was summed up as the 'liquidation of bandit–terrorist gangs penetrating from nearby states into Kyrgyzstan's Osh Region and Uzbekistan's Ferghana Region or forming in those territories'.[43] It was followed up by the CIS Southern Shield 2000 exercise in early April 2000, which aimed at preventing military incursion by extremists from Afghanistan into Central Asia.[44] For the first time troops from all member states of the CIS Treaty of Collective Security participated, plus Uzbekistan, in combat training.[45] In October 2000 the summit meeting of the Treaty of Collective Security took the general decision to set up collective forces, to be used against external aggression and for anti-terrorist operations.

By the end of the 1990s the Central Asian states fell into different categories depending on the degree and scope of their cooperation with Russia in this field: (a) Turkmenistan and Uzbekistan, which were outside the CIS Treaty on Collective Security; (b) Kazakhstan and Kyrgyzstan, who remained in the Treaty but were scaling down their participation; and (c) Tajikistan, the close ally. Thus Tajikistan, the weakest link in Central Asia, had become the main ally of Russia in Central Asia, and this indicated the weakness of Russia's position in the region as the century closed. However, by the time Vladimir Putin was inaugurated as president in May 2000 Russia seemed to be increasing its influence and had managed to reorient Uzbekistan into operational military cooperation.

Whether the dynamics from within the region will allow Russian engagement and influence in the region to increase in the long-term perspective remains an open question for the future.

Russia and regional dynamics

Within the Central Asian region there is a great potential for conflicts. With loyalties divided along ethnic, regional and religious lines, conflicts may cut across borders. An ethnically complex population, regional differences, harsh socio-economic conditions and an ongoing Islamic revival create the breeding ground for conflicts and extremism in all the Central Asian countries. In this context some factors are more likely than others to cause conflicts to spread and escalate, thereby changing the main variables of the region. Among these are the 'Tajik factor', the 'Uzbek factor' and the 'Afghan factor'. Russia has tried to control and influence all three of them.

The *'Tajik factor'* follows from the instability of the fragile Tajik society, torn by years of civil war. It threatens a breakdown of society and a radicalization of political forces with consequences for the wider region. The roots of the Tajik civil war were mainly regional, and these divisions remain in society. A religious–political dimension is present as the otherwise moderate Muslim opposition includes some radical Islamist elements. A large Tajik population in both Uzbekistan and Afghanistan adds a wider ethnic dimension to the Tajik factor.

Russia intervened in Tajikistan as civil war erupted in 1992 and together with Uzbekistan helped Rakhmonov to take power the same year. Russia maintained its influence after the peace agreement was signed in June 1997. The agreement made the Islamist forces, which Russia had wanted to destroy, a partner of Russia's ally, the Tajik Government. In the 1999 presidential election Rakhmonov was re-elected in unfair elections and in the parliamentary elections in early 2000 he consolidated his basis of support. The peace process continued but the situation remained extremely volatile.

Russia had used political pressure to make the Rakhmonov regime sign the peace agreement.[46] The implementation of the agreement threatened to create new problems for Russian policy. On the one hand, the presence of Islamist forces in a Central Asian government creates a precedent in Central Asia, and the Russian and Tajik governments were therefore hesitant to implement the agreement. On the other hand, the failure of the peace process could radicalize the UTO and make radical Islam a political force in Tajikistan.[47] The fact that the agreement dealt only with the former warring parties and excludes the northern Leninabad region remains a main weakness. The Leninabad region has a large

Uzbek population, is the economically most developed area of the country, is economically oriented towards Uzbekistan and is cut off from the rest of Tajikistan by high mountains. Excluding it meant reducing Uzbek influence on the peace process. This gave Russia a freer hand over Dushanbe but involved the risk that the prospects for the successful development of the peace process would be reduced. A major problem for Tajikistan remains the lack of government control over large parts of the country, especially its eastern part. This opens its territory for use as a refuge for Islamic fighters from neighbouring countries, as happened in spring 1999 when Uzbek Islamists fled to Tajikistan.

The prospects for Russia influencing the situation in Tajikistan are diminishing. Russia seems determined to maintain its troops there but will have difficulties with this in the future. Tajikistan is situated far away from Russia and Russia has access only via Uzbek and Kyrgyz territory and the vast expanse of Kazakhstan.

The 'Uzbek factor' includes the potential for Uzbekistan to become a regional power in Central Asia, thereby shifting the power balance in the region. It also implies the risk that growing tensions in Uzbek society between the regime and its critics, first and foremost radical Islamists, will complicate the situation for the neighbouring states as well.

With large Uzbek minority groups in Tajikistan and Kyrgyzstan, Uzbekistan keeps an interest in events in these countries. Russia's policy of excluding the northern region of Tajikistan from the peace process contributed to Uzbekistan becoming an outspoken critic of Russia in the region. The Uzbek authorities have been accused of supporting armed rebellions in Tajikistan, including the one led by Colonel Khudoberdiyev, an ethnic Uzbek, in 1998. Khudoberdiyev demanded that the Leninabad region be included in the governing bodies.[48]

Uzbek President Karimov fears the influence of the UTO in Tajikistan, just as he feared his own, more radical, Islamists on Uzbek territory. Even if radical Islam so far remains a limited phenomenon in Central Asia in general, fundamentalist Islam has a stronghold in the densely populated Uzbek part of the Ferghana Valley. The bombs in Tashkent in February 1999 (for which Islamist extremists were blamed) resulted in Karimov's determination to destroy all opposition to his rule, Islamist or non-Islamist. Socio-economic conditions and an unemployment rate of more than 50 per cent among young people in Ferghana provided a breeding ground for popular discontent but also for radical Islam.[49]

Fear of Islamist extremists activated the Uzbek authorities, which during 1999 ordered the Uzbek security services to act on the territories of Kyrgyzstan and Kazakhstan to pursue ethnic Uzbek Wahhabites there.[50] After the 1999 bombings in Tashkent Uzbekistan closed the Tajik–Uzbek border and the authorities referred to reports of a Tajik connection in the bombings.[51] When in summer 1999 Uzbek Islamists left Tajikistan, where they had found refuge, and in August entered south Kyrgyzstan and took control of mountain villages and hostages close to the Tajik border, the Kyrgyz authorities responded with force and the Uzbek authorities actively assisted them in their response. Uzbek aircraft bombed the area, with permission from the Kyrgyz authorities, but also bombed villages on the Tajik side of the border, which led to protests from the Tajik Government.[52] Karimov criticized the Kyrgyz authorities for not demonstrating greater urgency and 'resolution' in resisting the militants.[53]

In August 2000 a new offensive by Uzbek Islamists was initiated in southern Kyrgyzstan and in Uzbekistan proper. In Uzbekistan three areas were infiltrated—in the south near Tajikistan, and in the east close to Kyrgyzstan, and also to Kazakhstan.[54]

The internal problems of Uzbekistan thus became a factor of instability for its neighbours. Simultaneously the Uzbek authorities' readiness to carry on the struggle against 'terrorists' outside the national borders demonstrated Uzbekistan's potential and determination to act as a strong power in the region.

Russia has tried to counter Uzbek influence in the region, in Tajikistan as well as in Kyrgyzstan, but also to find a common ground for cooperation with Uzbekistan. The struggle against religious extremism and international terrorism offered a common denominator. Russia's capacity to influence the Uzbek factor in the long run seems, however, to be very limited.

The 'Afghan factor' is another source of instability and of the spread of radical Islam into Central Asia.[55] There was indirect reference to the turmoil in Afghanistan as a threat to Central Asia when in September 1993 Russia, Kazakhstan, Kyrgyzstan and Uzbekistan decided to set up the CIS collective peacekeeping force in the Tajik civil war. At that time Russia, keeping a low profile with regard to Afghan internal affairs, supported the government of President Burhanuddin Rabbani, which assumed power as a result of the negotiations in the early 1990s after the Soviet forces left Afghanistan.

The Taliban takeover of Kabul in September 1996 changed the Afghan political scene. Russia reacted strongly and tried to rally the Central Asian states against the threat of the Taliban crossing the border into Central Asia and to use the situation to encourage Russian military integration with Central Asian states.[56] The Central Asian reaction was not as expected. Turkmenistan refrained from any joint measures, referring to its status as a neutral country, calling the issue an internal Afghan one, and trying instead to find a role as a possible arbitrator between the warring Afghan factions. Kazakhstan displayed concern but since its frontiers are far from Afghanistan this concern was less urgent than that of Uzbekistan, Kyrgyzstan or Tajikistan.

When the Taliban advanced north in the summer and autumn of 1996 Uzbekistan initiated active measures to fortify its southern frontier. At that time Russia's General Staff, in cooperation with Uzbekistan's Defence Ministry, began to elaborate plans to resist possible aggression by the Taliban. Over the following years Russia assisted Uzbekistan in equipping the military forces of Dostum, the Afghan war leader and ethnic Uzbek, opposed to Taliban rule. However, when areas controlled by Dostum in northern Afghanistan were taken over by the Taliban in 1998 and Dostum was ousted, Uzbekistan stopped referring to a 'Taliban threat'. In August 1998, Uzbekistan joined Turkmenistan in claiming that the war in Afghanistan was of a domestic character and that the only real reason for concern was the possible influx of fugitives to the CIS countries, and Uzbekistan became a firm supporter of a negotiated solution to the war.[57] Russia, which had had common interests with both Uzbekistan and Iran to oust the Taliban from power in Kabul, thus lost the chance of influencing the situation in Kabul with the help of Tashkent.

Russia maintained its support for the Afghan war leader Ahmad Shah Massoud, who still controlled a small part of northern Afghanistan, in his struggle against the Taliban. Russian analysts explained the continued Russian support for Massoud and refusal to recognize Taliban rule by Massoud's support for national reconciliation in Tajikistan.[58] There is an 'Afghan factor' in Tajikistan, therefore, which Russia seeks to control.

The Islamist attacks in 1999 and 2000 increased Russia's concern about Afghanistan as a refuge for terrorists in a belt from Chechnya over Central Asia into Xinjiang in China. As the Taliban in autumn 2000 threatened to oust Massoud's forces from northern Afghanistan, Russia nervously responded. In May 2000 official Russian representatives, among them Sergei Ivanov, Secretary of the mighty Russian Security Council, did not exclude the possibility of air strikes against Afghanistan.[59] The threats of air strikes were criticized by Uzbek President Karimov and were not carried out.

The complicated ethnic composition of Tajikistan, Uzbekistan and Afghanistan with their large diasporas encourages ideas of joining together the different ethnic kin in greater states. Such ideas constitute a threat to existing state borders. The 1994 report by the Russian Foreign Intelligence Service mentioned the threat from political forces which wanted to separate northern Afghanistan and include it together with Tajikistan in a new state entity.[60] With twice as many Tajiks living in Afghanistan as in Tajikistan, and significant minorities in Uzbekistan, a 'greater Tajikistan' would create a continuous Persian-speaking belt from the borders of China to the Persian Gulf, 'a belt that would rival the Turkish belt to the north'.[61] In Uzbekistan unofficial Pan-Turkic ideas in favour of a 'greater Uzbekistan' or 'Turkestan' give rise to worry and concern among neighbouring states. In the Russian political debate it has been argued that Russia has to balance between these two political–cultural spheres.[62] The offensives by radical Islamists in Kyrgyzstan and Uzbekistan raised the fear of the prospect of an Islamic state being created around the Ferghana Valley, covering Central Asia, northern Afghanistan and Chinese Xinjiang.

Russia's ability to influence these regional dynamics has been reduced. The Tajik, Uzbek and Afghan factors create dynamics in the region which may easily escape control, and their complexity works to further undermine Russia's influence in Central Asia.

Russia and the strategic scene in Central Asia

Russia's policy on the international level in Central Asia can be understood in the context of its efforts to maintain regional stability and to prevent 'outsiders' from gaining influence in the Central Asian states.

Russia's relations with Iran, Turkey and China normalized after the break-up of the Soviet Union. The former ideologically based division was gone, and the fact that Russia no longer shared borders with Iran and Turkey, and that the border with China was now shorter, contributed to a relaxation of relations. During the 1990s, however, a new element of rivalry entered as these states became potential competitors of Russia for influence in Central Asia.

It was important to Russia to create an understanding among other regional powers that its strategic and national interests in Central Asia must be respected. Russia watched with concern the change in the strategic situation in the Caspian region and Central Asia as the USA became engaged in the region. Investments first of all in the exploitation of oil and gas and the prospects of new transport routes began to influence the foreign policy orientation of the region.

As early as 1994 the report by the Russian Foreign Intelligence Service accused US policy of trying to weaken and isolate Russia on former Soviet territory. At that time this view was not yet the predominant one in the Russian leadership. But by November 1999, when Russian Defence Minister Igor Sergeyev argued that 'Western policy constitutes a challenge to Russia, a challenge aimed at weakening its international positions and edging it out of the strategically important regions of the world, primarily from the Caspian region, Transcaucasia and Central Asia', his words reflected a widespread opinion within the Russian political elite.[63] The US engagement in the Caspian region and Central Asia stimulated a Russian rapprochement with Iran and China, which made the latter states more disposed to respect Russian interests in Central Asia.

Iran is an important actor in the wider Central Asian region. At the time of the break-up of the Soviet Union, the Islamic revolution in Iran seemed to Moscow to constitute a serious threat. Iranian influence was feared when Russia intervened in Tajikistan as civil war erupted there in 1992. This initial phase of distant relations between Russia and Iran during Boris Yeltsin's presidency did not last. When Iranian President Rafsanjani toured Central Asia in October 1993, Radio Moscow stated that Iran had given up exporting Islamic fundamentalism and was instead seeking mutually beneficial commercial ties with all the countries in the region.[64] Iran did not exploit the turbulence in Central Asia or in Tajikistan. Instead it kept a low profile on ideological issues and tried to develop economic and cultural relations with the Central Asian states.

The ethnic composition of Iran contributes to its interest in maintaining stability in the whole Caspian Sea region. Almost one-third of its population is ethnically Azeri and there is also a relatively large group of ethnic Turkmen. With a 'Moscow-centric' policy, Iran became more understanding of Russia's interests in the region, and Russia in turn accepted a greater role for Iran in Central Asia. Iran played an important role when the inter-Tajik negotiations started in April 1994. Moscow thus became 'cognizant of the fact that a more balanced Moscow policy in Central Asia (and also the Persian Gulf) needs a more balanced policy towards Tehran'.[65] Russia and Iran gradually moved towards a closer relationship on the basis of pragmatic and strategic considerations.[66]

During the late 1990s, the growing US influence in the Caspian area contributed to a common understanding between Russia and Iran. The US policy of isolating Iran prevents the construction of major new oil and gas pipelines across Iran. Furthermore, Russia and Iran share a fear of the consequences of the Taliban maintaining control of Afghanistan.

Russia, however, found itself in a delicate situation. On the one hand it denied US claims that Russian nuclear and missile technology was illicitly being exported to Iran and sought commercial advantage from building nuclear power plants in Iran.[67] On the other hand it did not want to antagonize the USA, which has a crucial voice in international credit institutions. The Russian Government was therefore careful to maintain a balance in its approach to Iran. When the then Foreign Minister Kozyrev visited Tehran in 1993, he first called Iran a 'strategic partner', but after his visit stressed carefully that friendship with Iran need not be based on an anti-Western or anti-American policy.[68] This explicit denial that Russian friendship with Iran is directed against the USA has been repeated.

At the end of 1998 the Russian Duma declared Russia's interest in strengthening cooperation with Iran.[69] The Iran lobby within Russia, the core of which formerly consisted of communists and supporters of Vladimir Zhirinovsky with a strong anti-Western leaning, came to attract new groups. These groups were not driven by anti-Western sentiments, but instead included such people as the 'oligarch' Boris Berezovsky.

While most analysts have pointed to the common interests of Russia and Iran and noted the improvement in bilateral relations,[70] some have also noted the risk of competition for influence in Central Asia between the two states in the future. The visit by Iranian President Khatami to Italy in spring 1999 led to Russian media concern that a possible thaw in US–Iranian relations would have negative effects on Russian–Iranian relations. Radzhab Safarov, an expert in the Russian Duma, expressed concern that improved relations between Iran and the West would have as a result that Iran 'without any special care for Russia activates its national-religious policy on the territory of the former Soviet Union'.[71]

China. The normalization of relations between Russia and China was already initiated during the Gorbachev era. As pointed out in the chapter by Guangcheng Xing, in 1996 and 1997 agreements on border demarcation and confidence-building measures were signed between China, Russia and three Central Asian states—Kazakhstan, Kyrgyzstan and Tajikistan—in Shanghai. An arms reduction component to this process of confidence building was agreed in April 1997. The Russian Government's strategy with regard to economic relations with China shifted after 1993 to a focus on key industries such as energy, nuclear power, heavy machinery and defence.[72] Arms exports came to play a particularly important role.

To a great extent the improved relations between Russia and China result from their mutual concern to maintain regional stability in Central Asia. For China, Central Asia is an unpredictable zone from which Turkic nationalism and Islamist ideologies could radiate into Xinjiang. Mutual interests contributed to a regular framework being set up since 1996 by Kazakhstan, Kyrgyzstan, Tajikistan, China and Russia—the 'Shanghai Five'. In July 1999 they agreed to establish a permanent mechanism for high-level meetings on security issues in order to discuss such items as cross-border crime and illegal drug trafficking, but also transport cooperation and economic collaboration.[73] The common concern of fighting 'international terrorism and separatism' is clearly reflected in joint declarations and coordinated measures, especially since the Bishkek summit of August 1999.[74]

During the 1990s the issue of growing Western, and above all US, influence in Central Asia became prevalent in Chinese as well as Russian discussions. On this point there was a considerable degree of convergence between Chinese and Russian evaluations of a unipolar post-cold war world dominated by the USA. Russia and China are both interested in a stable Central Asia beyond Western influence and viewed each other as a factor of stability in this context.[75]

In the Russian debate during the 1990s there were voices in favour of a Russian rapprochement with China as an alternative to a foreign policy based primarily on developing relations with the West. During his visit to Beijing in November 1992, President Yeltsin announced that 'developing Russian–Chinese relations has priority in Russia's foreign relations'. In April 1996 this was further elevated to a proposal for a 'strategic partnership for the 21st century', which was accepted by China.

NATO intervention in Kosovo moved Russia and China closer together on strategic issues. Foreign Minister Igor Ivanov's visit to China in June 1999 was followed by statements on the 'common point of view' of the two countries 'on almost all international problems'.[76] Yeltsin's visit to Beijing in November 1999 further indicated this common interest. In Russia there are circles, especially in the military, that support the idea of an anti-Western alliance with China. However, neither country has opted for a relationship that directly challenges Western interests. More pragmatic considerations outweigh such strategic thinking. Chinese and Russian economic relations with the USA far outweigh bilateral relations between China and Russia.[77]

There also is a competitive element in Russian–Chinese relations in Central Asia. Its geography, size and long borders with Kazakhstan, Kyrgyzstan and Tajikistan make China a natural partner for these states. This has also been pointed out by voices in the Russian debate. China has developed into a major trade partner for Kyrgyzstan and Kazakhstan and has signed an agreement for the development of plans for a 3000-km long oil pipeline from Kazakhstan to Xinjiang, with a possible extension to the Chinese coast for transport on to Japan.[78] If this pipeline is ever built, in the long term Russia and Central Asia (Kazakhstan and Turkmenistan) may become competitors in exporting natural gas and oil to China.[79] If it is never built, competition for strategic influence over Central Asian states may prevail in Russian–Chinese relations.

Turkey. In the Russian political debate there has been a strong streak of Turkophobia since the break-up of the Soviet Union. Russia's nervousness about Turkish influence mainly reflects concerns about the Caucasus region rather than Central Asia. In spite of the fact that Central Asia (except for Tajikistan) is an area of Turkic language and culture, Turkey plays less of a strategic role in Central Asia than in the South Caucasus.

Russia's economic and energy relations with Turkey are expanding. Turkey is also a major player in the 'great game' of future pipeline routes to transport oil from the Caspian Sea. The Turkish proposal for an oil pipeline from Baku to Ceyhan has become a serious option for the future at the same time as Russia's route from Baku to Novorossiisk has become less feasible. Turkey already plays a crucial role for Russian oil exports as this oil passes through the Bosporus Straits, and can limit Russian tanker traffic through the straits. As Turkey is a NATO country its security cooperation with Central Asian and Caucasian states in the PfP programme is evaluated by Russia in the context of NATO.

Russia watches with concern the increasing engagement of external powers in Central Asia, especially that of the USA and Turkey. Even if there are grounds for competition and rivalry, as these states may become influential in Central Asia, there is also a basis for mutual understanding, especially between Russia, China and Iran. Not only do they share an interest in stability in the region; China and Iran also recognize Russia's principal interests in the region. The growing Western influence in

Central Asia has also become a factor for rapprochement between these states. So far, however, there are no conditions for a strategic anti-Western alliance emerging between Russia, China and Iran in the Central Asian context. Neither the Russian Government nor the governments of the other two states seem to be prepared for such an alliance.

Prospects for the future

Russia is losing its former role as the 'security manager' in Central Asia. In the 1990s it failed to build a voluntary security community with the Central Asian states. Instead, Russia and the Central Asian states developed diverging identities, values and interests. Russia offered traditional military cooperation and assistance in meeting external threats, the perception of which was no longer shared by the Central Asian states. Only three of the five states continued military cooperation within the CIS and the strongest state in the region, Uzbekistan, was not one of them. Russian military troops remained only in Tajikistan and Russian border guard troops in Tajikistan and Kazakhstan. Russia was left with the weakest of all the Central Asian states, Tajikistan, as its main military ally.

The attacks by Uzbek Islamists in 1999 and 2000 partly changed the situation. Russia managed a rapprochement with Uzbekistan and strengthened its security cooperation with Kyrgyzstan and Kazakhstan. Cooperation in fighting religious extremism and international terrorism provides at least a temporary impetus to military cooperation, but hardly to long-term cooperation or integration. Russia has a very limited capacity for assisting the Central Asian states in response to the most important factor for internal security—social and economic development. Russia's resource constraints limit the contribution it can make to sustainable economic development in the region. Failing an increase in trade and with the challenge of new options for the export of Central Asian oil and gas, Russia's economic influence in the region will weaken further. Russia is losing its capacity to influence the dynamics of the region—the most important of which are the 'Tajik factor', the 'Uzbek factor' and the 'Afghan factor'. The Uzbek factor in the politics of neighbouring countries—both Tajikistan and Kyrgyzstan—is growing. So far Russia has been able to control the Tajik factor, but this is possible only as long as the peace process between the former warring parties continues. In the long run the Afghan factor cannot be used to rally the Central Asian states in favour of Russian-led military cooperation.

Even if Russia's relations with Iran and China have improved and these states have been brought closer through a common concern about the growing Western influence in the region, anti-Western alliances seem unlikely. There seems to be no interest on the part of any of these other governments in provoking a reaction from the USA by creating such an alliance.

Russia's disregard of Western criticism of its efforts to bring Chechnya under control by military means in late 1999 and early 2000 demonstrated a preparedness to act forcefully when perceived core national interests were threatened. The Russian Government demonstrated firmness in dealing with Islamic terrorism in Kyrgyzstan in 1999 and 2000. However, Russia's preoccupation with its domestic problems, above all in the North Caucasus, means that scarce resources have to be devoted to domestic problems that are more urgent than concerns in Central Asia. The trend towards Russian disengagement from the region seems difficult to reverse for any Russian government in the foreseeable future. A major crisis or conflict in Central Asia in which the US and Western governments refrain from becoming involved would provide Russia with an opening to shift the security policy orientations of the key Central Asian states once again in its favour. Whether Russia's reduced capabilities would allow it to use such an opportunity successfully is a different question.

The changes which have taken place in the region since the break-up of the Soviet Union mean that Russia will have difficulty in restoring its position in Central Asia of the early 1990s as a dominant state and security 'guarantor' or 'manager'. Yet Russia remains a natural partner for Central Asian states, because of its geographical location, its long transparent border, and various shared security problems. As President Putin has argued, an economically strong Russia will be an attractive partner for cooperation with the Central Asian states. However, for the next five to 10 years Russia will be preoccupied with its own domestic problems. In this period Russia may realistically need to accept a role as one among a number of influential states which can contribute towards the creation of a new security framework in Central Asia.

Notes

1. Lena Jonson, *Russia and Central Asia: A New Web of Relations* (London: Royal Institute of International Affairs, 1998).

2. Interview with Nazarbayev in *Nezavisimaya gazeta*, 16 January 1997.

3. See Yeltsin's speech to Parliament in *Rossiiskaya gazeta*, 25 February 1994.

4. 'The Strategic Course of Russia in Relations with the CIS Member States', presidential decree, 14 September 1995. *Diplomaticheskii vestnik*, no. 10 (October 1995).

5. Central Asia has been regarded as important for Russia first and foremost from a strategic standpoint ever since these territories were conquered in the 19th century.

6. 'Rossiya i SNG: Nuzhdaetsya li v Korrektirovke Pozitsiya Zapada?', *Rossiiskaya gazeta*, 22 September 1994.

7. 'O Natsionalnoi Bezopasnosti. Poslanie Prezidenta RF Federalnumu Sobraniyu', *Nezavisimaya gazeta*, 14 June 1996.

8. 'Politika Natsionalnoi Bezopasnosti Rossiiskoi Federatsii (1996–2000)', *NG-Stsenarii*, no. 2 (May 1996).

9. 'Kontseptsiya Natsionalnoi Bezopasnosti Rossiiskoi Federatsii', *Nezavisimoe voennoe obozrenie*, 14 January 2000; and 'Voennaya Doktrina Rossiiskoi Federatsii: Proekt', *Krasnaya zvezda*, 9 October 1999.

10. *Voennaya mysl* (special issue), May 1992.

11. Mohiaddin Mesbahi, 'Russian Foreign Policy towards Central Asia: the Emerging Doctrine' in Ingmar Oldberg, ed., *Priorities in Russian Foreign Policy: West, South, East? Proceedings of a conference in Stockholm, 3 June 1996*, FOA rapport, R-97-00391-180 (Stockholm: Swedish National Defence Research Establishment (FOA), 1997).

12. Irina D. Zviagelskaya and Vitali V. Naumkin, 'Non-Traditional Threats, Challenges, and Risks in the Former Soviet South' in Rajan Menon, Yurii Fedorov and Ghia Nodia, eds, *Russia, The Caucasus and Central Asia: The 21st Century Security Environment*, Eurasia in the 21st Century, vol. 3 (Armonk, N.Y.: M. E. Sharpe, 1999).

13. Timothy Heleniak, 'Going Home: Migration among the Soviet Successor States', *Analysis of Current Events* 9, no. 6 (June 1997).

14. *Jamestown Monitor*, no. 4 (6 January 2000).

15. President Nazarbayev of Kazakhstan said that the CIS was falling apart and its members should seek greater cooperation. He also stated that trade turnover between the CIS countries had fallen by 70% since 1991 and that only 5–10% of the documents signed within the CIS framework were being implemented. Interfax Kazakhstan in BBC Monitoring, *Inside Central Asia*, issue 293 (20–26 September 1999).

16. BBC Monitoring, *Inside Central Asia*, issue 301 (15–21 November 1999).

17. *Jamestown Monitor*, no. 226 (7 December 1999).

18. S. Z. Zhiznin and P. I. Rodionov, 'Energicheskaya Diplomatiya v Kaspiisko-Chernomorskom Regione (Gazovye Aspekty)', *Diplomaticheskii vestnik*, no. 6 (June 2000), pp. 79–87.

19. Arkady Dubnov, 'Best Wishes for CIS Security', *Vremya MN*, 22 January 1999, p. 6 in *Former Soviet Union 15 Nations: Policy and Security*, January 1999, p. 31.

20. See, for example, Mohiaddin Mesbahi, 'Russia and the Geopolitics of the Muslim South' in Mohiaddin Mesbahi, ed., *Central Asia and the Caucasus after the Soviet Union* (Gainesville, Fl.: University Press of Florida, 1995).

21. Speech by Bakhadyr Umarov, Press Secretary of of the Uzbek Foreign Ministry in Vladimir Georgiev, 'Uzbekistan Takes a Separate Stand', *Nezavisimaya gazeta*, 4 February 1999, p. 1.

22. Arkadi Dubnov, 'Uzbekistan is Disengaging from the Tashkent Treaty', *Vremya MN*, 2 February 1999, pp. 1, 6 in *Former Soviet Union 15 Nations: Policy and Security*, February 1999.

23. Andrei Korbut, 'Krizis Sistemy Kollektivnoi Bezopasnosti', *Sodruzhestvo NG*, May 1999, p. 9; and Andrei Korbut, 'Integratsiya s Elementami Dezintegratsii', *Nezavisimoe voennoe obozrenie*, no. 21 (4–10 July 1999).

24. Karen Brutents, 'Rossiya i Aziya', *Nezavisimaya gazeta*, 22 June 1999, p. 8.

25. Yu. Golotyuk, 'Russia Is Joining the Union of the Three', *Izvestiya*, 13 October 1998, p. 1.

26. 'SNG. Khronika Sobytii iyun–iyul 1999', *Sodruzhestvo NG*, no. 7 (July 1999).

27. *Jane's Defence Weekly*, 22 December 1999. See also Mikhail Gerasimov, 'Russia: Relations on Upswing. Moscow's Strategic Partnership with Tashkent Implies Ensuring Mutual Security', *Nezavisimaya gazeta*, 17 December 1999.

28. Gerasimov, *ibid*.

29. Vladimir Georgiev, 'Turmeno-Afganskaya Granitsa Mozhet Stat' Beskontrol'noi', *Nezavisimaya gazeta*, 25 December 1999, p. 5. The two sides have agreed to set up a new treaty on future cooperation but this has not happened so far. BBC Monitoring, *Inside Central Asia*, issue 301 (15–21 November 1999). At most the Russian border troops in Turkmenistan numbered 1900 men. BBC Monitoring, *Inside Central Asia*, issue 282 (5–11 July 1999), p. 3.

30. Following talks in Ashgabat with the head of NATO's Partnership Coordination Center, the Turkmen leadership finalized and agreed to sign an individual country programme for 1999–2000 within the framework of the PfP. *Jamestown Monitor*, no. 92 (12 May 1999).

31. Interview with Kazakh Defence Minister in Vadim Soloviev and Sergei Sokut, 'The Safety of the Commonwealth Is Our Common Cause', *Nezavisimoe voennoe obozrenie*, no. 42 (6–12 November 1998), p. 1.

32. See the interview with the Kyrgyz Chief of Staff who answered the question on CIS cooperation with regard to conflicts by referring to the PfP. Aleksandr Alf, 'Rossiya—Glavny Partner', *Nezavisimaya voennoe obozrenie*, no. 27 (16–22 July 1999), p. 3.

33. In the case of Kyrgyzstan the Russian side decided to withdraw.

34. In 1998 there were 3000 Russian servicemen in Kyrgyzstan along the 1000-km Kyrgyz–Chinese border and at the border control at Manas airport in Bishkek. Before 1998 they also protected the Kyrgyz–Tajik border. Saidkasym Kiyampur, 'Russian Border Guards Will Leave Kyrgizia', *Russkii Telegraf*, 26 August 1998, p. 8. Russia will transfer practically all its military equipment and vehicles to Kyrgyzstan, except for certain types of arms.

35. Russian TV in BBC Monitoring, *Inside Central Asia*, issue 301 (15–21 November 1999).

36. Iranian radio, Reuters, 21 November 1999.

37. According to the Russian commander, Major-General Aleksandr Markin, in the Russian border troops in Tajikistan 14% of the officers, 40% of the ensigns and 100% of the rank and file are Tajik nationals. Interfax, 22 July 1999 in BBC Monitoring, *Inside Central Asia*, issue 284 (19–25 July 1999), p. 2.

38. Rakhmonov has signed a decree stipulating the resubordination of Tajik border guards to the operational command of the Russian border guards in the event of emergency. Yurii Golotyuk, 'Russia Will Keep Its Military Units at Tajik–Afghani Border', *Izvestiya*, 23 October 1998, p. 2. The Director of the Russian Federal Border Service, Colonel-General Konstantin Totskii, said in October 1998 that the Tajik authorities were asked to prepare themselves to independently protect the border more actively. Alexander Korostkii, 'Russia Is Reducing Its Presence on CIS Borders', *Segodnya*, 24 October 1998, p. 2.

39. According to an agreement of 2 October 1999 signed in Bishkek, Russia, Uzbekistan, Tajikistan, Kazakhstan, Armenia and Belarus undertook to provide weapons and ammunition to the Kyrgyz military. BBC Monitoring, *Inside Central Asia*, issue 294 (27 September–3 October 1999). Russia provided the Kyrgyz Army with military equipment and brought equipment and weapons to Osh for the fight against the Islamists. ITAR-TASS in *Inside Central Asia*, issue 293 (20–26 September 1999).

40. Yurii Golotyuk, 'Russia Is Not in a Hurry to Open a "Second Front"', *Izvestiya*, 22 September 1999, p. 3.

41. Ostankino Radio Mayak, Moscow 26 January 2000/BBC Monitoring, *International Reports*, 26 January 2000.

42. ITAR-TASS in *Jamestown Monitor*, 5 November 1999, no. 206.

43. ITAR-TASS in *Jamestown Monitor*, 5 November 1999, no. 206.

44. 'Ex-Soviet States to Hold Anti-Terrorist Exercise', Reuters, 20 March 2000.

45. Vladimir Georgiev, *Nezavisimaya gazeta*/Reuter, 7 April 2000.

46. On Russian policy in the Tajik civil war, see Lena Jonson, *The Tajik War: a Challenge to Russian Policy*, Discussion Paper 74 (London: Royal Institute of International Affairs, 1998).

47. Saodat Olimova, 'Political Islam in Tajikistan' in Lena Jonson and Murad Esenov, eds, *Political Islam and Conflicts in Russia and Central Asia*, Conference report (Stockholm: Swedish Institute of International Affairs, 1999).

48. Dimitrii Petryakov, 'What Stands behind the Mutiny in Khudjand on November 4–5 of 1998' in *Former Soviet Union 15 Nations: Policy and Security*, November 1998, pp. 29–32; Oleg Odnokolenko, 'Dushanbe Accuses Uzbekistan and Russia of Supporting Rebels', *Segodnya*, 10 November 1998, p. 3; and Viktoria Panfilova, 'The Controversies Have Deep Roots', *Nezavisimaya gazeta*, 25 November 1999, p. 5.

49. Bakhtiyar Babadzhanov, 'The Ferghana Valley: Source or Victim of Islamic Fundamentalism?' in Lena Jonson and Murad Esenov, eds, *op. cit.*; and Igor Lunev, 'Uzbekistan', *Nezavisimaya gazeta*, 17 April 1999, p. 5.

50. In an interview Kyrgyz President Askar Akayev commented on this behaviour by Uzbekistan more or less in terms of a small country having to accept this kind of act by a larger neighbour. Igor Rotar, 'Neprostoe Sosedstvo', *Nezavisimaya gazeta*, 2 July 1999, p. 5. Similar problems along the Uzbek–Kazakh border led the authorities of the Makhtaralskii border region in Kazakhstan to request that a military unit be deployed there. Igor Rotar, 'Mezhdu Otvergnutym Proshlym i Tumannym Budushchim', *Sodruzhestvo NG*, no. 7 (July 1999). See also Vladimir Georgiev, 'Moskva Obrela Novogo Soyuznika', *Nezavisimaya gazeta*, 17 April 1999, pp. 1, 5.

51. Gulfira Gayeva and Yurii Chubchenko, 'Russia Names Its Principal Ally in Central Asia', *Kommersant Daily*, 26 February 199, p. 3. *Former Soviet Union 15 Nations: Policy and Security*, February 1999, p. 85.

52. BBC Monitoring, *Inside Central Asia*, issue 294 (27 September–3 October 1999).

53. Uzbek President Karimov said: 'These things are happening because of the weak policy carried out by the Kyrgyz government. This kind of humane attitude towards terrorists will lead to this kind of incident'. BBC Monitoring, *Inside Central Asia*, issue 301 (15–21 November 1999).

54. *Jamestown Fortnight in Review*, issue 17 (8 September 2000).

55. With large Uzbek and Tajik minorities in northern Afghanistan there is an Uzbek as well as a Tajik factor in Afghan politics.

56. 'Taliban Raises Anxiety in the CIS', *Strategic Analysis*, vol. 19, no. 12 (1997).

57. On the eve of the summit meeting of foreign and defence ministers of the Central Asian Economic Community (CAEC) on 22 August 1998 in Tashkent. Vladimir Mukhin (Professor of the Russian Academy of Military Sciences), 'Extension of the Zone of Taleban's Influence May Significantly Infringe upon Russia's Interests in Central Asia' in *Former Soviet Union 15 Nations: Policy and Security*, August 1998, pp. 18–23.

58. In the words of Russian analyst Alexander Umnov, '[Russia's] assistance to Massoud, whose close contacts with Dushanbe are well known, helps maintain the brittle reconciliation between secular and religious–political forces in Tajikistan, which Russia needs. That is why Moscow supports the Talebin's enemy . . . ' Alexander Umnov, 'Why Does Russia Need Akhmed Shakh Massoud?', *Nezavisimaya gazeta*, 21 November 1998, p. 6.

59. Radio Free Europe/Radio Liberty (RFE/RL), *RFE/RL Newsline*, no. 101 (25 May 2000).

60. 'Nuzhdaetsya li v Korrektirovke Pozitsiya Zapada?', *Rossiiskaya gazeta*, 22 February 1994, p. 6.

61. Anthony Hyman, 'Afghanistan and Central Asia' in Mehdi Mozaffari, ed., *Security Politics in the Commonwealth of Independent States. The Southern Belt* (London: Macmillan, 1997), p. 125.

62. See analyses by Alexander Umnov.

63. Russian NTV, 12 November 1999 in BBC Worldwide Monitoring/Reuter, 12 November 1999.

64. Alvin Z. Rubinstein, 'Moscow and Tehran' in Alvin Z. Rubinstein and Oles M. Smolansky, eds, *Regional Power Rivalries in the New Eurasia. Russia, Turkey and Iran* (New York and London: M. E. Sharpe, 1995).

65. Mohiaddin Mesbahi in Adeed Dawisha and Karen Dawisha (eds), *The Making of Foreign Policy and the New States of Eurasia* (London: M. E. Sharpe, 1995), p. 224.

66. Adam Tarrock writes, 'For example, the catalysts for the present "strategic alliance" are Russia's needs for foreign currency and the desire to have a friendly neighbour to the Muslim states in Central Asia, and Iran's need for Russian arms, new technologies and, perhaps more importantly, for political support at both regional and international levels. In addition, both countries have common security concerns and economic interests in the development of oil and gas in the Caspian Sea'. Adam Tarrock, 'Iran and Russia in "Strategic Alliance"', *Third World Quarterly*, vol. 18 (winter 1997).

67. 'Credible reports continue to suggest that the Russian government has either turned a blind eye to the activities of Russian defense firms in this area or has actually assisted their efforts.' Fred Wehling, 'Russian Nuclear and Missile Exports to Iran', *Nonproliferation Review*, Winter 1999.

68. *Izvestiya*, 1 April 1993.

69. A statement was adopted 'On broader cooperation between the Russian Federation and the Islamic Republic of Iran'. Vitalii Naumkin, 'Rossiya i Iran v Tsentralnoi Azii i Zakavkaze', *Sodruzhestvo NG*, no. 7 (July 1999), p. 12.

70. Israeli scholar Galia Golan writes: 'Nonetheless, the relationship cannot be dismissed as purely tactical. There are abiding geopolitical interests which, barring drastic changes in either country or in the international arena, promise to sustain—possibly even strengthen—the positive relationship that has developed'. Galia Golan, *Russia and Iran: A Strategic Partnership?* Discussion Paper 75 (London: Royal Institute of International Affairs, 1998), p. 54.

71. Radzhab Safarov, 'Tegeran Prinyali na Zapade', *Nezavisimaya gazeta*, 12 March 1999, p. 6.

72. Jennifer Anderson, *The Limits of Sino-Russian Strategic Partnership*, Adelphi Paper 315 (London: International Institute for Strategic Studies, 1997), p. 35.

73. ITAR-TASS, 3 July 1999 in BBC Worldwide Monitoring/Reuter, 3 July 1999.

74. The summit of 25 August 1999 on strengthening security in the region and combating religious and separatist extremism and the international flow of drugs supported the idea of a nuclear-free Central Asia and the plan to revive the ancient Silk Road. The resulting joint declaration can be seen as a warning to the USA and NATO as it spoke of the need for a 'multipolar world' and opposed the use of force on the international scene unless it was sanctioned by the UN Security Council. BBC Monitoring, *Inside Central Asia*, issue 289 (23–29 August 1999).

In December 1999 a permanent body, the Bishkek Group, was set up comprising the chiefs of the law enforcement agencies who will meet at least once a year to coordinate activities with regard to fighting terrorism, separatism and cross-border crime. BBC Monitoring, *Inside Central Asia*, issue 303 (29 November–5 December 1999).

75. Rajan Menon, 'The Strategic Convergence between Russia and China', *Survival*, vol. 39, no. 2 (1997), pp. 101–25; and Yuri Peskov, 'Russia and China: Problems and Prospects of Cooperation with CIS Members in Central Asia', *Far Eastern Affairs*, 1997.

76. ITAR-TASS, 3 June 1999 in BBC Worldwide Monitoring/Reuter, 3 June 1999.

77. Anderson, *op. cit.*; and 'Russia and China. Can a Bear Love a Dragon?', *The Economist*, 26 April 1997.

78. O. Reznikova, 'Tsentralnaya Aziya i Aziatsko-Tikhookeanskii Region', *Mirovaya Ekonomika i Mezhdunarodnye Otnosheniya*, no. 4 (1999), pp. 100–108.

79. Keun-Wook Paik and Jae-Yong Choi, *Pipeline Gas in Northeast Asia: Recent Developments and Regional Perspectives*, Briefing Paper no. 39 (London: Royal Institute of International Affairs, January 1998).

CHAPTER SIX

The United States
and Central Asia

STEPHEN BLANK

Introduction

Central Asia represents a new frontier for the policy of the United States. Since the Central Asian states became independent, US economic, political and military interests there have steadily grown. Until 1994 US interests were restricted to economic and political pursuits; military interests were nowhere in sight.[1] However, that has all changed. The USA now deploys all its instruments of power to establish itself as a major player in Central Asia and across the entire Commonwealth of Independent States (CIS). Still, despite its enormous power, it remains an open question whether US policy can realize those interests and make the United States a 'core state' in the region.

To answer this question we must delineate both the rhetoric and the actuality of US national security policy—a term which better connotes the breadth of policy instruments, economic, political and military, and the scope of US involvement here, than does the traditional term 'foreign policy'. Thus we must realize that the Clinton Administration does not distinguish and has not distinguished between its defence of US values, such as promoting democracy abroad, and more concrete interests.[2] Major works on US policy insist that unless a policy is rooted in American values, even if it serves realpolitik interests of a balance of power, it will nei-

The views expressed here do not necessarily represent those of the US Army, the US Department of Defense or the US Government.

ther succeed nor earn domestic or foreign support.[3] Even if outsiders see a gap between rhetoric and reality, the Administration denies this perception and continues to insist that its policies conform to the promotion of interests and values. This imbrication of today's liberal ideology of globalization, democratization and reform with the use of America's formidable instruments of power applies particularly to Central Asia. Strategic interests, energy access, the denial of a resurgent Russian empire and a value-laden international policy to promote democracy as the main goal appear in both the rhetoric and the actuality of the USA's regional presence, making it difficult to distinguish between the motives of policies towards and programmes to aid Central Asian institutions.[4]

The US vision of Central Asia

The US national security strategy has made the integration of the new independent states into Western economic, political and military institutions and practices the fundamental regional policy aim of the Clinton Administration.[5] Practically speaking, this means that the US regional 'shaping strategy' for the future Central Asian security environment should combine all these forms of power in relations with each country of the region in order to induce them to move towards laws and institutions that provide a framework for market economies and democratizing, if not democratic, polities. As Stephen Sestanovich, Ambassador to the CIS, acknowledges, US policy begins not from an assessment of economic interests but rather from a strategic standpoint.[6] Yet he also simultaneously proclaims that America's highest goal is to create and sustain democratic political institutions.[7] Earlier, Under-Secretary of State Strobe Talbott said that 'job one' was conflict resolution—hardly the same thing, but certainly a worthwhile interest and value.[8] Whatever difference exists between these goals is subsumed in the overriding national security strategy. As a recent Government Accounting Office (GAO) report states,

> Specifically the strategy calls for competitive, market-oriented economies in which the majority of economic resources are privately owned and managed and transparent (open) and accountable governments and the empowerment of citizens, working through civic and economic organizations that ensure broad-based participation in political and economic life.[9]

Similar ideals animate the military relationship. As part of the US shaping strategy, the US military increasingly participates in bilateral relationships and through NATO's Partnership for Peace (PfP) with the Central Asian militaries. This engagement strategy is part of the USA's global strategy, to shape the regional security environment, institutionalize civilian democratic control over the military, as in Latin America, or foster multilateral defence cooperation in South-East Asia. These are key aspects of those regions' multilateral engagement with the United States.[10] The PfP programme, which includes all the Central Asian states as members, shares that focus. As the former NATO Secretary General, Javier Solana, said:

> What we are expanding is a European, indeed Atlantic, civil space. I deliberately include our military arrangements into this definition of 'civic space'. The postwar experience in Western Europe suggests that political and economic progress and security integration are closely linked. Once their security is taken care of, countries can devote themselves with more confidence to their long-term evolution. And a responsible military, firmly embedded in our democratic societies and under civil control, is part and parcel of that civic space, as are the military structures that are transparent, defensive, and multinational.[11]

However, the strategic value of engagement does not end with democratization. It also represents an attempt to work with partner and/or allied armies to provide stable, competent, peacetime military professionalism and enhance both sides' capability for successfully making the transition to war and participating in the initial stages of any future conflict.[12] Certainly that cooperation through joint and multilateral exercises, symposia, training and so on is supposed eventually to produce military forces that can actively collaborate with the United States and NATO in peace operations and are better able to defend their homelands against various kinds of conflicts.

Ideally the promotion of democracy, conflict resolution, civilian democratic control of the armed forces and open market economies should serve not just US values, but also the interests of the Central Asian and US governments. Talbott spelled out the rationale for this approach in a major 1997 speech:

If reform in the nations of the Caucasus and Central Asia continues and ultimately succeeds, it will encourage similar progress in the other newly independent states of the former Soviet Union, including Russia and Ukraine. It will contribute to stability in a strategically vital region that borders China, Turkey, Iran, and Afghanistan, and that has growing economic and social ties with Pakistan and India. The consolidation of free societies, at peace with themselves and each other, stretching from the Black Sea to the Pamir mountains, will open up a valuable trade and transport corridor along the old Silk Road, between Europe and Asia. [On the other hand] . . . If economic and political reform . . . does not succeed, if internal and cross-border conflicts simmer and flare, the region could become a breeding ground of terrorism, a hotbed of religious and political extremism, and a battleground for outright war. It would matter profoundly to the United States if that were to happen in an area that sits on as much as 200 billion barrels of oil.[13]

Thus Talbott outlined some of the vital strategic interests of the United States and the rationale for supporting democratization, open markets and conflict resolution as the most effective way to pursue those interests. He also depicted the situation there as a race between virtuous circles of peace and economic and political reform, on the one hand, and vicious circles of war, strife within and between states, ethnic conflict, authoritarian regimes, poverty and closed or semi-closed economies, on the other. His speech makes clear too that access to energy markets in oil and gas is the most vital US interest in the area.

Indeed, US involvement across the entire Transcaspian has taken off since 1994–95 when Washington conclusively rejected Russia's claims for an energy monopoly. By then the international financial institutions had embraced the so-called Washington consensus and were putting great pressure and sizeable resources into Central Asian and other CIS states to move them along the lines of a basically US model towards liberal markets and democratic governance.[14] The US decision of 1994–95 to keep Russia from monopolizing Central Asian energy holdings reflected the coincidence of two major US policy goals. On the one hand it was closely tied to security and defence issues, to prevent further Russian depredations on the sovereignty and independence of the Central Asian and Transcaucasian states. On the other hand it reflected the success of business interests in persuading the US Government of the centrality of access to oil and Washington's acceptance that for the energy-producing countries their oil and gas offered the only road to economic and political independence and prosperity.[15] Despite constant charges to the contrary, energy is not seen in isolation from US strategy but rather is vitally linked to US security objectives.[16] The 1995 decision reflects that coincidence of objectives.

In February 1995 the United States decided to support pipelines running through Turkey and not Russia. At the time,

> State Department sources have told *Newsweek* that the endorsement reflects a major shift in US policy toward Central Asia. The new approach, coordinated by the National Security Council, is designed to break Russia's grip on Central Asia's oil export. The objective is both to help ensure the survival of independent states in the region and to protect US corporate interests.[17]

By then Washington had already intervened in Central Asia's energy economy by urging Turkmenistan to send gas to Ukraine despite Ukraine's failure or inability to pay for it. Washington also offered Kazakhstan certain guarantees if Moscow 'turned off the oil tap'. This was one of the first decisions by the USA to interpose itself as an arbiter between Russia and the Central Asian states if disputes arose between them over the commonly used Russian pipeline system. In May, 1995 Under-Secretary of Energy William White toured Central Asia, urging the republics to regard themselves as important producers of oil and natural gas and to treat Russia and Iran as rivals.[18] Also in 1995, Glen Rase, head of the State Department's energy policy section, bluntly rejected Russian efforts to dominate the Caspian, stating that Russian talk of condominium there was 'a guarantee of inaction'. He further said that 'The Russian position must not be imposed on the states that prefer a more normal division of the Caspian . . . Washington does not recognize any spheres of influence'.[19]

Since then policy interest has grown almost exponentially. The only constantly functioning inter-agency working group led by the National Security Council monitors Transcaspian energy deposits and trends. US investors are flooding the region with capital, searching for contracts, leverage and influence. The United States has announced its readiness to use its good offices to mediate the dispute on the legal regime for drilling for energy resources in the Caspian Sea. It now insists that any new pipeline must bypass Russia and go from Central Asia, underneath the Caspian Sea, through Azerbaijan and Georgia to Ceyhan on Turkey's Mediterranean coast. Its officials and diplomats are unrelenting in their efforts to achieve this goal.[20] The US commitment to multiple pipelines clearly aims to exclude Russia and Iran as far as possible from dominating (although in Russia's case not necessarily from participating in) all future pipeline decisions. The United States also offered to send peacekeepers to Nagorno-Karabakh as part of an international operation under the Organization for Security and Co-operation in Europe (OSCE) and leads manoeuvres in Kazakhstan and the Black Sea.[21]

Thus, in order to preserve Central Asia and the Caucasus as a 'zone of free competition' and deny either Iran or Russia any lasting hegemony there, Washington has become the arbiter or leader on virtually every local interstate and international issue. These include the Minsk process to negotiate a resolution of the Nagorno-Karabakh conflict and the opening of a 'new Silk Road' and/or East–West trade corridor, in addition to the US involvement with oil and gas pipeline routes. And the focus on energy issues obscures the USA's leading role in the international financial institutions which play a major role in channelling foreign resources to Central Asia. The consuming interest in pipeline routes has also led Washington to adopt public positions on the international status of the Caspian Sea, to arbitrate on or mediate competing Azeri and Turkmen claims, and to take the lead in organizing or guaranteeing regional investment projects.[22]

This process reached its apogee in November 1999 when Washington orchestrated the signature of protocols on the construction of the Baku–Ceyhan pipeline for oil, which bypasses Russia, Iran and the Straits. Washington had led the process through all its stages, arranging financing, ironing out disputes, and winning commitments from as many of the participating states as possible. Contrary to the USA's stated intention that NATO enlargement and associated trends would not further embroil it in all kinds of local issues, the exact opposite is happening. Washington is becoming the main centre of international adjudication and influence for local issues.

The First Lady, Hillary Rodham Clinton, former Energy Secretary Frederico Pena and Vice-President Albert Gore have claimed that proper use of Kazakh energy resources can promote not only stability but even democracy—an outcome not known to be high on Kazakh President Nursultan Nazarbayev's agenda.[23] Washington has also told Georgia that any oil shipped out of the Caspian through its ports should go in part to

Ukraine to alleviate its energy dependence on Russia. Clearly energy and security jointly dominate the agenda as means to achieving broader Westernization, to the point where little pressure is effectively being directed towards democratizing local governments. Political conditionality as a condition of investment, trade and aid is fast losing its visibility, throughout the area and in US policy as well.[24]

US interests and policies are easy to analyse. The United States views three aspects of the Transcaspian equation as crucial: increasing the supply of energy to consumers; excluding Iran from influencing the exploration, shipment, development and marketing of energy products; and preventing any one state from monopolizing the local energy supply. Certain fundamental corollaries flow from these objectives.[25] Officially US policy aims to enhance local states' capability to produce and ship oil abroad; to obtain equal (that is, competitive) access for US energy firms and other firms that want to invest in these republics; to negotiate settlements to local wars; and to create stable, democratic governments as an ultimate outcome of these processes.

The United States strongly opposes Russian efforts to obtain a monopoly and an exclusive sphere of influence over conflict resolution, economies, politics, military agendas and energy supplies in the Caucasus and Central Asia. Indeed, it professes that it simply wishes to counter any regional monopoly and does not see the area as a region for competition with Russia.[26] US officials from President Clinton down reiterate their belief in a 'win-win' solution to the problems of the South Caucasus and Central Asia and deny that they see these regions in terms of competition vis-à-vis Russia.[27] They insist that US policy aims not to divide Central Asia and the South Caucasus into rival spheres of influence or to exclude Russia, but rather at a 'win-win' solution for all parties. Russia and the United States supposedly share a common interest in extracting the region's mineral wealth and prospering from it, and Washington should graciously integrate or include Russia in its plans to integrate the region into the West because its interests are above suspicion.[28] Accordingly the Clinton Administration rejects the concept of a sphere of influence for Russia or anyone else there, while local governments acknowledge that US interests and policies there are much more benevolent than Russian interests appear to be.[29]

Still, support for democratic values and the principles of liberal market economies and polities is hardly disinterested, nor is it as successful as Washington would like to proclaim. Undoubtedly energy policy and programmes of democratic assistance support the US goals of democratization, regional cooperation, conflict resolution and strengthening the region against efforts to create Iranian or Russian spheres of influence.[30] And assisting regional security integration and cooperation through institutions like the Central Asian Battalion (Centrasbat) exemplifies the military dimension of this policy.[31]

Nonetheless Central Asia is torn by conflicts, governed by authoritarians and no more stable now than before—indeed it may well be less stable. US policy must take some of the responsibility for this situation. For example, although the State Department strongly criticized President Nazarbayev's high-handed suppression of opposition to his re-election in 1999, on his next visit to Washington he and his Foreign Minister expressed great satisfaction with the aid they had received and pointed out that the United States is the leading investor in Kazakhstan.[32] Similarly,

> In raw money terms, the quantity of aid disbursed to Kyrgyzstan by the United States annually is meager although Kyrgyzstan is probably the least authoritarian and most forward-looking of the region's states. Yet Uzbekistan, one of the most repressive and economically closed societies of Central Asia, gets much more aid from Washington and the European Union.[33]

Outside observers are naturally disappointed about this, but these facts confirm long-standing US precedents. As Thomas Carothers observed,

> Democracy promotion has not become the central organizing principle of US policy as Clinton's rhetoric often suggests. The Clinton approach in practice is a moderate, semirealist one in which democracy promotion alternately surfaces and submerges depending on the context. Where US economic and security interests correlate with the advance of democracy and a democratic trend is occurring, US policy incorporates democracy promotion. Where US interests necessitate working relationships with non-democratic governments and where no democratic trend is evident, US policy largely eschews it.[34]

Central Asia clearly falls into the latter category. Strategic interests are coming to the fore and few, if any, democratic trends are observable. In part this is due to official repression. But that has bred a situation where the only effective opposition groups are Islamic insurgents or Russian separatists, or disaffected elites which may be critical of their governments but would hardly be reckoned as democrats. US policy reflects those facts just as Carothers predicted. Thus programmes in support of open markets and democracy undertaken by the US Agency for International Development (USAID) have encountered severe difficulties due to government repression, not just the structural consequences of backwardness and Soviet rule.

While the State Department considered privatization of state-owned enterprises the most important element in regional economic transformation, Central Asian governments either retreated from privatization in order to keep their holds over enterprises' 'rents' or never pursued it seriously in the first place.[35] In Kazakhstan and Kyrgyzstan tax collection has not notably improved despite USAID's programmes of technical support and advice for fiscal decentralization and modernization.[36] Similar defects plague programmes for banking reform and reform of intergovernmental fiscal management.[37]

Political democratization has not fared much better. Local governments, except for that of Kyrgyzstan, have impeded US reform activities for democratization, forcing USAID to target other areas where it might achieve positive results. Although USAID tried to finance non-governmental organizations (NGOs), independent media outlets and local governments, its programmes were blocked and have not amounted to very much at all.[38] Surveys of Central Asia therefore report region-wide authoritarian rule, albeit to varying degrees.[39] It is also unlikely that the many security challenges afflicting the region in 1999 will induce liberalization. Probably if anything more repression, not less, will be the outcome.

Energy relations

The USA's standing as Kazakhstan's leading foreign investor reflects the importance of energy-related investments and the critical US interest in securing the unimpeded flow of energy resources from these states to world markets. Apart from US security goals, exports of energy appear (perhaps tragically so in view of the comparative history of other *rentier* states which depended on oil and gas for their foreign currency) to be the only relatively short-term way in which these states can defend their economic, political, and thus strategic independence. Diversification of their foreign economic relations as well as their larger security relations may be the only way out. Such diversification coincides with at least the rhetoric of US energy policy.

Because these governments were catapulted into competitive international relations with few instruments of power or cards in their hands, the intense 'great game' that is now taking place in the area from Europe to China gives them little choice but to stress energy. This competition for leverage over energy and thus the destiny of Central Asia (and the South Caucasus) makes US energy policy a strategic policy in the full sense of the term. As General Anthony Zinni, USMC, Commander-in-Chief of CENTCOM (the US Central Command) has said, access to energy drives all US policy in the region.[40]

Rhetorically, geo-economic rivalry is allegedly supplanting the classical forms of geo-strategic competition, but the intensifying struggle over Caspian energy sources also reveals a much more bare-knuckled and traditional rivalry than mere economic rivalry. For Russia, the United States, Turkey, Iran, Pakistan, China and Eurasia's oil- and gas-producing states, control of those energy sources and of their transport to market means leverage, if not control, over the producer states' destinies. Politics, not economics, dominates current and future decisions about pipelines and major investment projects. Very likely a similar policy process is occurring among all the contenders for influence and leverage over Central Asia.

Since the entire Caspian area is riddled with intrigues and wars, this hard-headed assessment suggests that the pacific, liberal paradigm of geo-economics that dominates much writing about international affairs is misplaced. Notwithstanding its rhetoric about win-win outcomes, the United States in practice does not share the view of an automatically benevolent new world order that is tirelessly proclaimed by many US academics and officials. The growing US involvement in the Caspian region is in the highest degree strategic or even geopolitical and aims to enhance US and not other states' influence. It combines all the traditional instruments of power, superior economic potential and military prowess, and a commitment to integrating the area more fully into the West in terms of both defence and economics. The quest for energy, which is the source of all the talk of a new great game between Russia and the United States, cannot be understood apart from or separated from more traditional competitive geo-strategies aiming to integrate the Transcaspian into a Western or Russian *ecumene*.

Strategic calculations of energy prices and accessibility through pipelines, the uniquely American sensitivity to oil and gas prices, and traditional security issues in Europe, the CIS and the Middle East drive US policy. Economically and politically—particularly in terms of expanding investment and trading opportunities for the new states with the West and devising conflict resolution mechanisms that involve Europe's security organizations—the increase in US interest in the Caspian region coincided with that area's emergence onto Europe's security agenda after 1992.

Western goals entail a break with Russian domination of the southern CIS as a whole. That domination would inevitably diminish regional security by attempting to create, in the face of determined local opposition, an exclusive Russian sphere of influence, perhaps even a restored union, albeit not a Soviet [re]Union. Perhaps equally, if not more importantly, it would mean the practical acceptance of Russia's view that these states have only a diminished sovereignty, an aim fundamentally at odds with the US insistence on preserving their independence as a key policy goal.[41]

Consequently the Caspian region has become perhaps the most important area of direct Western–Russian contention today. Europe put the area on its agenda through the OSCE, and the US determination to prevent Russia gaining a sphere of influence here had become public by 1995. Moreover, after NATO's Kosovo campaign the Russian elites expect NATO to strike at Russian interests here, probably because of the large energy deposits in the region and the handy pretext of ethnic conflicts.[42] The rivalry with Russia embraces economic issues of energy routes, pipelines and so on as well as the classical issues of security, the territorial integrity of states and defence. As the oil-producing states are now members of the PfP, and Azerbaijan, Kazakhstan and Georgia are overtly seeking NATO's direct participation in the area, the contest with Russia and Iran has assumed a more overt military aspect to parallel the economic–political rivalry.[43] Furthermore, given the spiralling strategic stakes here, the engagement of NATO and specifically the USA in the region is likely to grow.

In September 1995, US experts on Central Asia meeting at NATO headquarters went so far as to cite the extensive US interests in Caspian energy deposits as a reason why Washington might have to extend its Persian Gulf security guarantees to this region.[44] This has not happened to date. However, US writers increasingly call this area and the 'greater

Middle East', of which it is deemed to be part, the 'strategic fulcrum of the future' or the 'strategic high ground' because of its energy resources.

Military–security cooperation and conflict resolution

It is mistaken to see the US and/or Western engagement in the Caspian region in strictly economic or strategic terms alone. Just as values and interests are intertwined, so are these policy motives. Elizabeth Sherwood-Randall, Deputy Assistant Secretary of Defense for Russia, Ukraine and Eurasia in 1994–96, observes that a coherent Caucasus policy began to emerge in 1994. The Pentagon's main concern was the role of local armed forces, not least Russia's efforts to subvert the new states and intervene there. Washington therefore sought to supplant the primacy of bilateral ties to Russia with other (i.e., US and Turkish) and multilateral relationships. It aimed to support democratization, liberal market economies and integration with the European community of states, to remove weapons of mass destruction and nuclear materials, and to open the area for US business investment.[45]

The Pentagon ultimately allocated areas of responsibility (AORs) to US commands for the Caspian region. The US European Command (USEUCOM) got the Caucasus and CENTCOM received Central Asia. Although this is as much an administrative device to supervise the ongoing programmes of bilateral and NATO military cooperation, it also represents a major step for contingency planning, and Russia knows it.[46]

All these actions signal an ever-deepening and broader US regulation of the region's security agenda. Thus the potential for using truly coercive diplomacy in support of the West in the area is growing. Indeed, the fear that NATO will encroach upon the CIS is one of the major reasons for the anger which NATO enlargement arouses in Moscow.[47] Accordingly most observers, and even some official US statements, view the totality of the diverse forms of the US regional engagement as intended to further the goals of breaking Russia's monopoly, demonstrating the USA's power projection capability, tying the region to the West through the PfP, enhancing local military capabilities for self-defence, preventing a military reliance on Moscow, excluding Russia from acting as the only mediator in conflict resolution in the region—its main means of asserting its power—and cementing an enduring local presence to defend US energy interests.[48]

However, these objectives are accompanied by the risk that the United States could relatively easily be drawn into local ethnic conflicts in a peacemaking or peacekeeping role. In 1999 President Islam Karimov of Uzbekistan discovered the virtues of both Russian protection and the OSCE in the struggle against terrorism because he now faced a real security threat.[49] It is unlikely that the OSCE is eager to intervenc in Uzbekistan's internecine struggles but it is also not impossible that some crisis in Central Asia could draw in other external powers.

For the time being Washington has wisely eschewed the direct commitment of US troops to any of the many conflicts in the area, but that does not reflect a policy principle. Clearly, US regional military involvement is growing. General John Sheehan, USMC, Commander-in-Chief of the US Atlantic Command (ACOM) and NATO's SACLANT (Supreme Allied Commander Atlantic), announced the USA's willingness to take part in regional peace support operations involving Central Asian forces under UN authorization, further extending the US offer of security cooperation to those states.[50]

NATO and the US military's increasing involvement go beyond conducting PfP programmes with local states and exercises with states in the region. NATO's expanding interest also reflects the broader process by which the entire area has entered the European security agenda since the collapse of the Soviet Union. This too is not just a question of conducting PfP programmes with local states and exercises in Central Asia. Turkey's provision of military training to Central Asian states and Azerbaijan, its intention to organize a Caucasian peacekeeping force, and its desire to play a larger and visible role as a kind of regional gendarme are only the most prominent of such examples.

This deepening political, economic and military involvement raises the region's stakes for key US constituencies, perhaps including the armed forces. Central Asia's heightened importance could lead the US Government in the event of a challenge to security there to determine that critical or even vital interests were threatened. US military analysts speak frankly of their vision of the activities contained under the rubric of engagement and the PfP, not only in Europe or Central Asia, as essential aspects of the US strategy of 'extraordinary power projection'. US engagement programmes take the form of joint exercises, staff visits, training, increasing interoperability and so on to help shape the peacetime environment.[51] These activities also facilitate the transition to war and if necessary participation in its initial stages.

Nevertheless, the stated US policy of not challenging Russia and the policy of dollar diplomacy in its current form imply that in the Caspian region the United States will rely on economic influence and military exercises, but avoid costly, protracted military involvements in resolving conflicts. It will not definitively commit resources to peace operations in the South Caucasus or Central Asia unless Russia approves—or so it says, even though the logic of this stance is contradicted by the logic of its previous military exercises there.

Thus the previous offer to provide peacekeepers to Nagorno-Karabakh was only possible with Russian troops' participation there as well in an international force under OSCE control—an obvious non-starter for Russia.[52] Likewise, the United States has done little or nothing to criticize or penalize Russia's military interventions in Central Asia or the wars in Chechnya. It displays an ability to airlift thousands of troops into Central Asia, but, what happens if a new crisis breaks out and there is the real prospect of force being used? Will the USA then commit itself to use this capability and can it sustain forces in those theatres?

The USA and the strategic scene in Central Asia

The USA's disavowal of any regional competition with Russia in Central Asia and the CIS does not sort well with the programme of military exercises through the PfP, whose avowed aim is to integrate the region firmly with the West in both economics and security. This is where the ambivalence in US policy sets in. Because the US regards Russia as a potential or even actual stable democratic partner, it has also cautioned Georgia, Azerbaijan, Kazakhstan and presumably other regional states not to infringe on Russia's interests.[53]

Unfortunately the true logic of the evolution of US policy comes close to converting the entire South Caucasus and Central Asian region into an arena of great-power rivalry. Even as the US engages in actions to 'prepare the theatre', it is unlikely to deploy or sustain those forces after building up expectations to the contrary. However, as long as the Caspian Basin is a major energy producer, a stake of this magnitude justifies the USA's compelling interest in the Caspian region. Thus US policy is impaling itself on a contradictory logic. Moreover, there is good reason to believe that its underlying fundamental assumptions are also untenable.

US policy leads to the following situation. On the one hand the USA is determined to use economic power to integrate the Caucasus and Central Asia into Western economic and security systems and attain geopolitical mastery even in Russia's claimed backyard. Military forces will follow in the now approved guise of peacekeepers or peace enforcers, a sure confirmation of the fact that peace operations have now replaced gunboat diplomacy as the main military instrument for the establishment of great-power spheres of influence.[54] US statements have previously claimed that it can successfully and cheaply isolate both Iran and Russia and manage those two strategic challenges in the energy area, not to mention Iraq. Pursuit of the Caspian policy will continue along with a search for a way to maintain this strategy cheaply, for instance, by a very protracted reappraisal of policy towards Iran.[55]

These pursuits will probably intensify along with the search for alternatives to the insecure Middle East oil supply, even though the United States can neither secure the local 'peaces' that are crucial to a stable energy regime across Eurasia, nor secure oil and gas lines if they are threatened, nor secure access to these lines if unfriendly elements take power locally.[56] Nor is it clear how stable any government in the Caspian Basin is, and the strife in Uzbekistan and Kyrgyzstan shows little sign of resolution. Thus Washington is overextending itself at a time when its resolve, intelligent understanding of the region and resources, as shown in Iraq, are insufficient to bring pressure to bear even on its allies, not to speak of its rivals and adversaries.

The second drawback of the policy is that it drives Iran and Russia to cooperate on regional policies and Russia to sell Iran arms and technology, including nuclear missile technology. Yet, because Washington will do little to counteract Russia's official complicity in challenging key US interests in energy and arms sales, we cannot discern that any costs accrue to Russia from its close relationship with Iran, which has deep roots in their strategic convergence.

This strategic failure highlights a third, deeply embedded aspect of US foreign policy which has led to failure. As Sestanovich wrote before his appointment, it is impossible to discern any strategic context for the US Administration's Russia policy. That policy remains astrategic or devoid of any geopolitical context.[57] Or at least the United States remains unwilling to admit that strategy plays any role in its Russian policy, a failing that in practice amounts to much the same thing. Consequently Russia has no reason to accommodate US pressure on Iran and much to lose by doing so. Nor does Russia have sufficient *external* incentive to desist from coercive measures in the Caucasus and Central Asia, whether economic or military. Indeed, US probes only enhance Russia's sense of regional threat and propensity to reply in kind while not preventing it from doing so. Russian leaders are convinced that they must do more to resist US penetration here, not support or tolerate it.[58]

The fourth failing of US policy is that Washington, for all the instruments of global policy it possesses, remains singularly unable to use them to obtain a comprehensive and insightful understanding of regional trends and their implications in much of the Third World. All the unforeseen crises since 1990, the unexpected Iraqi attack on Kuwait, Somalia and the continuing Iraqi crisis suggest that this is a structural failing of US policy. Information has not brought deeper understanding or foresight.[59] The USA's burgeoning economic, political and military presence in the Third World upsets older relationships and regional structures which it may not grasp and does so in ways that it does not fully comprehend or to which it cannot easily reply.

Specifically, Washington could trigger renewed military pressure in the CIS region, either directly or through Moscow's surrogates. Or it could contribute, as in the Shah's Iran, to the destabilization of fragile and traumatized Caucasian and Central Asian societies. It is by no means clear that US presence and influence will help local states develop energy policies that increase stability and economic progress, rather than following the usual pattern of misrule and misconceived economic policy. Those outcomes characterize too many oil-producing states. Past experience of the effects of large-scale US influence is not altogether encouraging, for if the oil producers follow Nigeria's example, as current trends unfortunately suggest, Washington has bought a large stake in long-standing crises and the potential for failed states and perennial violence.[60]

The regional structure of political forces hardly engenders optimism about the strategic outcome. Given the uncertain domestic political outcomes among the oil and gas producers, the US ambivalence about committing forces and the dangerous regional situation of rival alliances create the potential for wider and more protracted regional conflicts which could become proxy wars for the great powers, like the Third World conflicts of the 1980s. There is a risk that polarization is being fostered along traditional lines.[61] In conjunction with its second war in Chechnya, Russia is renewing its determination to assert its Caucasian and Central Asian prerogatives together with China and against the United States.[62]

Russia's warnings about US efforts to gain military, political and economic leverage in the South Caucasus and Central Asia and the Russian elite's extreme sensitivity regarding the region show that Moscow too will resolutely contest the expanded US presence. This is explicitly expressed in Russian official statements under President Vladimir Putin. Russia's new draft military doctrine and security concept suggest that it will use nuclear deterrence against Western military action in the CIS region.[63]

The danger is that Russia and the USA could be drawn into a confrontation in an effort to rescue their allies or close partners from defeat in local conflicts. Many structural conditions for conventional war or protracted ethnic conflict where third parties intervene now exist in the Caucasus and Central Asia. Violent action by disaffected Islamic groups, drug trafficking and the unresolved ethnopolitical conflicts that dot the region, not to mention the undemocratic and unbalanced distribution of income in states with corrupt governments, provide plenty of dry timber for future fires. Recent history indicates that many Third World conflicts generated by local structural factors have had great potential for unintended escalation. Major powers often feel obliged to rescue their proxies and protégés. One or other of them may fail to grasp the nature of the stakes for the other side, since interests here are not as clearly defined as in Europe. Commitments involving the use of nuclear weapons or perhaps even conventional war to prevent the defeat of a client are not well established or clear as they are in Europe. For instance, in 1993 a suggestion by Turkey that it might intervene militarily on behalf of Azerbaijan during fighting over the Nagorno-Karabakh region led to a Russian threat of nuclear retaliation against such intervention.[64]

There exists an 'arc of crisis' from the Balkans to China where the danger of conflicts and conflict escalation remains real. An assessment in the late 1980s by Richard Betts is still insightful, even if in the post-cold war period Russia's military resources have greatly declined. Betts observed that the greatest danger lies in areas where: (1) the potential for serious instability is high; (2) both superpowers perceive vital interests; (3) neither recognizes that the other's perceived interest or commitment is as great as its own; (4) both have the capability to inject conventional forces; and (5) neither has willing proxies capable of settling the situation.[65]

This analysis implies that for each side the interest or area in question is a vital one. This does not imply that conflict between the dominant powers in a region or their proxies is foreordained. Rather this analysis underlines the dangerous structural conditions in the region. Great-power rivalry does not necessarily impart stability to an already troubled region, quite the contrary. Russian and Chinese efforts at the Bishkek summit meeting of the 'Shanghai Five' group of states in 1999 to develop a new bloc with the Central Asian states and Russia's new military doctrine demonstrate that such rivalry stimulates efforts to create spheres of influence but also provides smaller states with the means to resist them by balancing competing rivals.[66]

In Central Asia Russia is unlikely to be restrained by any local institution or state in its pursuit of unilateral advantage and CIS reintegration.[67] The only restraints it now accepts are objective ones like the limits of its faltering economic and military power, which preclude the easy attainment of its goals of regional hegemony and compel it to pursue its aims by more pacific and less coercive means. And even the perceptions of waning power are difficult for Russian leaders to accept and translate into policy. Russia is disinclined to accept limits on its capability to achieve its perceived vital interests. And where it has moved from using military coercion to economic efforts to retain its pre-eminence, it has done so as much for lack of a viable military option as from the insight that it stands to gain more from a more purely economic approach.[68]

While the balance of assets to influence policy in Central Asia remains in Russia's favour, this hardly means that Russia can succeed at will in advancing its interests throughout Central Asia. But it does mean that if any regional balance, on energy or other major security issues, is to be achieved, another major state or coalition of states must lend power to the smaller littoral states to anchor that balance. But to achieve this that outside balancer must be ready to play a protracted, potentially even a military role in the region to ensure stability and peace. Yet this risks the kind of conflict described above. There is little to suggest that the United States can or will play this role over the long term. This suggests that ultimately its bluff can be called. For an outside regional balancer to succeed, it must reinforce the local states' current efforts to diversify foreign investment in local energy deposits, encourage the growth of these states' economic and military power, promote regional economic and military cooperation, and stabilize them from within and without.

The USA can only achieve part of this challenging agenda. This implies that the balancing role cannot be served by a unilateral US commitment. A multilateral commitment would be more effective, for instance under the auspices of the UN or NATO as through the PfP programme, even if this commitment is still dependent on US leadership. The record of the UN and the OSCE gives few grounds to hope that a regional balance to counteract Russian designs in Central Asia could emerge through the actions of these multilateral structures in the absence of a firm US commitment.[69]

Prospects for the future

The new Central Asian states deserve peaceful and unencumbered development, and Russian attempts to restrict their sovereignty and perpetuate colonial relationships have been a factor prompting the assertion of US power in the region in ways that Washington at first refused to countenance.[70] But by now it is by no means certain that Washington knows the limits of this regional engagement. There is no doubt that cheap energy is immensely important to the US and Western economies and polities. But it remains unclear if the Caspian region will produce oil and gas on a scale that is of truly strategic interest for the USA (even if it is of clear strategic interest to the local states). It also remains unclear whether Washington can cheaply sustain an entire European, South Caucasus/Central Asian and Middle Eastern international order against the multifarious threats in any of these regions, let alone in all of them. The possibilities for conflict between or among local governments and ethnic movements in Central Asia are very high and there is no reason to believe that the great powers involved can easily escape indirect or even direct participation in those struggles.

Furthermore it appears that support for democratization, which features so prominently in US rhetoric and policy in the region, will be blocked by the competing imperatives of supporting existing regimes against threats to their stability and that of their energy supplies. Although the US rhetorical thrust for democracy is unabated, it is clear that these programmes have foundered on the rocks of the opposition of the incumbent regimes and of competing US priorities. Consequently success in developing more democratic polities and more open market economies can only be described as limited. The local states are characterized by personalist authoritarian regimes with shaky control over their multiple militaries and little interest in democratization.

At the same time the enormous and accelerating projection of US investment and military presence into these states represents a form of power projection. But the large involvement of foreign governments and economies in the Central Asian states prompts internal destabilization because it provokes demands for greater democratization or for greater foreign penetration than troubled regimes can sustain. Therefore, should crises break out in Central Asia and pro-Western governments fall or become still more repressive, it remains unclear whether the US and Western presences can be sustained in their present form. The USA is enlarging its commitment in the region absent-mindedly even though it lives in a post-colonial era and as a country has no tolerance for colonial wars.

It is questionable whether the USA has the capacity to achieve simultaneously and cheaply the objectives of forging lasting, legitimate, democratic political structures, market economies and regional stability in Central Asia. The trajectory of US policy brings into sharp relief a basic dilemma: while many Americans believe that it is almost a law of international affairs that democratic states remain at peace with each other, it can be argued that states undergoing the protracted phase of democratization are prone to violence and regressions along the way.[71] Unquestionably the dual-track approach of the USA in supporting democratization and seeking the integration of these states' economies and militaries into Western-led structures creates a laboratory for testing these propositions. At present the energy resources of the region are the priority interest of US policy and democracy building has lower priority. However, should US policy fail to achieve its principal goals of integration and democratization and Central Asia fail to achieve either internal or external security, then it will revert to being a peripheral region in US strategy.

Notes

1. The former director of the Strategic Studies Institute of the US Army War College, Col Richard Witherspoon (Ret), related to the author that during 1992–93 the Pentagon's only interest in countries like Kazakhstan was in getting nuclear materials and weapons out of them.

2. S. Neil MacFarlane, *Western Engagement in the Caucasus and Central Asia* (London: Royal Institute of International Affairs, 1999), pp. 1–21.

3. For example, William Bundy, *A Tangled Web: The Making of Foreign Policy in the Nixon Presidency* (New York: Hill & Wang, 1998), pp. 291–292. More recently, see Liam Anderson and Michael Beck, 'US Political Activism in Central Asia: The Case of Kyrgyzstan and Uzbekistan' in Gary K. Bertsch, Cassady Craft, Scott A. Jones and Michael Beck, eds, *Crossroads and Conflict: Security and Foreign Policy in the Caucasus and Central Asia* (New York and London: Routledge, 2000), pp. 75–79.

4. MacFarlane, *op. cit.*, *passim*; and the summary of the remarks to the Seminar on the Caucasus and the Caspian of the Strengthening Democratic Institutions Project given by Steven Young, Director of the State Department's Office of the Caucasus and Security Affairs of the Newly Independent States, 28 October 1996, *The Caucasus and the Caspian 1996–1997 Seminar Series II* (Cambridge, Mass.: Harvard University, John F. Kennedy School of Government, Strengthening Democratic Institutions Project, 1997), p. 82.

5. President William J. Clinton, 'A National Security Strategy for a New Century' (Washington, DC: The White House, 1997), p. 18; and President William J. Clinton, 'A National Security Strategy for the Next Century' (Washington, DC: The White House, 1998), pp. 32–33.

6. Statement of Stephen Sestanovich, Ambassador-at-Large, Special Adviser to the Secretary of State for the New Independent States, before the House International Relations Committee, 30 April 1998, *Turkistan Newsletter,* vol. 98-2:089-06-May-1998.

7. Frank T. Csongos, 'Central Asia: Official Outlines US Policy', Radio Free Europe/Radio Liberty, *RFE/RL Newsline,* 18 March 1999.

8. Deputy Secretary of State Strobe Talbott, 'A Farewell to Flashman: American Policy in the Caucasus and Central Asia', Address at the Johns Hopkins School of Advanced International Studies, Washington, DC, 21 July 1997.

9. United States General Accounting Office (GAO), *Report to the Chairman, Committee on International Relations, House of Representatives: Foreign Assistance, US Economic and Democratic Assistance to the Central Asian Republics* (Washington, DC: USGPO, 1999), p. 10.

10. William H. Lewis and Edward Marks, *Searching for Partners: Regional Organizations and Peace Operations,* McNair papers, no. 58 (Institute for National Strategic Studies, National Defense University: Washington, DC, 1998), pp. 105–107, 123.

11. Quoted in Sean Kay, *NATO and the Future of European Security* (Lanham, Md.: Rowman and Littlefield, 1997), p. 108.

12. Major-General Kenneth R. Bowra and Colonel William H. Harris, Jr., 'Regional Engagement: An ARSOF Approach to Future Theater Operations', *Special Warfare,* fall 1998, pp. 2–23.

13. Talbott, *op. cit.*

14. MacFarlane, *op. cit., passim.*

15. Anderson and Beck, *op. cit.,* pp. 85–86; and Elizabeth Sherwood-Randall, 'US Policy and the Caucasus', *Contemporary Caucasus Newsletter* (Berkeley Program in Soviet and Post-Soviet Studies: University of California, Berkeley), issue 5 (spring 1998), pp. 3–4.

16. Anatol Lieven, 'The (not so) Great Game', *The National Interest,* no. 58 (winter 1999–2000), pp. 69–81.

17. Steve LeVine, 'High Stakes', *Newsweek,* 17 April 1995, p. 10.

18. Boris Rumer, 'Disintegration and Reintegration in Central Asia. Dynamics and Prospects' in Boris Rumer, ed., *Central Asia in Transition: Dilemmas of Political and Economic Development* (Armonk, N.Y.: M. E. Sharpe, 1996), p. 10; and Oksana Reznikova, 'Transnational Corporations in Central Asia' in Rumer, pp. 82–83.

19. 'If We Clash It'll Be on the Caspian', *Current Digest of the Post-Soviet Press,* vol. xvii, no. 21 (21 June 1995), p. 21.

20. 'The Fortnight in Review', *Prism,* vol. iii, no. 15, Pt. 1 (October 1997); Rachel Bronson, 'NATO's Expanding Presence in the Caucasus and Central Asia' in Stephen Blank, ed., *NATO after Enlargement: New Challenges, New Missions, New Forces* (Carlisle Barracks, Pa.: Strategic Studies Institute, US Army

War College, 1998), pp. 229–254; and Glen Howard, 'NATO and the Caucasus: the Caspian Axis' in Blank, pp. 151–228, give full accounts of NATO's deepening involvement in this region.

21. ITAR-TASS (Moscow), 16 April 1998 (in English) in Foreign Broadcast Information Service, *Daily Report–Central Eurasia* (hereafter *FBIS-SOV*), FBIS-SOV-98-106, 21 April 1998; and *Statement of Undersecretary of State Thomas Pickering to the Senate Foreign Relations Committee,* 3 March 1998 in *Johnson's Russia List,* no. 2092 (4 March 1998), davidjohnson@erols.com.

22. Bronson, *op. cit.*; Howard, 'NATO and the Caucasus: the Caspian Axis', *op. cit.*; and MacFarlane, *op. cit., passim.*

23. Glen E. Howard, 'NATO Expansion and Azerbaijan's Search for Security', unpublished paper presented to the CSIS Project on Russia and the CIS, Washington, DC, 15 July 1997.

24. Martha Brill Olcott, 'The Caspian's False Promise', *Foreign Policy,* no. 112 (summer 1998), pp. 101–102.

25. Voice of America, Testimony of Secretary of Energy Frederico Pena to the House International Relations Committee, 30 April 1998; Statement of Stephen Sestanovich, *ibid.*; and Pickering, *Statement of Undersecretary of State Thomas Pickering to the Senate Foreign Relations Committee, op. cit.*

26. Talbott, *op. cit.*; and Interview with US President Bill Clinton, *International Affairs* (Moscow), no. 2 (1997), p. 5.

27. Talbott, *op. cit.*; Ambassador Alexander Vershbow, US Permanent Representative on the North Atlantic Council, 'NATO–Russia: Promise of Partnership or Problems?', Remarks at the Moscow State Institute for International Relations (MGIMO), 28 October 1999, *Johnson's Russia List,* no. 3506 (5 November 1999), djohnson@erols.com; and Interview with President Bill Clinton, *op. cit.*, pp. 2–5.

28. Stephen J. Blank, 'The OSCE, Russia, and Security in the Caucasus', *Helsinki Monitor,* vol. vi, no. 3 (1995), pp. 69–71; and Bradford R. McGuinn, 'From the Caspian to the Gulf: The Assertion of US Power', *Middle East Insight,* November–December 1997, pp. 10–14.

29. Statement of Stephen Sestanovich, *op. cit.*

30. Statement of Stephen Sestanovich, *op. cit.*

31. Talbott, *op. cit.*; US Department of State, Office of the Spokesman, 'Remarks by Secretary Madeleine K. Albright to Students at Vilnius University and Question and Answer Session', 13 July 1997, published by the US Information Agency; 'The End of the Beginning: The Emergence of a New Russia', Address by Strobe Talbott, Deputy Secretary of State, Stanford University, Stanford, Calif., 19 September 1997, from *Johnson's Russia List,* djohnson@cdi.org, no. 1220 (23 September 1997); US National Security Council, *Caspian Region Energy Development Report,* 1997, p. 17; and Floriana Fossato, 'Russia: the Amount of Change Has Been Extraordinary', Radio Free Europe/Radio Liberty, *RFE/RL Report,* 12 December 1997, as transcribed in *Johnson's Russia List,* no. 1428 (12 December 1997), djohnson@erols.com.

32. *Nezavisimaya gazeta,* 21 December 1999 (in Russian) in *FBIS-SOV,* 21 December 1999; and Presidential Bulletin, Interfax, 23 December 1999.

33. Anderson and Beck, *op. cit.*, p. 86.

34. Thomas Carothers, 'Democracy Promotion under Clinton', *Washington Quarterly*, vol. xviii, no, 4 (autumn 1995), p. 18.

35. GAO, *op. cit.* (note 9), pp.17–18.

36. *Ibid.*, pp. 18–20.

37. *Ibid.*

38. *Ibid.*, pp. 26–31.

39. Karen Dawisha and Bruce Parrott, eds, *Conflict, Cleavage and Change in Central Asia and the Caucasus*, Authoritarianism and Democratization in Post-communist Societies, no. 4 (Cambridge: Cambridge University Press, 1997).

40. 'Anthony Zinni: Avoid a Military Showdown with Iraq', *Middle East Quarterly*, vol. V, no. 3 (fall 1998), p. 64.

41. This view emerges clearly in Russia's new national security concept. 'Kontseptsiya Natsional'noi Bezopasnosti Rossiiskoi Federatsii', *Nezavisimoe voennoe obozrenie*, 14 January 2000.

42. Conversations with Russian officers and analysts in Moscow and Helsinki, June 1999; Interfax (Moscow), 12 November 1999; and Igor Ivanov, 'West's Hypocrisy over Chechnya', *Financial Times*, 16 November 1999, p. 19.

43. Howard, 'NATO and the Caucasus: the Caspian Axis', *op. cit.*, pp. 151–229; Jan S. Adams, 'The US–Russian Face-off in the Caspian Basin', *Problems of Post-Communism*, vol. xlvii, no. 1 (January–February 2000), pp. 49–58; and *Jamestown Monitor*, 22 December 1999.

44. Dmitri Vertkin, *Kazakhstan Security and the New Asian Landscape*, Bailrigg Paper no. 26 (Centre for Defence and International Security Studies, Lancaster University, 1997), pp. 17–18; and Robin Morgan and David Ottaway, 'Drilling for Influence in Russia's Back Yard', *Washington Post*, 22 September 1997, pp. A1, 15.

45. Sherwood-Randall, *op. cit.*, pp. 3–4.

46. Reuters, 17 November 1997; *Pipeline News*, no. 79 (10–17 November 1997); 'Oil Rush', *Washington Post*, 20 November 1997, p. 24; and Adams, *op. cit.*, pp. 49–58.

47. Adams, *op. cit.*, pp. 49–58; and Ivanov, *op. cit.*

48. *Caspian Region Energy Development Report*, *op. cit.*; Gennady I. Chufrin and Harold H. Saunders, 'The Politics of Conflict Prevention in Russia and the Near Abroad', *Washington Quarterly*, vol. xx, no 4 (autumn (1997), pp. 40–43; and Viktor Israelyan, 'Russia at the Crossroads: Don't Tease a Wounded Bear', *Washington Quarterly*, vol. xxi, no. 1 (winter 1998), pp. 55–58.

49. Adams, *op. cit.*, p. 57; *Kommersant*, 3 December 1999 (in Russian) in *FBIS-SOV*, 3 December 1999; and *RFE/RL Newsline*, 13 December 1999.

50. 'The Fortnight in Review', *Prism*, vol. iii, no. 15, Pt. 1 (October 1997).

51. Roger W. Barnett, *Extraordinary Power Projection: An Operational Concept for the US Navy*, Strategic Research Development Report 5-96, US Naval War College, Center for Naval Warfare Studies, Occasional Papers, Newport, RI, 1996, pp. 7–8.

52. Stephen J. Blank, 'The OSCE, Russia, and Security in the Caucasus', *op. cit.*; and McGuinn, *op. cit.*, pp. 10–14.

53. *Izvestiya*, 23 December 1999 (in Russian) in *FBIS-SOV*, 23 December 1999; and Statement of Stephen Sestanovich, *op. cit.*

54. McGuinn, *op. cit.*, pp. 10–14.

55. In June, 1998 Secretary of State Madeleine Albright proclaimed an initiative to improve and normalize relations with Iran. It is too early to determine how successful that move will be, but clearly energy considerations were a factor behind it. Secretary of State Madeleine K. Albright, Remarks at the 1998 Asia Society Dinner, Waldorf-Astoria Hotel, New York, 17 June 1998, as released by the Office of the Spokesman, 18 June 1998, US Department of State, Washington, DC. URL <http://secretary.state.gov/www.statements/1998/980617a.html>.

56. *Ibid.*

57. Stephen Sestanovich, 'Why the United States Has No Russia Policy' in Robert J. Lieber, ed., *Eagle Adrift: American Foreign Policy at the End of the Century* (New York: Longman, 1997), p. 166.

58. Adams, *op. cit.*, pp. 49–58; and Stephen J. Blank, 'Every Shark East of Suez: Great Power Interests, Policies, and Tactics in the Transcaspian Energy Wars', *Central Asian Survey*, vol. xviii, no. 2 (1999), pp. 149–184.

59. Ephraim Karsh, 'Cold War, Post-Cold War: Does It Make a Difference for the Middle East?', *Review of International Studies*, vol. xxiii, no. 3 (September 1997), p. 281. On p. 283 he notes that Saddam Hussein's build-up prior to the invasion of Kuwait in 1990 was 'treated in Washington with the disbelief that commonly accompanies a warning that another government is about to break a basic international rule', exactly as occurred in Chechnya in 1994. See also Stephen J. Blank, 'Yugoslavia's Wars and European Security' in Stephen J. Blank, ed., *Yugoslavia's Wars: The Problem From Hell* (Carlisle Barracks, Pa.: Strategic Studies Institute, US Army War College, 1995), pp. 123–159.

60. Alec Rasizade, 'Azerbaijan and the Oil Trade: Prospects and Pitfalls', *Brown Journal of World Affairs*, vol. iv, no. 2 (summer/fall 1997), pp. 277–294; Olcott, *op. cit.*, pp. 95–113; and Dawisha and Parrott, *op. cit., passim.*

61. *Rossiiskaya gazeta*, 13 September 1997 (in Russian) in *FBIS-SOV*, 15 September 1997; and Howard, 'NATO and the Caucasus', *op. cit., passim.*

62. See the joint communiqué issued at the Bishkek summit, Beijing. Xinhua Domestic Service, 25 August 1999 (in Chinese) in *FBIS-SOV*, 26 August 1999.

63. 'Kontseptsiya Natsional'noi Bezopasnosti Rossiiskoi Federatsii', *Krasnaya zvezda*, 9 October 1999 (in Russian) in *FBIS-SOV*, 8 October 1999.

64. Dmitry Volsky, 'The Explosive Karabakh Conflict', *New Times*, no. 16 (1993), p. 24; and J. D. Crouch II, William van Cleave, *et al.*, 'The Politics of Reform in Russia', *Global Affairs*, vol. vii, no. 3 (summer 1993), p. 197.

65. Richard Betts, 'Nuclear Peace and Conventional War', *Journal of Strategic Studies*, vol. xi, no. 1 (March 1988), pp. 90–91.

66. *FBIS-SOV*, 26 August 1999.

67. Paul d'Anieri, 'International Cooperation among Unequal Partners: The Emergence of Bilateralism in the Former Soviet Union', *International Politics*, vol. xxxiv, no. 4 (December 1998), pp. 417–48.

68. Gerhard Simon, 'Russia's Identity and International Politics', *Aussenpolitik* (English edn), no. 3 (1997), pp. 245–256; and Tatiana Parkhalina, 'Of Myths

and Illusions: Russian Perceptions of NATO Enlargement', *NATO Review*, May–June 1997, p. 14.

69. S. Neil MacFarlane, 'The UN, the OSCE, and the Southern Caucasus', *Caspian Crossroads*, vol. iii, no. 1 (1997), pp. 18–22.

70. For the earlier US view, see Stephen J. Blank, *Energy, Economics and Security in Central Asia: Russia and Its Rivals* (Carlisle Barracks, Pa.: Strategic Studies Institute, US Army War College, 1995), p. 30.

71. Edward Mansfield and Jack Snyder, 'Democratization and the Danger of War', *International Security*, vol. xx, no. 1 (summer 1995), pp. 5–38.

CHAPTER SEVEN

China and Central Asia

GUANGCHENG XING

The vision of Chinese–Central Asian relations

In its efforts to modernize, China has concentrated on economic reform and development and pursued a policy of 'opening up'. A long-term peaceful and stable international and regional environment has therefore become a necessity, and this has encouraged a policy of good-neighbourly relations.[1] In developing relations with the newly independent Central Asian states—Kazakhstan, Kyrgyzstan, Tajikistan, Turkmenistan and Uzbekistan—China has considered five main aspects.

First, Chinese strategists realize that the strategic importance of the Central Asian states will increase and that the region will have a considerable influence on the world of the 21st century. Economically, Central Asia and its surrounding areas will play an important role in the world's supply of energy. Politically, the Central Asian states are increasingly manifesting their own style, different from that of Russia or Ukraine and even more from that of Eastern and Central Europe. They will not follow the example of Iran, where religion and state form one political structure. Although the Central Asian leaders are interested in the political system of Turkey, with a secular state and where religion and state are separate, they are not likely to introduce the 'Turkish model' either.

Chinese observers consider that the future role of Central Asia is dependent not only on the strength of the five individual states but also on how they cooperate with their neighbours and what issues they pursue. An alliance between the Central Asian states and any one of the regional powers would influence the structure of the international system. If the Central Asian states and the Islamic states to their south were in harmony, this would disturb the Western world and its interests. If the Central Asian states were to 'gang up' with Russia, the United States and the Western powers would find it very difficult to engage in the region and the potential economic benefits of engagement would be reduced. If the Central Asian states were to largely ally themselves with Western states, then the economic and political interests of Russia would suffer.

Second, China considers the Central Asian states in the context of Eurasia. They have a linking role, not only in a geographical sense but also in the political and cultural senses. Central Asia can be called a 'bridge' between East and West. China is closely interested in the stability and prosperity of the region. If there were turbulence around that bridge, the future of political and economic cooperation in the whole Eurasian continent would be seriously affected. Political and economic cooperation with Central Asian states is therefore very important for China. It supports them in any move aimed at safeguarding stability and prosperity, and is against any behaviour or trend of thought aimed at undermining that stability and prosperity.

Third, China gives high priority to the development of bilateral and cross-border relations with the Central Asian states. The more these relations develop and tighten, the more it will benefit bilateral interests and contribute to stability and prosperity in the region.

Fourth, China considers its relations with the Central Asian states from the point of view of the stability and development of Xinjiang. China will expand the framework and the dynamics of cooperation across the border from Xinjiang and develop relations according to the principles of equality and mutual benefit.

Fifth, China has had friendly contacts with the Central Asian states since ancient times. The Silk Road created close ties between it and the peoples of Central Asia. Facing the new century, these states together have the need, the ability and indeed the responsibility to construct a Silk Road of modern times.

Since the Central Asian states became independent in 1991 they and China have come to share several security concerns in the region. The Chinese Government stresses the Five Principles of Peaceful Coexistence in its relations with them. These principles include peace, cooperation, development, exchange, mutual prosperity, progress and understanding.

The normalization of relations

China's relations with Central Asia improved steadily during the 1990s. As early as 1986, Mikhail Gorbachev had initiated a gradual rapprochement between China and the Soviet Union.

At the time there were a number of unsettled issues between the Soviet Union and China, one of them being the border question. An agreement of 1991 basically resolved the issue of the eastern part of the border, except for a few stretches which were still disputed, but the question of the western part of the border was left unresolved. China also has borders 3000 km long with three Central Asian countries—Kazakhstan, Kyrgyzstan and Tajikistan. The border question is thus an important part of the relations between China, Russia and these three states. In February 1992 in Minsk a decision was taken to set up a joint group with representatives from Russia and the three countries. In joint communiqués issued by China and Kazakhstan in February 1992 and by China and Kyrgyzstan in May 1992 the parties agreed to negotiate on the border areas in accordance with the general principles of the 1991 Sino-Soviet agreement.

When Prime Minister Li Peng visited Kazakhstan in April 1994, he and President Nursultan Nazarbayev signed an agreement concerning their joint 1700 km-long border. The agreement defined the border legally and declared that it would be a 'link of friendly cooperation and mutual prosperity'.[2] In September 1997 and July 1998 additional agreements were signed which essentially resolved the Chinese–Kazakh border issue.[3] An agreement signed on 4 July 1996 by Chairman Jiang Zemin and President Askar Akayev of Kyrgyzstan to a great extent resolved the issue of the Chinese–Kyrgyz border. At a summit meeting with the leaders of the five Central Asian countries in Bishkek (Kyrgyzstan) in 1999, Jiang Zemin, Nazarbayev and Akayev signed an additional agreement on the border question which reinforced previous treaties.

However, the Chinese–Tajik border issue has not yet been resolved. This is a very complex dispute over an area of about 20,000 square kilometres in the mountainous region of Pamir. Both sides are eager to resolve it.

Negotiations between China and the Soviet Union on reducing military forces in the border region were initiated in November 1989 (involving what are now China's borders with Kazakhstan, Kyrgyzstan and Tajikistan). In April 1990 China and the Soviet Union signed an Agreement on Mutual Reduction of Military Forces in the Border Region and the Guiding Principles of Increasing Mutual Trust in Military Affairs. After the break-up of the Soviet Union in December 1991, Russia, Kazakhstan, Kyrgyzstan and Tajikistan formed a new group to hold talks with China in this field; these started in March 1992.

Another issue of concern in relations between China and the Central Asian states is nuclear safety. Kazakhstan inherited a part of the Soviet nuclear weapon stocks. Under an agreement reached by the Commonwealth of Independent States (CIS) countries in May 1992, it agreed to relinquish to Russia all its tactical nuclear warheads. However, it took a different approach to the question of strategic nuclear weapons. President Nazarbayev stated clearly that Kazakhstan would not transfer its nuclear weapons and would remain in possession of nuclear technology. He argued that Kazakhstan 'feels the threat from the US, China and Russia. If they destroy their nuclear weapons so shall we'.[4] He also clearly said that Kazakhstan had the right to join the 'nuclear club',[5] and asked the USA to accept Kazakhstan as a 'temporary nuclear weapon state' and create a strategic alliance with it. However, Kazakhstan finally chose to give up its nuclear weapons. Three factors facilitated this. First, the surrounding countries exercised strong pressure by linking the nuclear weapon issue directly to the question of economic aid. Second, both Ukraine and Belarus stated that they would give up their nuclear weapons and hand them over to Russia. Third, Kazakhstan received security guarantees from the USA, Russia and China, which declared that they would not use or target their nuclear weapons against Kazakhstan when it gave up the strategic nuclear weapons on its territory. On 8 February 1995 the Government of China issued a declaration on providing a security guarantee to Kazakhstan.[6]

Economic and energy relations

Trade and economic cooperation have come to play the main role in relations between China and the Central Asian states. During his visit to Kazakhstan in 1994, Li Peng declared the following guidelines for developing this cooperation: (a) to observe the principles of equality and mutual benefit; (b) to diversify the forms of cooperation; (c) to take realities into account and make full use of local resources; (d) to improve transport conditions and construct a new Silk Road; (e) to provide a small amount of economic aid, as a sign of friendship, to the Central Asian states; and (f) to develop multilateral cooperation and promote common development. Li Peng declared that in the Central Asian region China will not seek either a political or an economic sphere of influence.[7]

In 1993 China became a net importer of oil and it is increasingly reliant on energy imports. Central Asia is especially important to it in this respect. In June 1997 the China National Petroleum Corporation (CNPC) won the right to own and operate the Uzen oilfield in western Kazakhstan, although this subsequently lapsed. China also contracted to open up the Zhanazhol, Kenjiyake and Wujing oilfields in Aktyubinsk. In September 1997 the agreement for its largest potential investment in economic cooperation with Central Asia was signed: China planned to construct a 3000-km long oil pipeline from western Kazakhstan to western China. In September 2000 the Chinese discussed the possibility of a feasibility study for the pipeline. Kazakhstan is already supplying China with modest amounts of oil by rail. The CNPC also agreed to construct a pipeline from the Uzen region of Kazakhstan to the Turkmenistan border.[8]

China regards the development of contacts with the Central Asian states as being soundly based, both nationally and internationally, for four reasons. First, at the national level China and the Central Asian states are undergoing a period of economic transition. Their economic goals are very ambitious and they all need interaction with the wider world. Second, geopolitical factors indicate a high priority for economic and trade contacts between them. Third, their economic structures are complementary. Fourth, the opening of the 'second Eurasian bridge' and the improvement of other transport connections have provided a solid material basis for contacts.

Trade between China and the neighbouring Central Asian states increased during the 1990s, especially during the second half of the decade. China is the second largest trading partner of Kazakhstan and Kyrgyzstan. Trade between China and the Central Asian states is diversified: there is intergovernmental, local, barter, remittance and frontier trade. Economic cooperation between them is also diversified: there are enterprises with sole ownership as well as joint ventures in a great variety of areas and there is provision for the Chinese Government to make loans to all the Central Asian states.

The infrastructure between China and Central Asia has developed significantly. In 1992 the railway between Urumchi and Almaty was opened. In addition to this link, 14 other ports of entry were open in Xinjiang in April 1993, most of them simple road routes. There are also two airports which provide international links.[9]

There are, however, some problems in this economic cooperation. China and the Central Asian states have to find more suitable and effective methods of trade than barter. As the Chinese Minister for Foreign Trade has said, 'As our trade with neighbouring countries is developing, it is changing from barter and frontier trade to the international norm, remittance trade, and this creates a more stable basis for long-term development'.[10] The conditions for investment in the Central Asian states are also bad. The relevant statutes have not been improved and the laws are changing, so that foreign businessmen face difficulties in adjusting. Industry and commerce are not sufficiently attuned to the market economy, and their narrow thinking in terms of self-interest and protectionism complicates relations for Chinese businessmen.

The foreign economic management systems and mechanisms of both China and the Central Asian states are at present in a transitional stage. The interests of the centre and rural areas can conflict. The fact that China's north-west is one of the backward parts of the country, that its economic basis is weak and that the quality of its human resources is poor has a major effect on economic cooperation and trade contacts between China and the Central Asian states.

China takes a strategic perspective on economic cooperation with the Central Asian states. However, if economic relations are to develop fully, China should take the following factors into consideration.

First, China cannot enter the Central Asian market with large-scale investments. That market has serious deficiencies. It is only gradually maturing and the proper laws and regulations are only slowly being issued. However, market mechanisms and the conditions for investment in some areas are improving. If Chinese entrepreneurs do not see these changes in time they may miss the opportunity. China's investment principles are such that, as soon as improvements occur in investment conditions, research should be carried out and investments made.

Second, it is a mistake to believe that economic cooperation with the Central Asian states should be maintained through and by the north-west part of China. Central Asia is a big market with genuine prospects, and north-west China is not adequate to deal with it. Instead China should introduce policies to attract strong Chinese companies and economic entities to the north-west of China and Central Asia. The Central Asian states for their part want to develop economic cooperation not only with north-west China but also with the developed areas of the country. China should concentrate on its best and strongest business to open up Central Asia.

Third, Central Asia's natural resources are very rich and China should cooperate to take advantage of and open up those resources. It is obvious that the Central Asian states will rely on their natural resources for invigorating their economies, that the speed of restructuring in other economic sectors will remain slow, and that light industry will not be a priority sector for them. They will need to import large amounts of consumer goods for daily use. China should therefore invest in building light industry either in the Central Asian states or in north-west China to produce consumer goods for the Central Asian markets. In this way it can complement their economies and participate in the Central Asian economic circulation system.

Fourth, China needs to be aware of the competitive situation. In entering the Central Asian markets it may face strong competition from other former Soviet republics, Western countries, Turkey, Iran and so on. China should act on the basis of mutual benefit in economic cooperation and try to win this economic space through appropriate efforts and good preparation.

Finally, China must take advantage of all relevant factors, historical, political, economic and especially geopolitical. It should become a guide and a kind of courier station for the Central Asian states in their dealings with the Pacific countries and guide them to more active economic cooperation and trade contacts in the Pacific region. The 'second Eurasian bridge' is an important route for China to guide the Central Asian states through to the Pacific. China should adopt a much wider perspective in its dealings with Central Asia. In the 21st century economic cooperation within Eurasia will develop, and the Central Asian states are at the centre of the Eurasian axis. The rich economic zone of western Eurasia and the rapidly rising Pacific countries are at the western and eastern ends of Central Asia: Eurasia looks like a 'saddle' with a dip between the peaks. The economies of the Central Asian states will recover. China should ensure that the economic development of its north-western part is connected not only with that of Central Asia but also with overall economic development in Eurasia. Looked at in this way, there is stronger motivation and greater scope for its economic relations with the Central Asian states.[11]

The Central Asian states should also consider economic and trade cooperation with China from the strategic point of view. China has a number of irreplaceable functions for them. First, as noted above, increased cooperation with China and the Pacific states would enable the

Central Asian states to join the economy of Asia faster. The projected oil and gas pipelines between China and Central Asia will further benefit Central Asia. Second, just as Central Asia is a large market for China, so is China for Central Asia. The markets should be considered from the point of view of mutual benefit. The Central Asian states should enter the Chinese market and the Chinese market should allow them room to do so. Third, in the process of economic recovery the Central Asian states have to rely on China to provide ordinary consumer goods. This mutually complementary set-up of their economies will connect China and the Central Asian states closely. Successful recovery in Central Asia will be possible only by means of strengthened economic cooperation with China.

In the long term, the Central Asian states should maintain equally close relations with the CIS countries and Asia. At present Asia has a rapidly growing economy, and the emergence of the Pacific 'economic ring' will have a further great impact on the economies of Central Asia. The sooner the Central Asian states move away from the hinterland of Eurasia and join the dynamic Asian heartland, the better. A North-East Asian economic circle is also appearing, and this is prompting Russia to make a strategic choice whether or not to enter it. Active interaction with both West and East will create the necessary impetus for the economies of both Russia and the Central Asian states.

Military and security cooperation

After the break up of the Soviet Union, diplomatic and military experts representing China, Russia, Kazakhstan, Kyrgyzstan and Tajikistan undertook negotiations on disarmament and confidence building in military affairs in the border region, and a common understanding was achieved. In 1993 a Chinese–Kazakh communiqué on the principles for bilateral military contacts was signed'.[12] Another joint communiqué in 1995 stated that: 'Concerted efforts will be made to formulate an agreement on the reduction of armaments and the increase of mutual trust in military affairs in the border region. The atmosphere of friendship will be strengthened and confidence and cooperation in the two countries' common border region will be maintained. Military–technical cooperation will be developed.'[13]

In April 1996 in Shanghai the presidents of Kazakhstan, Kyrgyzstan and Tajikistan, the State Chairman of China, and Russian Foreign Minister Yevgenii Primakov signed an agreement on confidence building in military affairs in the border region. The agreement specifies that: 'the armies of the two sides deployed in the border area shall not attack each other; no military manoeuvres aimed at each other should be carried out; the limit, scale, range and frequency of military manoeuvres shall be limited, both sides have to inform each other about important military activities taking place 100 km in depth; observers must be invited to military exercises; any dangerous military action shall be prevented; friendly contacts strengthened between the troops on each side deployed in the border region. . . .' The agreement was a breakthrough in confidence building between China and the Central Asian states and in efforts to maintain peace and security in the wider Asia–Pacific region.

Negotiations on arms reduction in the border regions, which started in 1992, intensified in September 1995, when experts from China, Russia, Kazakhstan, Kyrgyzstan and Tajikistan met in Moscow, and continued throughout 1996. Finally in Moscow in April 1997 the five countries signed an Agreement on Mutual Reductions of Military Forces in the Border Region. The agreement includes the following undertakings: (a) to reduce military forces deployed near the border region in all five countries to defensive troops only; (b) not to use weapons or threaten to use them or seek to maintain military superiority; (c) to reduce numbers of ground forces, air forces, air defence and border defence forces, and the numbers of major weapons deployed to 100 km on either side of the border; (d) to define the size of the forces remaining after the reduction and the manner and timetable of this reduction; (e) to exchange relevant information on their forces deployed in the border region; and (f) to conduct regular verification of the implementation of the agreement. The agreement is valid until December 2020 but can be extended. The information exchanged on the military forces in the border area will be kept secret from third countries.

This agreement is an important achievement, marking the change of attitude of the parties since the cold war and their progress towards mutual understanding and trust.

In July 1998 Jiang Zemin, the presidents of Kazakhstan, Kyrgyzstan and Tajikistan, and Yevgenii Primakov, representing the Russian President, met in Almaty to discuss the strengthening of regional peace, stability and economic cooperation. The meeting focused on common efforts to fight separatism, religious fundamentalism, terrorism, illegal arms trafficking and the illegal drugs trade as common threats to the region's stability and security. It also stressed the need for consultation and coopcration between the five countries' ministries for foreign affairs, security, defence and customs.[14] The communiqué issued at the end of the meeting emphasized that the expansion and strengthening of bilateral and multilateral cooperation between the five countries will play a crucial role in the stability, enhanced security and prosperity of the whole of Asia. It stressed that cooperation between the five countries is not targeted against any other country.

Many different aspects of cooperation between China and the Central Asian states in military affairs and security have been proceeding at different levels: for example, in November 1993 an agreement on cooperation was signed between representatives of the Ministry of Internal Affairs of Kyrgyzstan and the Chinese Ministry of Public Security. An intensive exchange of visits has also taken place between representatives of all levels and all branches of the Chinese Army and the chiefs of staff of the Central Asian armies.[15]

Islamism and separatism in Central Asia and Xinjiang

The part of China that borders on Central Asia is the Xinjiang Uighur Autonomous Region (XUAR). The largest ethnic minority of the region, the Uighurs, who are ethnic Turks and Muslims, constitute 7 million out of a population of 16.6 million. There are demographic similarities with Central Asia, since Xinjiang is home to about 1 million Kazakhs and smaller numbers of Kyrgyz and Tajiks. Growing unrest and separatism in Xinjiang are the top priority on the Chinese domestic security agenda.

The religious issue did not become serious until the 1970s but has since become more complex and prominent. Political Islam in Xinjiang has gone through three stages of development. The first stage was between the late 1970s and the mid-1980s, when the number of believers in Islam in Xinjiang rose sharply. Many people who were not originally believers or had lapsed took up religion again. Even Communist Party officials and young people, including university students, began to profess Islam, to the concern of the authorities. Religious activity increased rapidly and a movement to build mosques reached a peak. By the mid-1980s the Muslims of Xinjiang had the highest number of mosques per capita in the world—on average one for about 150 people. This overheated situation was related partly to the crisis in belief after the Cultural Revolution, but also to insensitivity on the part of the authorities responsible for the administration of religious affairs and their unawareness of the growing role of religion.

The second stage was the second half of the 1980s, when radical Islamism appeared, opposing the government's principles of the separation of state and religion and interfering with public administration and with the work of the judicial bodies in the areas of marriage and education. Believers built mosques and extended premises for Islamic activities without permission. The radical Islamists opened schools for the study of religious literature to train cadres for religious institutions, and incited believers to wage a jihad (holy war) and engage in terrorism. Religious activities were extensively used as a cover for separatist activities, and the radical Islamists and separatists formed alliances.

The third stage covers the period from the early 1990s to the present. It is characterized by very obvious signs of religion becoming politicized and by the violent activities of extremist fundamentalist sects. The influence of fundamentalism is spreading fast in Xinjiang. Radical Islamists and terrorists are uniting. Assassinations and revolt have become more frequent. Fundamentalist influence in the 1990s has thus brought an element of instability to Xinjiang, and radical Islamists have become a political force opposed to society and government.

The Government of China and that of the XUAR took stronger action against the radical Islamists and—in conformity with the law—tightened control over religious activities. In 1988 a decree was issued regulating the administration of places for religious activities in Xinjiang. This was the first regulation of a local nature, marking the legalization of religion in Xinjiang.[16] In the 1990s two more decrees were issued, on the management of religious professional workers and on the administration of religious affairs, providing the necessary foundation for legal control of the religious affairs of the XUAR. The Chinese Government was firmly opposed to politics being influenced by religion or vice versa.

Separatism in Xinjiang is a second problem for the Chinese authorities. China has always considered Xinjiang an inseparable part of its territory. The fight against separatism there has a long history. Ideas of Pan-Islamism and Pan-Turkism, with the goal of separating Xinjiang from China, appeared as early as the 1930s. Separatist concepts such as the Republic of East Turkestan and the National Liberation Movement followed in the 1940s. After the founding of the People's Republic of China, the government cracked down on separatism and its leaders, including the East Turkestan National Revolutionary Party. The separatist movement was brought to its lowest level in the 1970s. In the 1990s, influenced by the new international environment, it received new impetus. The '9th of April' movement in Aksu in 1980, the '30th of October' movement in Kashgar in 1981 and the '5th of February' movement in Yining (Gulja) in 1997 are examples.

The Chinese Government's policy is to fight separatism and pursue saboteur and terrorist groups without setting itself against the Uighur minority as a whole. It does not regard separatism as an ethnic issue, nor does it regard issues arising between different ethnic groups as ethnic issues. If it were to respond in any different way, extreme ethnic feelings stimulated by political Islam might turn into a powerful social force, resistant to any control.

The independence of the Central Asian states has in certain ways encouraged the separatists in Xinjiang. Furthermore, the latter carry out operations from the Central Asian states. At present they are most active in Kazakhstan, where they founded the East Turkestan Committee, the Uighuristan Liberation Foundation and the Uighur Trans-National Union. These later united to form the Uighur Political Union Committee. This organization together with the International East Turkestan Committee (the International Ethnic Consultative Committee) in Turkey and the East Turkestan National Liberation Union in Munich are the main organizations abroad. The situation in Afghanistan has also had great influence on Xinjiang. A small number of radical Islamists from Xinjiang went to Afghanistan for terrorist training. Since returning secretly they have instigated a series of terrorist actions.

The activities of Uighur separatists abroad have increased. In March 1999 the English-language edition of the *Journal of the World Muslim Union* published a letter of appeal by the separatist elements to the US President, Bill Clinton, in the name of the Uighur Political Union Committee.

Terrorism has brought an element of instability not only to Xinjiang but to the Central Asian region. The incursion by terrorists into Kyrgyzstan in August 1999 shows that the problem must be tackled urgently. The governments of China and the Central Asian states have therefore made common cause in the struggle against separatists and Islamist radicals. Thus, in July 1999 Jiang Zemin and Nazarbayev declared that measures against terrorism should be reinforced in order to stabilize the region.

The meeting in August 1999 in Bishkek between the leaders of China, Russia, Kazakhstan, Kyrgyzstan and Tajikistan stressed the crackdown on terrorism, religious radicalism and separatism.

Separatism and economic development

Economic development is a central component of China's approach to fighting separatism and maintaining long-term stability in Xinjiang. In the 1990s the regional government initiated a policy of expanding foreign trade, attracting foreign businesses to joint ventures with local firms, and building trading centres jointly with foreign partners. In September 1993 representatives from China's five north-west regions and provinces (Xinjiang, Ningxia Hui Autonomous Region and the provinces of Gansu, Shanxi and Qinghai) met in Urumchi to discuss cooperation, the joint construction of a main transport link and coordinated efforts to open up the Central Asian states. This allowed Xinjiang to become the main economic actor cooperating with the Central Asian states, and gave an impetus for the Chinese regions and provinces to expand their economies. In September 1995 all Xinjiang's 16 areas, prefectures and cities were given state ratification and licences allowing them to engage in foreign trade. Previously only a few entities had been allowed to do so. This was an important adjustment in foreign trade policy.

By the end of 1997 China had opened nine centres for land communications with Central Asian states, most of them in Xinjiang—Huoerguosi, Dulata, Muzhaerte, Baketu, Aheitubieke, Jiemunai, Alatau Shankou, Torugart and Yierkeshitan. Huoerguosi is one of the oldest centres for trade with Kazakhstan: it is 100 years old and now has the principal road link between China and the Central Asian states. Because of its advantageous geographical position, Xinjiang has carried out the greater part of China's trade with the Central Asian states, especially in the first few years after they achieved independence.[17]

During the cold war period China's strategy with regard to its northwest was one of defence. This inhibited the development of the area. After relations with the Soviet Union were normalized, China adopted a new strategy of opening up Xinjiang. This represented a major strategic adjustment and gave new opportunities to the north-west, especially Xinjiang. After the break-up of the Soviet Union, China established trade and economic contacts with all the CIS countries and formulated a strategy for the development of foreign economic cooperation. The policy is to open up not only to the West but also to the CIS countries.

In 1992, in the new international situation, the Party Committee and the People's Government of Xinjiang submitted a Report on the Expansion of the Opening-Up Policy in Xinjiang to the Communist Party of China and the State Council. The State Council responded officially to this report. Xinjiang was allowed to benefit from a policy similar to that enjoyed by the coastal areas and the special economic zones. The State Council ordered Xinjiang to implement a policy of opening up in all directions, with a special focus on the west. Xinjiang was also required to create a network for local firms and to attract foreign businessmen with the purpose of networking in the east in order to make progress in the west. The goal was to create an open structure with Urumchi as the 'door' and Yining, Bole and Tacheng (Qaramay) as the 'windows'. The open zones of the neighbouring countries should serve as forward positions, the opening up of railway links would provide logistic support, and the eastern provinces and areas would form a hinterland. In order to create a genuinely open region the whole area should be covered by a network of cooperation on many levels, in different channels and forms and in diversified markets. In this way Xinjiang can become a channel between the East and the West and a link between East Asia, Central Asia and Eurasia, as well as an important point on the contemporary Silk Road.[18] The opening wide of the north-west 'door' marks an important strategic change in the attitude of the Chinese Communist Party and Government.

China and the strategic scene in Central Asia

The Central Asian states are unquestionably subject to some adverse influences from external powers. The interests of these powers are contradictory. In general, the following groups of powers play a particular role: (a) Russia; (b) the West, led by the USA; (c) the Islamic world; and (d) China and some other Asian countries. Russia, China and Iran have obvious concerns or advantages since they border on Central Asia. The USA is projecting itself because of global strategic circumstances. Turkey inclines to the USA and major Western countries, and Iran to Russia. However, neither Turkey nor Iran is likely to play a major role in Central Asia. They are more likely to maintain normal relations or perform an intermediary role. Turkey is an old adversary of Russia and Iran has had hostile relations with the USA for nearly 20 years. The USA is trying to use Turkey to encourage the Central Asian states to resist Russia and Iran and, without doubt, to constrain China's intentions and strategic considerations.

China regards Russia as a guarantee of the stability of the Central Asian states, and perhaps also of the stability of the surrounding areas. All the senior officers of the Central Asian armies were officers under the Soviet Union, and their military equipment and skills date from the Soviet period. Although there are some complaints against Russia, the Central Asian states cannot manage without it. They prefer to be protected within Russia's defence area and for most of the 1990s relied on Russian border troops in protecting their own outer—former Soviet—borders. In this respect Tajikistan is the most dependent. On the other hand, Russia is also helping them to build up their own armies, to train officers, and even to handle ecological crises.

In their strategic approaches to Central Asia, both China and Russia seek peace and stability, are opposed to great-power influence in the region, and support regional cooperation. There are some contradictions between them. Russia traditionally views the Central Asian states as being within its sphere of influence and does not wish to see China become deeply involved there; China is opposed to Russia considering the Central Asian states as a region of its own, and supports their sovereignty and independence and their cooperation with all other countries. Nevertheless, China expresses understanding of Russia's strong role in the region and acknowledges that its military cooperation with the Central Asian states is helpful for stability there. The possibility cannot be excluded that this cooperation could be directed at a third country. Russia's role in Central Asia can be contained or stimulated. If, for example, the USA expands its influence in the region, cooperation with the Central Asian states might become more urgent for both China and Russia.

The USA perceives the Central Asian states from the perspective of its strategic interests in the broadest sense. First, it considers that they have rich energy resources, and it is through energy resources that the USA usually attempts to control the world. Second, it intends to oppose fundamentalism by active involvement in Central Asia and is concerned that Central Asia and the Middle East might unite to become a dynamic region of Islamic radicalism. Third, it intends to contain Russia. By means of strong political, economic and military influence in Central Asia it might eventually weaken Russia's strategic influence. Fourth, in entering Central Asia the USA intends to contain China's strategic plans and as part of this to exert influence on Xinjiang.

The USA sees Turkey as its best partner in becoming engaged in Central Asia. It has been helping Turkey in its negotiations to join the European Union and supporting its efforts to achieve oil and gas pipelines linking the Central Asian states via Azerbaijan to Turkey.[19] The US element in Central Asia will be the most dynamic, but also the most indefinite. It is very possible that US influence is responsible for the present instability in the region.

As regards their interests in the Central Asian states, the USA and Russia regard themselves as antagonists. Increased US power in Central Asia could greatly affect Russia's influence and damage its interests. The USA through its aggressive competition might unbalance the fragile strategic interests in the Central Asian region. In view of the specific character and complexity of the region, the USA must also consider the interests of the countries that surround it.

China is opposed to any US scheme to build military bases in the Central Asian states, carry out joint military manoeuvres there or use the Central Asian states as a tool to contain China because it considers this as endangering the safety of its own north-west regions. The USA is encouraging NATO to expand eastwards and compete with Russia in Central Asia. In August 1998 the USA launched an unauthorized military attack on Afghanistan, threatening security in the region around China. It is strengthening its security cooperation with Japan and considers itself a protector of Taiwan. Part of the purpose of its military cooperation with the Central Asian states is to threaten China's security.

China has not explicitly expressed opposition to the participation of the four Central Asian states (Tajikistan is not a member) in the NATO Partnership for Peace (PfP) programme. Nonetheless, it is watching closely how NATO influence increases in the Central Asian states. NATO's penetration in the region has brought an element of instability: it will undermine the strategic balance and the (otherwise improving) security environment for the neighbouring countries, and hinder the consolidation of their independence and normal development. China is a neighbour of the Central Asian states and does not wish to see NATO conduct military manoeuvres there year after year near its borders. This is causing China serious anxiety, especially after the Kosovo crisis.

Since the Central Asian states became independent, Turkey has signed agreements on friendship and cooperation with all of them. It has two roles in the region—to become the 'big brother' of the Turkic nations and to be a strategic partner for the USA. The latter role will be the more important. Iran for its part entered Central Asia comparatively early and is actively supporting the construction of the Asia–Europe land bridge. In spite of its Islamic profile, Iran will have only limited influence in Central Asia.

China is not against the Central Asian states developing military cooperation with other countries. It supports them in their task of developing their own armies and defence systems, and welcomes the efforts of relevant countries and international organizations to support their peace and stability. However, China retains its own principles and security interests. In its view the involvement of large countries should not allow an arms race or military confrontation to develop between the states of Central Asia, and other countries and external forces should not be able to interfere in the internal politics of the states in the region or harm their independence and sovereignty. China will neither seek to obtain a sphere of influence among the Central Asian states nor force its will and ideas on these states. It does not, however, allow activities to take place in the Central Asian states that harm its own sovereignty or are directed at breaking up China. Any cooperation should be aimed at serving the interests of peace and the development of Central Asia and the whole of Asia.

Prospects for the future

In the increasingly fluid international situation, the strategic importance of Central Asia for China will grow. Stability, development and cooperation are the main pillars in China's relations with its neighbours. This includes stability and development in each Central Asian state, between these states, and between Central Asia and other regions.

If stability is to be achieved the following have to be taken into consideration: (a) the economy. The crucial questions here are how Central Asia can overcome the post-independence crisis, choose a policy for economic growth and reform, exploit its inner potential to tackle the crisis, and bring about prosperity and revival; (b) the ethnic issue. There are two levels of this issue in Central Asia: the friction between the local people and the Russians, which has led to many Russians migrating to the Russian Federation; and the tensions between the different local nationalities; (c) relations between the Central Asian states; and (d) penetration by the major powers and other countries and their influence on stability in the region.

Stability is a prerequisite for development and development is a guarantee of stability. The governments of the Central Asian states realize this. Their efforts to maintain stability have the ultimate goal of providing the necessary conditions for overcoming the economic crisis and consolidating their independence.

Relations between China and the Central Asian states must be built on a stable foundation. The basic principles for developing such relations, the Five Principles of Peaceful Coexistence, have already been established. Now these general principles should be further elaborated and the norms of action and a stable mechanism of joint development defined.

From the Chinese perspective, the main requirements for developing its relations with the Central Asian states are as follows.

—The Central Asian states should support China's standpoint on Taiwan.

—China should support the independence and independent development of each Central Asian state.

—China and each of the Central Asian states should regard each other as security partners.

—China and the Central Asian states should stand together against separatism, Islamic extremism and terrorism.

—China and the three neighbouring Central Asian states should take advantage of cross-border ethnic links in order to strengthen friendship, understanding and contacts.

—Relations between China and the Central Asian states should be built on a firm economic basis.

—China and the Central Asian states should cooperate to defend peace and justice on the international scene.

Notes

1. Speech by Qian Qichen on 17 August 1992 at the Shanghai United Nations Asia–Pacific countries' meeting on questions of security and reduction of armaments, *Renmin Ribao* [People's Daily], 18 August 1992 (in Chinese).

2. [Strengthening good neighbourly relations, promoting mutually beneficial cooperation and congratulating Prime Minister Li Peng on the success of his visit to five countries], *Renmin Ribao*, 30 April 1994.

3. During Li Peng's working visit to Kazakhstan in September 1997, the two countries signed an Additional Agreement between China and Kazakhstan on Border Questions. On 4 July 1998, when Jiang Zemin visited Kazakhstan, he and President Nazarbayev signed the Second Additional Agreement between China and Kazakhstan on Border Questions.

4. President Nazarbayev, answering correspondents' question during his visit to India on 22 February 1992. Lotus Agency, New Delhi, 22 February 1992, telegram (in English).

5. Interview given by President Nazarbayev to the Italian *Newsletter* in [Kazakhstan entering the nuclear club], *Za Rubezhom* [Abroad], no. 13 (1992) (in Russian).

6. *Renmin Ribao*, 9 February 1995.

7. 'Premier Li Peng proposing six views', *Renmin Ribao*, 27 April 1994.

8. Mark Burles, 'Chinese policy toward Russia and the Central Asian republics', Rand Corporation, 1999, URL <http://www.rand.org/publications/MR/MR1045/>.

9. See note 8.

10. [The situation is gratifying and the prospects extensive: Foreign Economic Trade Minister Wu Yida answering questions from the *People's Daily* correspondent], *Renmin Ribao*, 21 December 1994.

11. Guangcheng Xing, [Relations between China and the newly independent Central Asian states] (Heilongjiang Education Press, 1996 edn), p. 157.

12. *Renmin Ribao*, 24 October 1993.

13. *Renmin Ribao*, 12 September 1995.

14. *Renmin Ribao*, 4 July 1998.

15. In March 1995 a delegation from the Chinese People's Liberation Army (PLA) visited Kazakhstan. In July 1995 representatives of the Xinjiang border defence army visited Kazakhstan and Kyrgyzstan. In November 1995 the Kyrgyz Minister of Defence, Murzakan Subanov, visited China and said that he hoped the armies of the two countries would establish direct contact. In October 1996 the Kazakh Minister of Defence, Alibek Kasimov, visited China. In May 1997 Chi Haotian, Deputy Head of China's Central Defence Commission, member of the State Council and Minister of Defence, visited Kazakhstan and Kyrgyzstan, met their leaders and discussed military cooperation. On 3 October 1997 the Kazakh Minister of Defence, General Mukhtar Altynbaev, visited China and met Li Peng and his colleagues at the Chinese Ministry of Defence. In May 1996 a Chinese military delegation headed by the Chief of the General Staff of the PLA, General Fu Quanyou, visited Kazakhstan and held talks with the Kazakh Minister of Defence and Prime Minister. In October the same year the military adviser of the President of Kazakhstan and former Minister of Defence, General Nurmajambetov, visited China and met PLA leaders.

16. Temporary Regulation on the Administration of Places for Religious Activities of the Uighur Autonomous Region of Xinjiang.

17. *1993 Sinkiang Statistical Yearbook*, pp. 231–233; *Sinkiang Social Economy*, 1994, 4th edn, p. 9; and *Research on Eurasia's Second Land Bridge*, p. 137.

18. *Renmin Ribao*, 6 July 1992.

19. Wan Guang, 'Meiguo de xin Zhongya zhanlüe' [The new Central Asia strategy of the USA], *Xiandai guoji guanxi* [Contemporary international relations], vol. 11 (1997), p. 11.

CHAPTER EIGHT

Iran and Central Asia

EDMUND HERZIG

Introduction

This chapter discusses Iran's relations with the states of Central Asia, and how these contribute to emerging patterns of regional security concerns and cooperation. The primary focus is on the view from Tehran—how Central Asian security matters affect Iran, and how Iranian policy makers and specialists perceive the Central Asian region and Iran's place in it. Afghanistan is discussed primarily as an issue in Iranian security policy and a factor in Iran's relations with the states of Central Asia. There is no attempt to give a Kabul or Kandahar perspective on Central Asian security.

By the beginning of the 1990s, when the Central Asian states became independent, the foreign and security policy of the Islamic Republic of Iran had already evolved significantly away from that of the early years after the 1979 revolution. The tendency (characteristic of revolutionary regimes) to prioritize ideological interests and to reject and oppose the international status quo—i.e., to export revolution—was eroded by a combination of internal and external developments. The Iran–Iraq War (1980–88) was a key factor in this process. The experience of invasion and the existential struggle for survival made Iran's leadership more aware of conventional vital national interests—independence, territorial integrity and national sovereignty—and of the ways in which the international system and its rules could be used to secure these. Following the war, the urgent need for reconstruction and more generally for social and economic development encouraged policy makers to focus more on material national interests in all areas; in foreign relations this was expressed in an emphasis on trade and attracting investment. Domestic political development, symbolized by the death of Ayatollah Khomeini in 1989 and the presidency (1989–97) of Hojatoleslam Ali Akbar Hashemi Rafsanjani, further reinforced the pragmatic trend.

Other external developments around Iran's borders also helped to shift Iranian policy towards seeking to promote regional peace and stability and normal state-to-state relations. In the early 1990s the Karabagh conflict threatened to spill over Iran's borders, to create a new refugee crisis, and potentially to draw Iran and other external powers into confrontation in the South Caucasus. The continuing civil war in Afghanistan posed a variety of threats (see below). Iraq continued to be the source of the gravest threats to Iran's security, whether in the shape of a possible renewed Iraqi attack on Iran or another of its neighbours—through Iraq's weapons of mass destruction programme, through its providing bases and support for the Mojaheddin-e Khalq organization (which continues to carry out terrorist attacks inside Iran)—or through the possible fragmentation of Iraq in a variety of post-Saddam Hussein scenarios. The nuclear proliferation and Kashmir conflict in South Asia and the unfriendly US naval presence in the Persian Gulf complete, in Tehran's eyes, the picture of Iran as an island of stability hemmed in by conflicts and threats.[1]

At the same time, the experience of the eight-year war with Iraq, as well as that of the 1991 Iraq–Kuwait War and Washington's subsequent policy of dual containment of Iraq and Iran, which it branded as the region's two 'rogue' states, reinforced Iranians' sense of being victimized by US global pre-eminence. This is revealed in a continuing distrust of the international system and its institutions and of broader processes such as globalization as vehicles for US hegemony. Countering Washington's efforts to isolate Iran became an important strategic objective in its own right. On the one hand this led Tehran to emphasize self-reliance in security, in order to develop the capacity to counter and deter likely threats. On the other hand there was a dawning realization that Iran's negative image abroad and international isolation stemmed at least in part from Tehran's inflammatory rhetoric and reliance on unconventional means (support for radical and revolutionary groups and alleged involvement in numerous acts of terrorism across the globe). And this in turn led to a prioritization of building trust and normal mutually beneficial relations with all but a handful of states that were still considered beyond the pale (primarily Israel and the USA). Tehran has looked to cooperation with neighbours, with other nearby and Muslim states, and with possible alternative major centres of power (Russia, China and Europe) to frustrate the US policy of containment. In this respect, Tehran has seen the value of regional and international organizations that are not susceptible to Western domination—for example the Non-Aligned Movement,[2] the Organization of the Islamic Conference (the OIC), and the Organization of Petroleum Exporting Countries (OPEC)—which can be vehicles for pursuing both ideological and material interests within the rules of the game. In short, by the end of the 1980s Tehran began to make a more coherent effort to balance deterrence and détente in a strategy to achieve its long-term security interests.[3]

In the 1990s the trend towards pragmatic national interest-based policy and towards working within the rules of the international system continued and was given further impetus by the election of President Mohammad Khatami in 1997. Soon after his election, Khatami stated that what Iran wanted in the international arena was peace, stability, and balanced and expedient development.[4] His watchwords in foreign policy have been 'détente' and 'dialogue of civilizations', reflecting a world view that is more pluralistic and less confrontational than that of the previous leadership. Like President Rafsanjani before him, he has laid particular emphasis on regional relations and cooperation—a priority that has paid dividends in a marked improvement in relations with Saudi Arabia and other Arab states. At the start of the 21st century the Islamic Republic of Iran no longer acts or is perceived primarily as a vanguard revolutionary state, but as an established regional power (although that also may cause anxieties among smaller neighbours).

If the broad trend towards pragmatism and moderation in foreign policy is clear and affects all the mainstream political groupings,[1] the pattern of Iran's international relations is more chequered. On some issues, notably Israel–Palestine, ideological priorities remain predominant, and the thoroughness of Tehran's conversion to working within the international rules of the game is open to question. The formulation and implementation of Iran's foreign and security policy is not the preserve of the President and Foreign Ministry alone: the Supreme Leader's office, the Supreme National Security Council, the Ministry of Information and Security, the Revolutionary Guard Corps, the armed forces and other state and quasi-state bodies are also involved. Some of these have travelled less far from the uncompromising ideals of the first years of the revolution and the anti-establishment means used to pursue them. These differences have, from time to time, been exacerbated by poor coordination between various actors and by the deliberate exploitation of foreign policy differences (for example over the possibility of an eventual resumption of relations with the USA) in intra-regime political and ideological competition.[6]

The normalization of relations between Iran and Central Asia

In the wake of the collapse of the Soviet Union, outside countries (including Iran), 'rushed in [to Central Asia] to offer co-operation, to advance their own interests and to prevent any possible ramifications'.[7] Like Turkey and the West, Iran was poorly informed about the Central Asian republics and was taken by surprise by their sudden acquisition of independence. Ignorance played to both Tehran's hopes and its fears. Like other international actors, it saw the Soviet collapse as giving rise to a vacuum in the former Soviet south, a vacuum that would inevitably be filled by some external power and ideology. In a worst-case scenario, the USA and its proxies, Turkey and Israel, would move in to encircle Iran's northern borders and complete the Islamic Republic's isolation. If things went well, however, the region's Muslim populations would rediscover their cultural roots, embrace Islamic government and provide Iran with a comforting northern cushion of small and friendly, if not client, states.[8] In any case, the creation of eight new states was seen as having a profound impact on Iran's strategic geography. Rather than being one of two non-Arab states on the northern periphery of a predominantly Arab Middle East, Iran (like Turkey) now saw the potential to be the centre of gravity of a new enlarged Middle East that included the non-Arab peoples of Central Asia and the South Caucasus.[9]

With these opportunities and dangers in mind, Foreign Minister Ali Akbar Velayati on a November 1991 tour of the Soviet Union visited Azerbaijan and the five Central Asian republics (the 'Muslim' republics) and reached agreement on opening consulates in all of them. This may be seen as marking Iran's first move in a brief intense competition with Turkey to provide the 'ideal model' for the new Muslim states. The competition was futile in that the presumptions of a vacuum were mistaken: Russia did not relinquish its position in the area and the new states were not looking for new 'big brothers', nor were they at all certain that they wished to reorient towards the Middle East. In any case, neither Iran nor Turkey had the resources or leverage to establish a pre-eminent position in Central Asia.[10]

An additional restraint on the competition was provided by the fact that for both Turkey and Iran the stakes in bilateral relations with Moscow were higher than those they were playing for in Central Asia. In the second half of the 1980s, relations between Iran and the Soviet Union had improved markedly, and throughout the 1990s relations with Russia remained a high priority. Agreements with Moscow were important for Iran's weapon purchases (10-year agreements of 1989–90) and nuclear programme (agreement of 1995), and Russian friendship is seen in Tehran as providing a vital strategic counterweight to American hostility.[11] In the run-up to the final collapse of the Soviet Union, Iranian leaders exhibited caution in developing relations with the union republics of the USSR in order not to antagonize the Soviet leadership (Moscow's approval was sought for the opening of consulates in the Muslim republics, for example), and throughout the 1990s Tehran refused to jeopardize relations with Moscow for the sake of less tangible and significant benefits that might be attained in Central Asia.[12]

Sensitivity to Moscow's concerns delayed Iran's recognition of the independence of the new Central Asian states until late December 1991, whereas Turkey had offered recognition in the middle of the month. Independence, however, opened the floodgates for diplomatic contact and formal relations (even before independence, in October 1991, President Saparmurad Niyazov of Turkmenistan had visited Iran). The presidents of Tajikistan, Kazakhstan and Uzbekistan all visited Iran in the course of 1992, and in 1993 Iran's President Rafsanjani visited all the Central Asian states (except Tajikistan, where civil war and the return to power of the ex-communists had set relations back to square one). There were many more exchanges at minister and deputy minister levels, a host of agreements were signed covering political, economic and cultural relations, and a number of new border crossings were opened and visa restrictions eased.[13] By June 1992 agreement had been reached with all the Central Asian states on opening embassies, although in some cases their actual opening was delayed by several years. The concrete achievements of this flurry of bilateral contacts have been less obvious, and many agreements have never been implemented, but, as Menashri notes, the diplomatic contacts and signature of accords were important in themselves—for the Central Asians in affirming their entry onto the world stage as independent actors, and for Iran in staking its claim to a role in the region and hence frustrating the US policy of isolation.[14]

It was also in this early period (roughly late 1991 to early 1993, which Deputy Foreign Minister Abbas Maleki subsequently described as the period of 'initial euphoria'[15]) that Iran—both the government and the quasi-state Islamic Foundations, such as the Bonyad-e Mostazafan and the Bonyad-e Shahid—made an effort to lead, encourage and shape religious revival in Central Asia.[16] They sponsored missionary activity, the distribution of religious books, the broadcasting of Iranian television and radio in Central Asia, the training of mullahs in Iran's madrassahs, and the opening of religious schools and mosques.[17] Tehran gave verbal, and by some accounts also material, support to the Islamic Revival Party in Tajikistan, but the ideological commitment was insufficient to sustain Iranian support once civil war broke out in 1992, with Russia and Uzbekistan firmly backing the ex-communists against the democratic–Islamist coalition.[18] Even for this early period it is hard to concur with Menashri's assertion that ideological and religious activities have been salient in Iran's engagement in Central Asia.[19] It is, of course, impossible to gauge the level and character of activities, a part of which remains undeclared, but available evidence suggests that Iran's cultural agenda has been as much Persian as Islamic and far from revolutionary in tone, and that it has never outweighed political, economic and security priorities.[20]

Quite early on, Tehran became aware of the intense suspicion and hostility that proselytizing activities aroused among Central Asian elites. President Islam Karimov of Uzbekistan was the most forthright in voicing alarm about Iranian support for Islamic radicalism and in excluding Islam from the agenda of bilateral relations. Nor was there any indication of an enthusiastic response from the vast majority of Central Asian Muslims. Conservative traditionalists and the secular-minded alike were repelled by Iran's image and reputation as a hard-line revolutionary state, while radicals, if they looked abroad for inspiration and support, turned to Sunni Islamists in Afghanistan, Pakistan, the Arabian Peninsula and Turkey.[21]

Another factor affecting Iranian perceptions and policies was the growing appreciation of the threats to regional stability and Iran's national security posed by developments in Central Asia and the South Caucasus (see section IV below). If in the immediate post-Soviet period Tehran had been most concerned about the danger of Central Asia being exploited by the USA in its global strategy to contain the Islamic Republic, attention now shifted to a series of more localized but immediate threats.

In the South Caucasus the conflict between Armenia and Azerbaijan over Mountainous Karabagh (Nagorno-Karabakh) was at its most intense in 1992–94. Fighting reached Iran's borders, there was the threat of a massive influx of Azerbaijani refugees, there was the danger of other external states (particularly Turkey) becoming engaged in the conflict, and there were strains on Iran's developing relations with both Armenia and Azerbaijan. In addition, at the time of the Azerbaijani Popular Front government in Baku (1992–93), the issue of irredenta and of the relations between independent Azerbaijan and Iran's Azerbaijani population threatened to destabilize relations.

In the Caspian Sea, the dispute among the littoral states over the legal status of the sea, and the related issues of oil and gas development and of the participation of international companies, became increasingly heated and apparently irreconcilable, especially following Azerbaijan's award of a major offshore contract to an international consortium, the Azerbaijan International Operating Company (AIOC), in 1994. From 1992 onwards Tehran has constantly reiterated its unease about the absence of an agreed legal regime for the sea, about the penetration of external powers into the Caspian, and about the possibility of an arms race among the Caspian states.

In Central Asia itself, apart from a series of violent inter-communal conflicts in the last years of Soviet rule, there was the civil war in Tajikistan, which was at its most intense in 1992–93, when the ex-communists supported by Russia and Uzbekistan ousted the democratic–Islamist coalition government, creating tens of thousands of refugees who fled to Afghanistan or other former Soviet republics. The linking of the Tajik and Afghan conflicts seemed to threaten the extension of long-term instability and armed conflict throughout the region. The Tajik conflict highlighted for Iran the risks of ill-judged engagement with opposition or Islamist forces in Central Asia. Tehran was faced with a stark choice between ideological and strategic/national interest priorities. Support for the Tajik Islamist opposition would seriously undermine the development of bilateral relations with the states of the region, would further damage the fragile prospects for regional stability, and would also pit Iran in an unequal contest against Russia, which it viewed as a strategic partner.

As early as President Rafsanjani's October 1993 visit to Central Asia, the period of initial euphoria was over and a pattern was set that characterized Iran's Central Asia policy throughout the rest of the 1990s. Islam occupied a very small part in Rafsanjani's discussions and agreements with Central Asian leaders; in this respect the visit drew criticism from radicals in Iran. Instead there was a heavy emphasis on regional peace and stability, and on developing mutually beneficial state-to-state relations and cooperation, particularly in the economic field (see following section).[22]

Iran now sought to play down its competition with Turkey, instead highlighting areas of common interest and cooperation, for example, in the export of Turkmen gas, and in the context of the Economic Cooperation Organisation (ECO). The realization that Russia still viewed Central Asia as an integral part of its sphere of vital interests, especially as regards security, also influenced Iranian policy. Tehran readily acquiesced in Russia's self-appointed role as the guarantor of security and stability in the region and was at pains to show that it saw its role in Central Asia as complementing rather than challenging that of Russia. Iran would help the Central Asians gradually to reduce their dependence on Russia, but recognized that Russia still provided for many of the region's needs, and that any attempt to wrest the Central Asians away from Russia would be against their own best interests.[23]

This second period of Iran's Central Asia policy could be termed the period of pragmatism and cooperation.

Economic and energy cooperation

As noted above, economic relations and trade have been important priorities in Iranian foreign policy since the late 1980s.[24] Tehran seeks to boost non-oil exports in order to help domestic economic development and job creation. No less importantly, however, Tehran has seen economic relations as contributing also to its political and security interests. At a declaratory level, Iran's leaders underlined the links between economic and political stability, and between the development of mutually beneficial economic relations and of trust and cooperation.[25] In the early 1990s these uncontroversial truisms had a specific relevance to Iran's regional predicament. Both in Central Asia and in the Persian Gulf the Islamic Republic was trying to engage with states whose leaders mostly had a negative and suspicious attitude towards Tehran, an attitude reinforced by US urging to steer clear of relations with Iran.[26] From this perspective, the success of economic relations is to be measured not only in terms of trade turnover, joint ventures and investment, but also in less tangible ways through building bilateral and multilateral relations, meshing Iran into the Central Asian region, and creating common interests.

The obstacles to developing economic relations between Iran and Central Asia were considerable. There was no existing pattern of trade relations, and there was almost no infrastructure to support the movement of people and goods—Central Asia's infrastructure was geared towards relations with Russia and the other Soviet republics. More fundamentally, the Iranian and Central Asian economies tended to be competitive rather than complementary. In all of them, exports were concentrated on a few primary products while imports comprised a more diverse 'basket' of manufactured goods. All have weak private sectors and manufacturing industries that cannot compete internationally. They share an urgent need for economic reform and investment, which is unlikely to come from within the region.[27] On the positive side, Iran's geographical location between Central Asia and the Persian Gulf (Iran's land and maritime borders with the former Soviet Union total 2670 km) and its relatively developed internal transport infrastructure offered the potential to develop an important role as a bridge to the world economy for the landlocked Central Asian states.

In the course of the 1990s Iran signed a great many bilateral and a few trilateral agreements and memoranda, as well as organizing trade exhibitions aimed at stimulating trade with the Central Asian states. Bilateral chambers of commerce and economic committees have been established and visa regimes eased. Numerous new border crossings were opened on the border with Turkmenistan. New shipping routes started up between Iran's Caspian ports and those of Kazakhstan and Turkmenistan, and air routes were established between Iran and the Central Asian states. Free trade zones were instituted at Sarakhs on the border with Turkmenistan and at the Caspian port of Anzali. A great many of these initiatives, however, have remained unimplemented, and they have not borne on Iran's relations with all the Central Asian states equally. Turkmenistan, the only one to share a land border with Iran, has been the subject of many more of these initiatives than any of the other states.

Two major infrastructure projects were completed in the 1990s. The first, a 300-km rail link from Mashhad, the capital of Iran's Khorasan province, to Tejen in Turkmenistan, was opened in May 1996, providing the first direct connection between the Iranian and Central Asian rail networks. The second, a 200-km pipeline between Korpedzhe in Turkmenistan and Kord-Kuy in Iran, allowed the export of Turkmen gas into the Iranian gas network. Iran financed the $160 million project, which was envisaged as the first step towards the export of Turkmen gas to Turkey and Europe via Iran, but to date the gas exported via the pipeline has been used to meet demand in Iran's northern cities. These new connections have undoubted economic value, even if none of them has yet been exploited to full capacity, but their symbolic significance in linking Iran to the Central Asian states and allowing the latter to turn south, away from Russia, has been emphasized by politicians and commentators alike. Eleven regional heads of state gathered at the opening of the Mashhad–Tejen rail link to hear President Rafsanjani extol the wider significance of the project: 'The world is moving towards greater regional cooperation, and sustained and regionally coordinated economic growth and development will consolidate peace and stability and pave the way for the enhancement of international relations'.[28]

One other major project is imminent: in 1999 the contract to construct a new 400 km oil pipeline from Neka on Iran's Caspian coast to Tehran was awarded to a Iranian–Chinese consortium. This pipeline will permit a big increase in the level of oil 'swaps' with Kazakhstan (an arrangement whereby Iran imports Kazakhstani oil for use in its northern refineries and exports an equivalent volume of Iranian oil on Kazakhstan's behalf from its Persian Gulf terminals). Swaps have been continuing intermittently and at a low level since 1996. There are other more speculative projects for the construction of oil and gas pipelines from the Caspian oil- and gas-producing states (Turkmenistan, Kazakhstan and Azerbaijan) to Iran, and via Iran to Turkey or the Persian Gulf. Iranian companies gained a modest share in Caspian oil and gas development, with 10 per cent stakes in two Azerbaijani consortia (although in 1995 Iran was excluded under US pressure from the largest consortium) and have cooperated in a limited way with Azerbaijani and Turkmen companies in exploration off Iran's Caspian coast. If Iran has so far failed to become a major player in the exploitation and export of Caspian energy resources, it has succeeded in staking a role for itself, in spite of vocal US opposition. The international oil industry and the region's oil and gas exporters agree that Iran's long-term prospects remain promising.

Iran has also sponsored two major multilateral projects directed towards facilitating economic and energy relations with the Central Asian states. The first and more important of these is the enlarged and revitalized ECO. At the 1992 Tehran ECO summit meeting the six Muslim former Soviet republics and Afghanistan joined the three original members (Iran, Turkey and Pakistan) to create a new intergovernmental regional organization whose mission is to promote economic, technical and cultural cooperation among its member states. The ECO has a permanent secretariat in Tehran, several technical committees, and, on paper at least, eight specialized institutions—a trade and development bank, a reinsurance company, a shipping company, an airline company, a college of insurance, a chamber of commerce, a science foundation, and a cultural–educational institute. The organization's members have agreed to reduce tariffs, promote the free flow of goods and capital, harmonize customs rules, establish free trade zones and border markets, and develop a framework for the reciprocal protection of investments and the elimination of double taxation. In 1998 they signed a declaration encouraging all ECO members to take steps to join the World Trade Organization (WTO), and the ECO has observer status at the WTO as well as at the UN General Assembly. The ECO Istanbul Declaration of 1993 set out the ECO Long-Term Perspective. This, and the 1994 Almaty Outline Plan for the Development of the Transport Sector in the ECO Region, represent efforts to develop long-term planning aimed at integrating the ECO member states into a functional region. At the 1998 Almaty summit the members endorsed a programme of action for the ECO Decade of Transport and Communication (1998–2007). The ECO has also promoted cooperation among members in the oil and gas sectors. The closest that the ECO has come to directly addressing security issues was in the 1998 Memorandum of Understanding on Cooperation against Smuggling and Customs Fraud, which has obvious relevance for narcotics and arms smuggling, although it was adopted in the context of efforts to facilitate and harmonize trade relations.[29]

For a variety of reasons, the ECO's concrete achievements are considerably less impressive than its declaratory record. Its members are in many ways a highly disparate group with widely varying perspectives on their interests and international orientations. Uzbekistan, which is a key link for all transport and trade promotion initiatives, has been lukewarm; Tajikistan experienced several years of civil war; and Afghanistan is still in the grip of conflict, with various ECO members supporting rival Afghan groupings. Azerbaijan's principal transport links to fellow ECO members Iran and Turkey are unusable because they pass through Armenia (which has been under Azerbaijani and Turkish blockade since early in the Karabagh conflict).[30] Nevertheless, as Pomfret notes, 'Most importantly in the present context, ECO provides a forum for discussion of regional disputes and for peaceful cooperation among the original members and the newly independent countries, including the Central Asian countries'.[31] He continues: 'Some of the ECO Summits, notably that of 1996 where the main debates featured disputes between Uzbekistan and Iran and delegates left a day earlier than planned, have been divisive. Nevertheless, it is an achievement of ECO to have kept such conflicts to the conference table . . .'.[32]

This evaluation of the significance of the ECO echoes President Rafsanjani's hopes for the organization, expressed at the 1992 Tehran Summit: 'Viable stability and peace are of great importance to our strategic and sensitive region. This important goal can only be achieved through the extensive collaboration of all regional countries'. He went on to cite the example of OPEC and the Association of South-East Asian Nations as models of organizations which in promoting economic cooperation have contributed also to regional security.[33] In similar vein, Foreign Minister Kamal Kharrazi claims that 'the ECO has contributed to the consolidation of amicable and promising relationships among its members'.[34]

At the same time as sponsoring the enlargement of the ECO at the 1992 Tehran summit, Iran took advantage of the occasion to launch a new multilateral intergovernmental initiative—for the creation of a Caspian Sea Cooperation Organization. This won the immediate backing of the other four littoral states (Azerbaijan, Russia, Kazakhstan and Turkmenistan), and although the Caspian Sea Cooperation remains a concept rather than an organization (ambitions to establish a permanent secretariat or any formal institutions remain unfulfilled) it has generated a considerable degree of interest and activity among the putative members. In October 1992 they agreed to form six committees with responsibility for: (a) the legal status of the Caspian; (b) environmental protection; (c) conservation and exploitation of biological resources; (d) prospecting for and exploiting mineral resources; (e) shipping and ports; and (f) marine research. In 1993 the littoral states agreed to establish a joint Caspian Sea research centre. There have been relatively frequent meetings at minister and deputy minister level, and agreements have been reached on environmental protection, biological resources and navigation. To date, however, the key issues of the legal status of the Sea and the exploitation of mineral (i.e., oil and gas) resources have proved insurmountable obstacles to multilateral agreement. The sharp, well-publicized disagreements of the littoral states over these issues may seem to make a mockery of the ideal of Caspian Sea Cooperation, but it could better be argued that they highlight the importance of a forum where differences and grievances can be aired around the table.[35] For Iran the Caspian Sea Cooperation concept has special significance in meshing Iran with the four other littoral states, all of which are former Soviet republics, and in a region which has been the focus of Western, especially US, business and policy initiatives. Tehran has been sensitive (doubtless with its Persian Gulf/Gulf Cooperation Council experience in mind) to the danger of being excluded from a future Caspian Sea regional grouping, to the risks of a possible future militarization of the Caspian and to the danger of hostile foreign penetration into the region—concerns that are not shared by all the other littoral states.[36] These specific concerns are reflected in the hopes Iran has expressed for Caspian cooperation, for example, in Kharrazi's urging that 'the littoral states strive to arrive at a suitable legal regime, excluding the interventionist designs of extra-regional actors'.[37]

In terms of the actual economic benefits derived from Iran's considerable outlay in bilateral and multilateral economic relations with the Central Asian states, the returns seem small. In 1990 the Minister of Economy and Finance, Mohsen Nourbakhsh, estimated that the South Caucasus and Central Asia were a potential $8–10 billion market for Iranian exports. From a starting point of next to nothing in 1990, Iranian exports to the Central Asian states grew to $349 million in 1996, while imports were a mere $111 million. These figures are trifling compared to the ambitions expressed at the start of the decade, insignificant compared to Iran's trade with, for example, Turkey or Azerbaijan (which itself is not great—over all ECO member states account for only 5.1 per cent of Iran's imports and 3.3 per cent of its exports), and of minor importance even to the Central Asian states, whose trade in the 1990s has reoriented away from Russia and the Commonwealth of Independent States (CIS), not towards Iran or other regional states, but towards new global partners.[38]

If, however, we focus on the political and security benefits derived from the developing economic, energy and transport relations, the balance sheet is more positive. Developing trade and transport links and deliberate multilateral initiatives have played a major role in bringing Iran and the Central Asian states closer together. They have helped their leaders to identify common interests in regional stability and security, and have prompted them to start perceiving their countries as belonging to the same region. Even President Islam Karimov, who throughout the 1990s remained intensely suspicious of Iranian engagement in Central Asia and who in 1995 initially expressed support for US sanctions against Iran, perceives benefits for Uzbekistan in expanded trade and transport relations with Iran.[39] For the Islamic Republic, bilateral and multilateral economic engagement with the Central Asian states helps to develop and give substance to the idea of a region of peace, stability and prosperity, facilitates cooperation in responding to specific security threats across its northern and eastern borders, and at the same time contributes to the ongoing effort to evade Washington's strategy of containment.

Security relations and Iranian responses to conflicts in Central Asia and Afghanistan

Threats

As noted in the introduction, from the outset Tehran saw the break-up of the Soviet Union as presenting threats as well as opportunities. Speaking in China in spring 1992, Deputy Foreign Minister Maleki warned that 'the emergence of a handful of undeveloped and poor states that continuously face the threat of rebellion and drought would severely affect the security and stability of the borders of the neighbouring countries'.[40]

Before elaborating on Tehran's perceptions of the threats emanating from Central Asia, it should be emphasized that neither individually nor collectively do the Central Asian states pose any conventional security threat to Iran. In terms of population, gross domestic product (GDP) and military strength, Iran is stronger than all the Central Asian states combined. There are no border disputes with Turkmenistan (the only Central Asian state with which Iran shares a land border), and Tehran and Ashgabat have generally managed to express common views about Caspian Sea legal regime and demarcation issues. By adopting a unilateral stance of permanent neutrality, Turkmenistan has allayed Iranian concerns about hostile penetration across its northern borders. Neither among Iran's Turkmen population (between 1 million and 1.5 million) nor in Turkmenistan has there been any expression of irredentist sentiment—in contrast to the situation in Iranian–Azerbaijani relations.[41] The dismantling of the last nuclear weapons in Kazakhstan in 1995 removed the only conceivable direct threat from any other Central Asian state.[42]

Iranian concerns focus, therefore, on softer and often indirect threats. The perception is that the Central Asian states are weak and fragile and unable to cope with their own security challenges, and that this may impact negatively on Iran's security. The risks that are commonly cited by Iranian analysts are that secessionism and extremist ethno-nationalism or the weakness of state- and nation-building processes and the failure of political institutions could lead to state failure or civil war. This in turn could lead to interstate conflicts and a more general regional crisis, as well as generating a humanitarian crisis and refugee flows. The example of civil war in Tajikistan and the perceived weakness and/or artificiality of the three smaller Central Asian states (Kyrgyzstan, Tajikistan and Turkmenistan) highlight these risks. The possibility of a humanitarian crisis caused by severe economic or environmental disaster has also been cited as a potential threat to which Iran would need to respond.

Tehran has also expressed concern about the extension into Central Asia of some of the 'soft' security threats generated by the Afghan civil war and the Taliban. (These are discussed further below.) The main issues here are the drugs trade, the associated spread of transnational armed criminal networks, and the influence of the extreme sectarian Islamism characteristic of the Taliban and of radical Pakistani Sunni groups. The latter phenomenon threatens to draw Tehran into the role of defender of persecuted Shi'i Muslims.[43] Regarding radical Islam in Central Asia, the Iranian position has been ambivalent. Tehran has attacked the repressive anti-Islamic policies of certain states, particularly Uzbekistan, and was critical of the 'troika' of Russia, Uzbekistan and Tajikistan, established in 1998 to combat Islamic extremism. Iran's Radio Mashhad, broadcasting into Central Asia, has aired the views of Uzbekistan's Islamist opposition.[44] But Tehran has not supported the Islamists' radical goals of overthrowing the existing regimes. The Islamic Movement of Uzbekistan's violent incursions into Kyrgyzstan and Uzbekistan in the summers of 1999 and 2000, its links with the Taliban and its alleged involvement in the drug trade have dissipated Iranian sympathy for Uzbekistan's radical Islamists. Nevertheless, the ideological difference between Iran and the Central Asian states over radical Islam remains fundamental, and as the threat of Islamist terrorism gains in prominence in Central Asian security concerns, so the prospect of any common security arrangement linking Iran with the Central Asian states grows more remote.

Iranian concerns about the 'soft' security threats emanating from Central Asia can only be understood in the context of the much more immediate threats of a similar nature posed by the situation in Afghanistan.

Tehran has perceived a danger of the situation in Afghanistan spreading via Tajikistan to other parts of Central Asia.[45] In the case of Afghanistan Iran is directly affected by state collapse and civil war in a neighbouring country. In the course of the 1990s and before, Iran became indirectly involved in the conflict through its support for the Shi'i Hazara of central Afghanistan and for a variety of other Afghan groups and warlords. Since the arrival of the Taliban in the mid-1990s, Iran, together with Russia, has been the major sponsor of the anti-Taliban Northern Alliance, which by 2000 had been reduced to a small patch of territory adjacent to Tajikistan. Afghanistan has brought Iran into a conflict of interest with its ECO partner Pakistan, and with Saudi Arabia and the United Arab Emirates— all states with which Tehran is seeking to improve relations—since these have been the main external supporters of the Taliban. Iranian lives have been lost in the fighting, most notably when 10 diplomats and a journalist were murdered during the Taliban capture of Mazar-i-Sharif in August 1998. This caused outrage in Tehran, with hardliners calling for punitive military action. In October there was a massive troop mobilization and manoeuvres involving some 70,000 Revolutionary Guards and 200,000 regular troops close to the Afghan border, but counsels of peace ultimately prevailed.[46] According to Iranian sources, there have been frequent instances of cross-border shelling and other provocations from Taliban-held territory. It has also been rumoured that the Taliban have offered to provide an alternative home for the Mojaheddin-e Khalq Organization and other groups committed to overthrowing the Islamic regime in Tehran.

In addition, Iran is still host to some 1.5–2 million refugees from Afghanistan, who are not only a burden on resources but are seen as the cause of a variety of social problems and tensions.[47] Opium and heroin trafficking from Afghanistan necessitates a constant high-level security presence along the 945-km border. Frequent clashes with well-organized and heavily armed drug smugglers inflict significant casualties on Iranian border guards.[48] Iran incurs costs not only as a front-line transit country, but also through an increasing domestic drug problem. The combination of the drugs trade, the civil war and state collapse in Afghanistan have affected Iran's entire eastern border region.[49] Transborder organized crime flourishes and has had an impact in a number of ways, for instance, in high-profile kidnappings of tourists in Iran, in the general disruption of economic life, and in progressive depopulation on the Iranian side of the border.

A final set of security threats is perceived in the danger of hostile penetration and influence in Central Asia. Tehran has strongly criticized the development of security relations between the Central Asian states and the USA and Israel, and has been more guardedly critical of NATO and Organization for Security and Co-operation in Europe (OSCE) engagement in the region. In the case of NATO, it is not so much the Central Asian states' engagement in the NATO Partnership for Peace (PfP) programme as the use of that framework by individual NATO member states, such as the USA and Turkey, to develop bilateral security relations in the region that perturbs Tehran. In the case of both NATO and the OSCE, Iranians have expressed concern about the long-term outcomes of these organizations' engagement in the region, fearing that the scope of current programmes may 'creep', and that the Islamic Republic may find itself on the wrong side of a new line in the sand drawn around an enlarged European or Euro-Atlantic security region.[50]

Responses

Among the regional and global states with major interests in Central Asia, Iran is distinguished by the almost complete absence of actual security relations with the countries of the region on either a bilateral or a multilateral basis. Russia, the USA, Turkey, other NATO member states and even China, through the Shanghai Forum, are all more directly and extensively engaged in Central Asian military and security affairs than is Iran.[51] In the light of the preceding analysis, which has emphasized that security is one of the main priorities in Iranian policy towards the region, this absence appears even more striking. Among the tens of agreements signed with Central Asian states, only two bear on security—one for military and border cooperation signed with Turkmenistan in January 1994, the other a letter of understanding on defence cooperation signed with Tajikistan in December 1997.[52] The details of these agreements have not been released, but there is no indication that either marks the beginning of a significant security relationship. Beyond these, there have been some limited initiatives with Turkmenistan towards cooperation and sharing intelligence in tackling the drugs trade and transnational crime, as well as the 1998 ECO Memorandum of Understanding on Cooperation against Smuggling and Customs Fraud mentioned above. Of course the absence of formal security relations does not mean that regional security issues are excluded from discussions between Iranian and Central Asian officials. Such talks contribute in a modest way to common understanding of issues in regional security.

Explanations for the absence of formal security relations can readily, if only speculatively, be suggested. Iran's willingness to leave Central Asian security matters to Russia and its CIS initiatives offers a partial explanation. The Islamic Republic's international isolation and general lack of experience of cooperative security relations may also be a factor, though it should be noted that the second half of the 1990s saw a number of initiatives to develop confidence-building measures with the Gulf Cooperation Council (GCC) states.

The specific character of the Islamic Republic's military institution, in which the Islamic Revolutionary Guard Corps has an important place in addition to the regular armed forces, and Iran's ideological and cultural peculiarities may also present obstacles in developing relations with the Central Asian militaries. Iranian military, security and intelligence officers, for example, would have a very different and much more sympathetic perspective on Islamic radicalism than would their Central Asian, Russian and indeed Chinese counterparts. It is noteworthy that in 1999–2000 the latter have readily developed common understandings and positions on religious extremism and Islamic fundamentalism through the Shanghai Forum. In other words, the security perspectives and interests of the Islamic Republic of Iran and of the Central Asian states remain too far apart to allow the adoption of common positions or the development of military cooperation. After a decade of gradually developing relations the Central Asians still do not have sufficient trust in Iran's motives and long-term ambitions to enter a close security relationship, especially as they have a number of alternative relationships on offer.[53] Even with Russia, in spite of the talk of strategic partnership and the mutually beneficial arms trade, Iran has no security relationship in the sense of military cooperation, joint exercises, or even confidence-building measures.

Another factor is that Turkmenistan, which as a neighbour might be expected to be the first focus for Iranian initiatives to build bilateral or multilateral security relations in Central Asia, has adopted a policy of permanent neutrality, which impedes the development of any relationship that could be construed as forming a bloc.

In the absence of substantive security relations, the Islamic Republic has responded to the perceived threats from Central Asia in a variety of other ways. This has been done partly through unilateral measures, by demonstrating a readiness to defend borders, and by taking measures to combat transnational crime, for example. There has also been informal undeclared cooperation in pursuit of specific goals: Iran's support for the Afghan Northern Alliance has been channelled through Turkmenistan, Uzbekistan, Kyrgyzstan and Tajikistan, and in all likelihood is coordinated also with Russia.[54] The perception of the threats posed by the situation in Afghanistan and by the Taliban is common to Iran, Russia and all the Central Asian states except Turkmenistan. That shared threat perception has been sufficient to draw these states into limited informal cooperation to support the forces opposed to the Taliban or to coordinate with international agencies for the purposes of conflict resolution and of combating narcotics trafficking, but it is essentially a temporary common interest, which is unlikely to lead to deeper cooperation, let alone to the formation of any formalized regional security grouping or organization.

As discussed in the preceding section, Tehran has developed a wide concept of regional security that emphasizes taking positive steps in the economic, social and cultural spheres, rather than concentrating on military–security relations. As Foreign Minister Ali Akbar Velayati expressed it in 1996, 'the Islamic Republic of Iran is convinced that regional cooperation is the only guarantor of regional peace, security and stability. It is in this light that bi- and multilateral relations are being forged with the countries of Central Asia'. In this connection, he highlighted the role of the ECO and the proposed Caspian Sea Cooperation Organization.[55] His successor as foreign minister, Kamal Kharrazi, echoes these ideas: 'We are of the firm conviction that the only way to ensure peace and regional stability is through regional cooperation'.[56] Another common theme in Iranian discussions of regional security is the need to exclude the interference of external powers. (In the context of Central Asia, this refers essentially to the USA, since both Russia and China are considered to be regional rather than external powers.)

If Iran has been passive in terms of security relations, however, it has taken an active role in conflict resolution and mediation. In the case of Tajikistan, as soon as civil war broke out in 1992, Iran shifted from a position of support for the Islamic Revival Party, one of whose top leaders, Ali Akbar Turajonzode, found refuge in Tehran, to one of peacemaker. Iran kept open relations with the ex-communist government, and eventually President Emomali Rakhmonov's hostility thawed; in 1995 he visited Tehran. Throughout the Tajik conflict Iran was a keen supporter of the United Nations' efforts to mediate a resolution (in this Iran was for a time at odds with Russia, which hoped that its military backing would secure victory for the ex-communists) and was instrumental in securing the Islamist-led United Tajik Opposition's acceptance of a 1994 ceasefire and of the eventual 1997 peace agreement.[57]

In the case of Afghanistan, while Iran is actively aiding the anti-Taliban forces, it simultaneously supports the United Nations' efforts to negotiate a settlement through the '6 + 2' group (the six neighbouring states—Iran, Pakistan, China, Tajikistan, Uzbekistan and Turkmenistan—plus Russia and the USA), and has also mooted a role for the OIC in mediating an end to the conflict.[58]

The Iranian approach to mediation in the cases of both Tajikistan and Afghanistan has been to argue that lasting peace can only be achieved through political negotiations and agreements to which all the main protagonists agree and which lead to a broadly-based representative government.[59] Iran has been keen to work within the framework of the United Nations and the OIC. Even while engaged in conflicts on the side of one or another party, Iran has shown willingness to maintain dialogue with the leaders of opposing parties, ideological differences and other grievances notwithstanding.

Iranian diplomacy in the 1990s achieved some success in peacemaking in the region, and Iran won international plaudits for its contribution to the Tajik peace settlement. It demonstrated the same propensity with regard to the Karabagh conflict also, although Iran's role in that case was marginalized when the OSCE became the main organization involved in mediating between the conflicting parties.

Unilateral measures to secure fundamental interests, informal cooperation with other states in pursuit of specific and limited shared objectives, a broad concept and approach for the promotion of regional security through cooperation in a range of fields, and an active diplomacy of conflict resolution and peacemaking have, in the first decade since the collapse of the Soviet Union, substituted for the development of substantive security relations with the states of Central Asia. These do not, however, disguise the fact that Iran, although it is affected by many of the same security challenges, is excluded from all of the new regional security groupings involving the Central Asian states. These either are intra-regional, involving only Central Asian states, or orient them towards Russia, or the West and Euro-Atlantic partnership, or, in the case of the Shanghai Forum, orient them eastwards towards China.

Prospects for the future: Iran and the strategic scene in Central Asia

The extent and nature of Iran's future participation in emerging patterns of Central Asian security cooperation will be shaped by a variety of factors. In Tehran there is an ongoing political and ideological struggle within the regime between reformers and conservatives. The outcome of that struggle will be important in determining Iranian domestic and foreign policy priorities in the short to medium term, and will affect the Central Asian leaders' perceptions of the Islamic Republic. Similarly, domestic political developments in Central Asia, where the first post-independence presidential successions cannot be indefinitely delayed, will have an inevitable, if as yet unpredictable, impact on relations with Iran. As the current ex-communist elite makes way for a new generation, will state policies towards political Islam, for example, become less uncompromisingly hostile? As long as the current ideological character of the Islamic Republic and the Central Asian states remains fundamentally unchanged, the marked differences between them will continue to work against the development of cooperative security relations and will weaken the prospects for Iranian participation in any emerging Central Asian security grouping.

Future developments in Afghanistan will also affect Iran's security relations with the Central Asian states. Throughout the 1990s, Iranian and Central Asian perceptions of the threats to regional stability posed by the Afghan civil war and by the Taliban have been broadly similar (only Turkmenistan has declared that it does not perceive the Taliban as a serious threat). The years 1999 and 2000, however, have seen some significant changes. The likelihood of an eventual Taliban victory has grown, prompting Iran and the Central Asians to begin to contemplate relations with a Taliban-dominated government in Kabul. The Taliban, moreover, have stated clearly that they have no intention to destabilize Central Asia. There have been a number of bilateral contacts between Tehran and the Taliban, and in autumn 2000 Uzbekistan's President Karimov began to adopt a less confrontational tone in talking about the Taliban. The establishment and international recognition of any effective government in Afghanistan (even one as ideologically unpalatable to most neighbours as the Taliban) would exert a positive influence on regional security. Nevertheless, it remains far from certain that a Taliban government offers a basis for a lasting political settlement of Afghanistan's internal conflict, or

that it would take steps to stem narcotics production and export, or to cur-
tail the international activities of the radical Islamist groups which it has
sheltered.

Peace in Afghanistan could affect Iranian–Central Asian relations in
other ways also. It would greatly enhance the prospects for the ECO to
become a more effective organization, but at the same time it would resurrect the prospect of Afghan competition to Iran in developing transport links (including oil and gas pipelines) from Central Asia to South
Asia and the Indian Ocean, and would remove a common threat which
has brought Iran and the Central Asian states closer to one another in
terms of security perceptions and cooperation.

Extra-regional developments will also be important in determining the
future of Iranian–Central Asian security relations. Chinese interests and
involvement in Central Asia have been growing, both in the economic
and energy fields, and in terms of security. Concerns about terrorism,
separatism and radical Islamism featured prominently in the July 2000
Dushanbe meeting of the Shanghai Forum countries (plus Uzbekistan),
indicating growing Chinese concern about the security links between the
Central Asian states, Afghanistan and Xinjiang (Chinese Central Asia).
Iran is not a member of the Forum, but there have also been important
developments in bilateral relations between Iran and China. A series of
meetings and exchanges culminated in President Khatami's June 2000
visit to China, when he toured Xinjiang. Tehran and Beijing share perspectives on some of the threats to their national security emanating from
Central Asia, and have expressed the desire to cooperate in developing
regional transport (including pipelines) infrastructure to link West and
East Asia. For Tehran, increasing Chinese engagement is welcome, both
as an indication of multi-polarity in the post-cold war era and as an additional counterweight to Western influence in Central Asia at a time
when Russia's commitments in the region are shrinking. Such strategic
motives probably prompted Tehran's award of the Neka–Tehran pipeline contract to a Chinese consortium.

The most important strategic factors for the future of Iranian–Central
Asian security relations concern Russia and the United States of America.

For most of the 1990s, Tehran essentially relied on Russia as a proxy
actor to secure Iranian security interests in Central Asia, both in terms of
preventing or containing threats arising within the region, and in terms
of limiting penetration by Iran's enemies and competitors—the USA,
Israel and, to a lesser extent, Turkey. At the turn of the 21st century, how-

ever, there are growing doubts as to whether Russia has the capacity or the will to continue to fulfil this role. As is argued elsewhere in this book, in the medium term, resource constraints and more important priorities in other arenas are likely to reinforce the trend of Russian disengagement from Central Asia, the 1999–2000 flurry of activity around Islamist terrorism notwithstanding. In addition, in the second half of the 1990s, the first cracks began to appear in the Irano-Russian 'strategic partnership'. It has become increasingly clear that the two countries are natural competitors in terms of export routes for Caspian oil and gas; the potential for rivalry in the Caspian was underscored when in 1996 Russia unexpectedly changed its stance on the issue of the legal regime, leaving Iran as the only sponsor of the 'condominium' approach. The second Chechen war also placed strains on Russian–Iranian relations. A combination of growing Russian disengagement from Central Asia and deepening divergence between Russian and Iranian interests will leave a gap in Iran's strategy for Central Asia—a gap that growing Chinese engagement may partly fill, but which Tehran may also consider demands a more active Iranian involvement in regional security matters.

Iran and Russia's close bilateral relations are in any case to a large extent a product of their common rejection of the USA's global hegemony in general, and of its encroachment into their Caucasian, Caspian and Central Asian backyard in particular. Shifts in Russia's or Iran's relations with the USA will, therefore, have an impact on relations between Tehran and Moscow, as well as directly affecting Iranian threat perceptions and opportunities for security engagement in Central Asia.

A normalization of US–Iranian bilateral relations will have the most significant and far-reaching effect on the character of Iranian–Central Asian security relations. At least since the election of President Khatami in 1997, there have been expectations and some indications of a thaw in US–Iranian relations. Few experts expect the Iran–Libya Sanctions Act to be renewed when it expires in 2002. The act underpins the entire US sanctions regime against Iran, which in turn is the principal remaining plank of the 1990s US 'dual containment' policy. In both Tehran and Washington the normalization of relations remains controversial, and how far and how fast the two sides move will depend to a great extent on domestic political dynamics, as well as on other factors extraneous to the Central Asian region (for example, developments in Israel–Palestine). In Central Asia the US Government takes a tough stance against Iranian engagement in Caspian energy development and export, continuing to deny the obvious benefits for the Caspian states of exploiting Iran's potential as a transit country, and refusing to exploit a loophole in the sanctions regime to allow US oil companies to engage in swap arrangements with Iran. But the USA did indicate tacit approval of Iran's constructive role in the Tajik peace process,[60] and the UN's '6 + 2' group for Afghanistan is one of the few forums where US and Iranian representatives work together for common goals. More broadly, there is a growing recognition in both capitals that there are a number of shared regional security interests: for example, in reinforcing the stability and viability of the Central Asian states, and in developing the region's links with the global community and the world economy. Those interests are not important enough to precipitate a major change in US–Iranian relations, but they suggest that when those relations normalize there will be scope for constructive dialogue and eventual cooperation—as is already the case in relations between Europe and Iran.

Most important, however, will be the shift in threat perceptions and strategic calculations that will result from a normalization of US–Iranian relations. Throughout the 1990s, for both Tehran and Washington, a major objective of policy in Central Asia was to limit and counteract the engagement of the other. When Iran's leaders cease to fear that the USA's long-term objective is to isolate and encircle Iran, it will remove, in their eyes, one of the major sources of threat in the region, as well as weakening the rationale for the Iranian leaders' reliance on Russia as security guarantor for the region. It will also knock-on to affect Iranian perceptions of the NATO and OSCE role in the region, and more broadly of the West's engagement (for example, through the TRACECA—Transport Corridor Europe Caucasus Asia—programme, which in Iran is currently seen as another instrument to wrench the region away from its 'natural' ties to the south). By the same token, the Central Asian elites' perceptions of Iran will be positively affected if the US Government no longer portrays the Islamic Republic as a threat to their interests and to regional stability. That will open the door for enhanced Central Asian–Iranian relations in a variety of fields, and will help to create a less competitive environment in which new patterns of regional security relationships can emerge.

Notes

1. For a slight variant on this list, see Ali Khorram, 'Afghanistan and the National Security of the Islamic Republic of Iran', *Amu Darya*, vol. 1, no. 2 (summer and fall 1996), p. 228.

2. Houman Sadri, 'An Islamic Perspective on Non-Alignment: Iranian Foreign Policy in Theory and Practice', *Journal of Third World Studies*, vol. 16, issue 2 (1999), pp. 29–46.

3. For a critical analysis of Iranian strategy, see Shahram Chubin, 'Iran's Strategic Predicament', *Middle East Journal*, vol. 54, no. 1 (winter 2000), pp. 10–24.

4. Saideh Lotfian, 'Iran's Middle East Policies under President Khatami', *Iranian Journal of International Affairs*, vol. 10, no. 4 (winter 1998/99), p. 423.

5. Lotfian, *op. cit.*

6. In the words of Nasser Hadian, a respected Iranian analyst, there has been, 'no consistency in foreign policy decisions either at the time of Dr Ali Akbar Velayati [former foreign minister] or at the time of Dr Kamal Kharrazi [current foreign minister]', cited in 'Roundtable: Iran's Foreign Policy during Khatami's Presidency', *Discourse: An Iranian Quarterly*, vol. 2, no. 1 (summer 2000), p. 11. For similar comments on security policy making, see Shahram Chubin, *Iran's National Security Policy: Capabilities, Intentions and Impact* (Washington, DC: Carnegie Endowment for International Peace, 1994), chapter 1.

7. David Menashri, 'Iran and Central Asia: Radical Regime, Pragmatic Politics' in David Menashri, ed., *Central Asia Meets the Middle East* (London: Frank Cass, 1998), pp. 73–97. For a discussion of Iranian–Central Asian relations, see R. K. Ramazani, 'Iran's Foreign Policy: Both North and South', *Middle East Journal*, vol. 46, no. 3 (summer 1992), pp. 39–412; John Calabrese, 'Iran and Her Northern Neighbors: At the Crossroads (Part 1)', *Central Asia Monitor*, no. 5 (1994), pp. 27–31; John Calabrese, 'Iran and Her Northern Neighbors: At the Crossroads (Conclusion)', *Central Asia Monitor*, no. 6 (1994), pp. 13–18; Eric Hoogland, 'Iran and Central Asia' in Anoushiravan Ehteshami, ed., *From the Gulf to Central Asia: Players in the New Great Game* (Exeter: University of Exeter Press, 1994), pp. 114–28; Edmund Herzig, *Iran and the Former Soviet South*, Former Soviet South Paper (London: Royal Institute of International Affairs, 1995); Mehrdad Mohsenin, 'Iran's Relations with Central Asia and the Caucasus', *Iranian Journal of International Affairs*, vol. 7, no. 4 (winter 1996), pp. 834–53; Hanna Yousif Freij, 'State Interests vs. the Umma: Iranian Policy in Central Asia', *Middle East Journal*, vol. 50, no. 1 (winter 1996), pp. 71–83; Adam Tarrock, 'Iran's Policy in Central Asia', *Central Asian Survey*, vol. 16, no. 2 (1997), pp. 185–200; Tchangiz Pahlavan, 'Iran and Central Asia' in Touraj Atabaki and John Kane, eds, *Post-Soviet Central Asia* (London: I. B. Tauris, 1998), pp. 73–90; Mehdi Sanayi Nahavandi, *Jaygah-e Iran dar Asiya-ye Markazi* [Iran's Role in Central Asia] (Tehran: Al-Hoda, 1376 A.H.s/1997) (in Persian); and Olivier Roy, 1999, 'The Iranian Foreign Policy toward Central Asia', available online from URL <http://www.soros.org/cen_eurasia/royoniran.html>; <http://www.soros.org/cen_eurasia/royoniran.html>.

8. Menashri, *op. cit.*, p. 78; and Farhad Ataee, 'Iran and Turkey in Post-Soviet Central Asia', *Discourse: An Iranian Quarterly*, vol. 2, no. 1 (summer 2000), p. 155.

9. This conception was elaborated by Deputy Foreign Minister Abbas Maleki in spring 1992. Ataee, *op. cit.*, p. 156.

10. Philip Robins, 'The Middle East and Central Asia' in Peter Ferdinand, ed., *The New Central Asia and its Neighbours* (London: Royal Institute of International Affairs/Pinter, 1994).

11. Galia Golan, *Russia and Iran: A Strategic Partnership?* Discussion Paper 75 (London: Royal Institute of International Affairs, 1998); and Abbas Maleki, 'Iran and Russia: Neighbours without Common Borders' in Gennady Chufrin, ed., SIPRI, *Russia and Asia* (Oxford: Oxford University Press, 1999), pp. 181–96.

12. Menashri, *op. cit.*, pp. 72, 82–83.

13. For a chronology of bilateral developments in the 1992–94 period, see Herzig, *Iran and the Former Soviet South* (note 7), pp. 21–24.

14. Menashri, *op. cit.*, p. 86.

15. *Tehran Times*, 22 February 1993, cited in Menashri, *op. cit.*, p. 89.

16. Ataee, *op. cit.*, pp. 156–57.

17. Ali A. Jalali, 'Islam as a Political Force in Central Asia: The Iranian Influence', *Central Asia Monitor*, no. 2 (1999), p. 4.

18. Mohiaddin Mesbahi, 'Tajikistan, Iran and the International Politics of the "Islamic Factor"', *Central Asian Survey*, vol. 16, no. 2 (June 1997), pp. 148–50.

19. Menashri, *op. cit.*, p. 86.

20. Jalali, *op. cit.*; Hoogland, *op. cit.*, pp. 116–17; and Herzig, *Iran and the Former Soviet South* (note 7), chapter 5, 'Culture and Religion'.

21. Edmund Herzig, 'Islam, Transnationalism, and Subregionalism in the CIS' in Renata Dwan and Oleksandr Pavliuk, eds, *Building Security in the New States of Eurasia: Subregional Cooperation in the Former Soviet Space* (Armonk, NY: EastWest Institute/M. E. Sharpe, 2000), pp. 236–57.

22. Menashri, *op. cit.*, pp. 89–91; and Ataee, *op. cit*, pp. 157–58.

23. Ataee, *op. cit*, p. 158.

24. For more general overviews of the development of economic relations, see Herzig, *Iran and the Former Soviet South* (note 7), chapter 4, 'Economic Relations'; and Sanayi Nahavandi, *Jaygah-e Iran dar Asiya-ye Markazi*, chapter 2, 'Alayeq-e eqtesadi' [Economic interests] (in Persian).

25. Herzig, *Iran and the Former Soviet South* (note 7), p. 32.

26. On Iran's regional policy, see Ramazani, *op. cit.*; John Calabrese, ed., *Revolutionary Horizons: Regional Foreign Policy in Post-Khomeini Iran* (Basingstoke: Macmillan, 1994); and Edmund Herzig, 'Iran and its Regional Relations' in Rosemary Hollis, ed., *Oil and Regional Developments in the Gulf* (London: Royal Institute of International Affairs, 1998), pp. 115–35.

27. Richard Pomfret, *Central Asia Turns South? Trade Relations in Transition* (London: Royal Institute of International Affairs, 1999), chapter 4, 'Trade Patterns in the 1990s', especially pp. 42–43.

28. *Inside Central Asia*, issue 121 (13–19 May 1996), p. 1.

29. Pomfret, *Central Asia Turns South?*, *op. cit.*, pp. 24–25; Bruno de Cordier, 'The Economic Cooperation Organization: Towards a New Silk Road on the Ruins of the Cold War', *Central Asian Survey*, vol. 15, no. 1 (March 1996), pp. 47–57; Richard Pomfret, 'The Economic Cooperation Organization: Current Status and Future Prospects', *Europe-Asia Studies*, vol. 49, no. 4 (1997), pp. 657–67; and K. L. Afrasiabi, 'The Economic Cooperation Organization Aims

to Bolster Regional Trade Opportunities', Parts 1 and 2, 2000, EurasiaNet available online at URL <http://www.eurasianet.org/departments/business/articles/>.

30. In addition to the works cited in the preceding footnote, see Elaheh Koolaie, [The Economic Cooperation Organization: Obstacles on the Way of Integration], *Central Asia and the Caucasus Review*, no. 16 (winter 1997), pp. 45–61 (in Persian).

31. Pomfret, *Central Asia Turns South?, op. cit.*, p. 24.

32. Pomfret, *Central Asia Turns South?, op. cit.*, p. 26.

33. Ramazani, *op. cit.*, p. 408.

34. Kamal Kharrazi, 'Role of Regional Powers in Conflict Resolution and Economic Development', *Amu Darya*, vol. 4, no. 1 (spring 1999), p. 11.

35. Ramazani, *op. cit.*, p. 408–09; Herzig, *Iran and the Former Soviet South* (note 7), pp. 38–39; and Elaheh Koolaie, [Active Involvement of the Caspian Littoral States] (sic: an accurate translation of the Persian title is 'Realizing a Council of the Caspian Littoral States: A Step on the Way to Reinforcing Regional Peace and Security'), *Central Asia and the Caucasus Review*, no. 14 (summer 1996), pp. 283–93 (in Persian).

36. Caspian issues have figured prominently in Iranian policy and specialist and public debate in the 1990s. *Amu Darya*, vol 4, no. 1 (spring 1999) includes five articles giving the perspectives of senior Iranian officials and analysts. On the risk of militarization, see Jalil Roshandel, [Demilitarization of the Caspian], *Central Asia and the Caucasus Review*, no. 14 (summer 1996), pp. 247–63 (in Persian); and Jalil Roshandel, [Militarism in the Caspian Sea, an Approach Arising from the Lack of Legal Regime], *Central Asia and the Caucasus Review*, no. 22 (summer 1998), pp. 21–33 (in Persian).

37. Kharrazi, *op. cit.*, p. 11.

38. Pomfret, *Central Asia Turns South?, op. cit.,* pp. 40–43 and table 8.

39. Kenneth Katzman and James Nichol, *Iran: Relations with Key Central Asian States* (Washington, DC: Congressional Research Service Report for Congress, 3 February 1998), p. 3.

40. Cited in Ataee, *op. cit.*, p. 155.

41. Shahram Chubin argues that, aside from the issues of Iraq and of the developing link between Israel and Turkey, 'Iran is basically without enemies. Unusually in a region of turmoil, Iran is relatively secure. Its core security as a nation state is not threatened. It is not about to disintegrate. It is not a failed state, threatened by ethnic dissension or secessionism'. Chubin, 'Iran's Strategic Predicament' (note 3), p. 15.

42. Saideh Lotfian, [Kazakhstan's Nuclear Status and Regional Security], *Central Asia and the Caucasus Review*, no. 14 (summer 1996), pp. 215–32 (in Persian).

43. There have been calls in the Iranian press for the government to take a more active role in supporting Central Asian Shi'i Muslims. *Inside Central Asia*, 1–7 July 1996, p. 6.

44. *Monitor: A Daily Briefing on the Post-Soviet States* [online], vol. 5, issues 60, 74 (26 March and 16 April 1999).

45. Nasser Saghafi Ameri, 'The Afghanistan Crisis: Geopolitical Aspects', *Amu Darya*, vol. 4, no. 1 (spring 1999), p. 70.

46. Ahmed Rashid, *Taliban: Islam, Oil and the New Great Game in Central Asia* (London: I. B. Tauris, 2000), p. 74–75, 204; and Ali Nasim Far, 'The Martyrdom of Iranian Diplomats and Journalist in Afghanistan from the Perspective of International Law', *Iranian Journal of International Affairs*, vol. 10, no. 4 (winter 1998/99), pp. 405–20.

47. Bahram Rajaee, 'The Politics of Refugee Policy in Post-Revolutionary Iran', *The Middle East Journal*, Volume 54, Number 1, Winter 2000.

48. 'International Meetings to Counter Narcotics Smuggling', Radio Free Europe/Radio Liberty, *RFE/RL Iran Report*, vol. 3, no. 36 (18 September 2000).

49. On the threats to Iran posed by Afghanistan, see Rashid, *op. cit.* (note 46), pp. 202–203; and Khorram, 'Afghanistan and the National Security of the Islamic Republic of Iran', *Amu Darya*, vol. 1, no. 2 (summer and fall 1996), pp. 225–30.

50. Robin Bhatty and Rachel Bronson, 'NATO's Mixed Signals in the Caucasus and Central Asia', *Survival*, vol. 42, no. 3 (autumn 2000), pp. 129–45; and Mansur Rahmani, 'NATO and OSCE: New Security Roles in Central Asia and the Caucasus', *Amu Darya*, vol. 4, no. 1 (spring 1999), pp. 89–98.

51. On Central Asia's emerging security relations, see Roy Allison, 'Subregional Cooperation and Security in the CIS' in Dwan and Pavliuk, *op. cit*, pp. 149–76.

52. Herzig, *Iran and the Former Soviet South* (note 7), p. 24; Hooman Peimani, *Regional Security and the Future of Central Asia* (Westport, CT: Praeger, 1998), p. 83; and Roy, 'The Iranian Foreign Policy towards Central Asia' (note 7).

53. Peimani, *op. cit*, p. 83.

54. Rashid, *op. cit* (note 46), p. 203.

55. Ali-Akbar Velayati, 'The Constructive Role of the Islamic Republic of Iran in Maintaining Regional Security', *Amu Darya*, vol. 1, no. 2 (summer and fall 1996), p. 188.

56. Kharrazi, *op. cit.*, p. 10.

57. Roy, 'The Iranian foreign policy towards Central Asia' (note 7). On the Russian role, see Lena Jonson, *The Tajik Civil War: A Challenge to Russian Policy*, Discussion paper 74 (London: Royal Institute of International Affairs, 1998).

58. Seyed Asghar Keivan Hosseini, [The Foreign Policy of the Islamic Republic of Iran in Afghanistan], *Central Asia and the Caucasus Review*, no. 22 (summer 1998), pp. 41–73 (in Persian); and Ahmed Rashid, 'Iran in Afghanistan: the Mission to Undermine Pakistan', *Central Asia–Caucasus Analyst*, 29 March 2000, available online at URL <http://www.cacianalyst.org/>.

59. Khorram, *op. cit.*; and Saghafi Ameri, *op. cit.*, pp. 69–70.

60. Katzman and Nichol, *op. cit.*, p. 2.

CHAPTER NINE

Turkey and Central Asia

GARETH M. WINROW

Introduction

With the break-up of the Soviet Union, Turkey quickly became involved in
Central Asia. Turkish officials have tended to perceive Central Asia as encompassing Kazakhstan, Kyrgyzstan, Tajikistan, Turkmenistan, Uzbekistan, Uzbek-populated territory in northern Afghanistan, and Xinjiang
in western China which is inhabited by large numbers of Turkic Uighurs.
Emphasizing the importance of so-called common ethnic, linguistic, cultural and religious ties, policy makers in Ankara have focused on the four
predominantly Turkic states of Central Asia and have given less attention
to largely Farsi-speaking Tajikistan, in spite of the substantial Uzbek
minority there. Turkish politicians and businessmen believed that involvement in Central Asia would boost Turkey's prestige, open up markets for
Turkish goods and provide alternative sources of raw materials and
energy. These interests corresponded with the official line that Turkey
was seeking to bolster the independence of the Turkic states, including
Azerbaijan.

Events in Central Asia do not pose an immediate threat to Turkey.
Likewise, in contrast to China, Iran and Russia, for example, what happens in Turkey will not necessarily have a direct impact on the security
concerns of the Central Asians. Nevertheless, Turkey has concluded military–security agreements with the Turkic states and is at the forefront of
NATO activities relating to Central Asia. Moreover, Central Asia and
the Transcaucasus cannot be treated completely separately, and events in
the Transcaucasus have a direct bearing on Turkey's defence interests.

Since the mid-1990s Turkish politicians and businessmen have become more aware of the Transcaspian linkage between Central Asia and the Transcaucasus in relation to possible east–west transport and energy corridors. For example, if built, a rail link between Kars and Tbilisi could form an important connection in a Central Asia–Europe rail network. Many in Ankara are eager to reap the economic and political benefits that would accrue if oil and gas pipelines joining Central Asia and Europe were constructed across Turkish territory. Turkish officials have increasingly focused on the energy-rich Caspian states—Azerbaijan, Kazakhstan and Turkmenistan. This is rendering outmoded the earlier distinction often made in Turkey between the post-Soviet states in the Transcaucasus and those in Central Asia. Turkish policy makers are more and more distinguishing between the western Central Asian/Caspian states—Kazakhstan and Turkmenistan—and the more remote and energy-poor states and territories in eastern Central Asia. It is not clear where Uzbekistan fits in this schema.

Many in Turkey oppose Russia's attempts to reassert its influence, if not dominance, in the Transcaucasus. Russia has maintained military bases in Armenia and Georgia, its troops continue to patrol Armenia's border with Turkey, and, to meet its defence needs, Armenia has become heavily dependent on Russian arms transfers. Turkish policy makers are anxious that Russia may exploit ethnic and regional disputes in the Transcaucasus, and in the North Caucasus in order to strengthen its presence in the Transcaucasus. The Turkish authorities were particularly concerned about the Russian assault on Chechnya which began in autumn 1999 after a spate of bombings in Russia and following armed clashes in Dagestan between Russian troops and local radical Islamic groups backed by Chechen guerrillas. Ankara would prefer a stable and peaceful Transcaucasus (and the North Caucasus) so that Russia would have less opportunity to meddle in regional affairs. A more secure, less volatile region would enhance the prospects for east–west transport and energy corridors. Increasing links between the Transcaucasus and Kazakhstan and Turkmenistan in particular may result in an overlap of military/defence and energy security concerns. This could have a significant bearing on Turkey's national interests.

This chapter examines Turkish policy towards Central Asia with a focus on Turkey's security interests. Security here includes economic and energy aspects as well as military and defence matters. Events in the Transcaucasus must not be overlooked because of the prospects for closer ties between states near to and bordering the Caspian. The impact of developments in Central Asia on Turkey's ties with states in the region will also be addressed. The importance of Turkey's relations with Central Asia is examined from a wider perspective, taking into account the interests of other states—China, Iran, Russia and the USA. The significance of Turkey's membership of NATO is also discussed, noting NATO's widening interest in Central Asia and the Transcaucasus.

The visions of a Turkic Commonwealth

There was a sense of euphoria among Turkish officials in December 1991. The unravelling of the Soviet Union gave Turkey an opportunity to establish and consolidate ties with long-forgotten Turkic cousins. The leaders of the newly independent Turkic states were eager to secure Turkey's political and economic backing. The US Administration, anxious that Iran might expand its influence in the power vacuum in Central Asia, urged the Turkic states to adopt the 'Turkish model'. This model was supposedly based on secularism, liberal democracy and a free market economy.

The then Turkish Prime Minister, Süleyman Demirel, boasted in February 1992 of a 'gigantic Turkish world' stretching from the Adriatic Sea to the Great Wall of China.[1] When touring Central Asia in May 1992, Demirel spoke of forming an association of independent Turkic states.[2] It seems that he had in mind a Turkic Commonwealth which may also have included Azerbaijan. Turkey appeared to have ambitions to become a leading or core state in Central Asia, even though geographically it is clearly not a part of Central Asia.

The bubble burst in October 1992 with disappointment in Turkey at the results of the first Turkic Summit, held in Ankara. The leaders of all the newly independent Turkic states attended. Immediately before the summit, Turkish President Turgut Özal had advocated the formation of a Turkic Common Market and the creation of a Turkic Trade and Development Bank. However, it was decided only to set up working groups to foster closer relations between the participating states.

Turkish officials had raised their expectations too high. This was perhaps not surprising given their lack of knowledge of Central Asia. Many Turks had tended to look down on their Turkic cousins and had failed to appreciate their educational and technical achievements. The Turkic leaders wanted to consolidate their states and build up national identities. The prospect of a Turkic Commonwealth did not attract them. Having recently secured independence from the Soviet Big Brother, they were not eager to surrender themselves into the embrace of a Turkish *Ağabey* (elder brother).[3] They sought to cultivate economic and political relations with other states, including Russia and Iran. Given its own economic problems, moreover, Turkey could only offer limited economic support.

Turkic summits continued to be held regularly. They focused on economic and cultural cooperation. Immediately before the Fifth Turkic Summit, in Astana in June 1998, Uzbek President Islam Karimov declared that the summits should not consider political or security matters. This was because of the absence of Iran and Tajikistan.[4] Noting calls for support from the Uighurs just before the Astana Summit, and not wanting to antagonize China, Karimov warned against the politicization of the summits.[5]

Turkey has nevertheless developed connections with the Turkic states. An extensive network of air and telecommunications links is in place. The Turkish Avrasya television channel broadcasts across much of Central Asia. Training courses for businessmen and diplomats from the Turkic states are being run. The Turkish Government has offered scholarships for up to 10,000 youths in Turkish schools and universities, although not all are taken up. The Turkish Ministry of Education and Turkish entrepreneurs have opened schools and universities throughout Central Asia. Contacts between religious officials in Turkey and Central Asia have developed.

Relations between Turkey and the Turkic states suffered when a coalition government led by the Islamist Welfare Party held office in Ankara from mid-1996 to summer 1997. The Welfare Party leader, Necmettin Erbakan, when Prime Minister visited Islamic countries such as Indonesia, Iran, Libya, Malaysia and Pakistan but travelled neither to Central Asia nor to Azerbaijan. The leaders of the secular Central Asian Turkic states, fearful of the possible spread of Islamic extremism from Tajikistan and Afghanistan, must have questioned the relevance of the Turkish model when the Turkish Government itself was reluctant to endorse secularism.

In spring 1999 a new government was installed in Ankara, led by Bülent Ecevit, head of the Democratic Left Party. One of the parties in his coalition was the Nationalist Action Party (MHP) led by Devlet Bahçeli. The MHP, when previously headed by the late Alparslan Türkeş, had established contacts with Pan-Turkic groups in Central Asia. Türkeş had helped form the Turkic States and Communities Friendship, Brotherhood and Cooperation Foundation (TÜDEV). Since 1993 this foundation has organized in Turkey annual conventions of Turkic states and communities. Delegates from the 'Turkic world', including the Russian republics of Bashkortostan, Tatarstan and Yakutia, attend these gatherings. President Demirel was a regular participant. In practice these meetings are of little political consequence. The small, fringe Pan-Turkic groups in Central Asia have scarcely any influence.

Has the MHP under Bahçeli moderated its ultra-nationalist stance? The coalition government protocol referred to the need to maintain good relations with China and further develop ties with Russia. Concerning the 'Turkic world', the protocol simply noted: 'The government will carry out an active and stable policy to improve economic, social and cultural cooperation with the Turkic republics'.[6] Bahçeli may have revealed his true colours at the Seventh Convention of TÜDEV at Denizli in July 1999. He called for the establishment of a Permanent Cooperation Assembly of the Turkic World and appealed again for the formation of a Turkic Common Market.[7] These remarks, though, were primarily aimed at Bahçeli's own constituents. In many of the statements of MHP officials there is much rhetoric but little substance.

The supposed bonds of Turkic solidarity have not always helped Turkey to promote its wider goals. For example, the Turkic states have not jeopardized their relations with the international community by recognizing the 'Turkish Republic of Northern Cyprus'. Turkish officials lobbied fiercely for its recognition immediately before the first Turkic Summit. At the Seventh Convention of TÜDEV, a clearly frustrated Rauf Denktaş, leader of the Turkish Republic of Northern Cyprus, noted: 'We regret the fact that the propaganda of those who want to eradicate us in Cyprus is given a place in brotherly countries'.[8]

By the late 1990s many Turkish officials, with the possible exception of members of the MHP, were aware that a degree of social and cultural homogeneity between Turkey and the Turkic states would not lead to the establishment of a Turkish/Turkic world. Even the formation of a looser form of cooperative arrangement such as a Turkic Commonwealth was not possible. Rather, business interests and military–political concerns have compelled Turkish decision makers to focus on developments in the Caspian region.

Economic and energy relations

Shortcomings in the Turkish economy have limited Turkey's involvement in Central Asia. Given its problems of high inflation, substantial budget deficits and difficulties in completing its privatization programme, it is questionable whether the Turkish economy is an appropriate model for the Turkic states. Genuine economic reforms in Central Asia are unlikely in the immediate future because of the negative impact of the Russian economic crisis of late 1998 and the slump in the prices of raw materials and minerals on the world market.

Shortly after the break-up of the Soviet Union, the Turkish Eximbank was prepared to extend up to US$900 million in government credits to boost trade between Turkey and the Turkic states and support the construction of hotels and factories in Central Asia. This was a substantial sum given the size of the Turkish economy. However, not all of the credits offered have been extended. This is in part because of cumbersome procedures and the incompetence of the parties involved. Credits extended have not always been properly used and the Central Asians have complained of the high rates of interest. Turkish businessmen have tended to take over from the Turkish state and have invested considerable sums in Central Asia. Nevertheless, Russia remains a more attractive market for Turkish entrepreneurs. By the end of 1997 Turkish construction firms had carried out work in the Central Asian Turkic states worth $5.75 billion. In comparison, the work undertaken by Turkish companies in Russia amounted to over $12.3 billion.[9]

Russia has also been a more important trading partner. In spite of its economic crisis, in 1998 Turkish exports to Russia totalled $1.35 billion and its imports from Russia $2.1 billion. In the same year, Turkey's exports to all the Turkic states (including Azerbaijan) were valued at $831 million and its imports from these states at $450 million.[10] Its exports to the Turkic states consist primarily of processed foods, textiles, machinery and transport equipment and its imports from them of textiles and metal products. Turkish officials and businessmen hope that trade between Turkey and the Central Asian Turkic states will increase substantially once several of these states generate earnings by exporting their energy to Turkey and other hard currency markets.

The energy issue links Central Asia and the Transcaucasus. Economic and military concerns are also interconnected with regard to the security of pipeline routes. Officials in Ankara have believed that the construction of pipelines across Turkey rather than across Russia and Iran would boost Turkey's influence and prestige in the Caspian region at the expense of its rivals. Kazakhstan and Turkmenistan would reduce their dependence on Russia if their energy were transported across Turkey. Turkey's increasing energy needs could also be satisfied.

Turkish politicians and businessmen have lobbied for international energy companies to finance the construction of a major oil pipeline connecting Baku in Azerbaijan with the Turkish Mediterranean port of Ceyhan.[11] Many in Turkey argue that if a Baku–Ceyhan pipeline is built fewer tankers will transit through the hazardous and congested Bosporus. However, other routes that bypass the Bosporus are possible, across the Balkans, Central Europe and Iran. Turkish experts believe that Turkey could consume up to 15 million tonnes a year of oil carried along a Baku–Ceyhan pipeline. However, for this route to be economically feasible there must be a guaranteed throughput capacity of at least 45 million tonnes a year. Azerbaijan will be reluctant to transport such large amounts of its oil along one pipeline. At least 20 million tonnes a year of Kazakh crude (the Turkmen oilfields are not yet developed) will therefore most probably have to be transported to Ceyhan along what would be a Tengiz–Baku–Ceyhan pipeline.

According to initial estimates, a Transcaspian oil pipeline carrying Kazakh oil may cost $3 billion. (This would be in addition to a similar sum required to construct the Baku–Ceyhan leg). Would energy companies finance such a project? Because of the great depth of the Caspian Sea near the Tengiz oil field in Kazakhstan, a pipeline would have first to extend overland to Turkmenbashi in Turkmenistan and then to run under the Caspian Sea to Azerbaijan. However, a Transcaspian pipeline along this route will not be laid until Azerbaijan and Turkmenistan resolve their dispute over the ownership of certain oilfields in the Caspian Sea. And will Kazakhstan have enough oil to export to Ceyhan? It is aiming to export by 2014 up to 67 million tonnes a year along a new pipeline from Tengiz to Novorossiisk which will be built by the Caspian Pipeline Consortium— a group of energy companies and governments in which Turkey is not represented. In summer 2000 initial surveys revealed that the East Kashagan structure in the Kazakh sector of the Caspian Sea has substantial oil reserves. However, the infrastructural development of this field will take time. It seems therefore that Turkey will not consume Kazakh oil or carry this crude across Turkish territory in the foreseeable future.

According to official Turkish figures, in order to meet its energy demands Turkey will need to import over 20 billion cubic metres of gas in 2000, more than 53 billion cubic metres per year in 2010, and up to 80 billion cubic metres by 2020. These figures may not be reliable. Such high estimates are in the interests of influential Turkish construction companies which are eager to secure lucrative contracts to build new gas turbine-driven power plants in Turkey. If these figures are exaggerated, the competition between Turkmenistan, Russia, Iran and other states to export their gas to Turkey will be much more intense. There appears to be fierce rivalry between the backers of the Blue Stream project and the US Government-supported Transcaspian gas pipeline project. The former aims to carry 16 billion cubic metres per year of gas from Russia to Turkey along twin pipes running parallel under the Black Sea. The latter is intended to carry 16 billion cubic metres a year of Turkmen gas to Turkey and a further 14 billion cubic metres per year across Turkey and on to Western Europe. In order to realize the Transcaspian gas pipeline project a pipe needs to be laid under the Caspian Sea and then extended across the Transcaucasus to Turkey.

Although an international consortium has been set up, it is not certain whether the Transcaspian gas pipeline project will be realized. Officials in Ashgabat and Baku need to agree over the division of oilfields in the Caspian Sea before a gas pipeline can be laid across the Caspian to connect Turkmenistan and Azerbaijan. And indicators suggest that there are extensive reserves of Azerbaijani gas in the Shah Deniz field in the Caspian Sea. Azerbaijan will want to export its gas from this and possibly other fields through any new pipeline across Azerbaijan and Georgia. The authorities in Baku may therefore not allow as much as 30 billion cubic metres per year of Turkmen gas to cross Azerbaijani territory en route to Turkey and Western Europe. It is quite conceivable that Turkmen gas may be squeezed completely out of the Turkish market.

In Ankara in June 1998 President Nursultan Nazarbayev of Kazakhstan announced that Turkey could import 20–25 billion cubic metres per year of Kazakh gas along another Transcaspian gas pipeline. This pipeline could run parallel to a Transcaspian oil pipeline carrying Kazakh crude. However, the Kazakh gas fields must first be developed. The largest is at Karachaganak. But in 2000 Kazakh officials were concentrating on exploiting the oil reserves of this field.

The importance of Kazakhstan and Turkmenistan in meeting Turkey's future energy needs may be exaggerated. More probably, in years to come Turkey will be consuming substantial amounts of Azerbaijani oil and gas. Kazakhstan and Turkmenistan, however, may still reduce their dependence on Russia by exporting their oil and gas along new routes—quite conceivably through Iran—avoiding both Russia and Turkey. Ironically, Turkey may become increasingly dependent on Iran and Russia to satisfy its energy needs. As of 1999 it was importing 7 billion cubic metres of gas from Russia and 5 million tonnes of Iranian oil per year. According to con-cluded agreements, Turkey intends to import 30 billion cubic metres of Russian gas and 10 billion cubic metres of gas from Iran per year by 2010. In practice, though, according to a de facto swap arrangement, once a Tabriz–Ankara gas pipeline is completed Turkey may actually be import-ing Turkmen gas resold to it by the Iranians at a higher price. Kazakhstan and Turkmenistan may still become important markets for Turkish prod-ucts if they export their oil and gas to a hard currency market.

However, Turkey will not be able to consume Caspian energy or transport it across its territory unless the security of pipeline routes is first assured.

Military and security cooperation

Turkey is not in a position to address many of the security concerns of the Central Asian states. Their leaders are primarily concerned with internal security issues, particularly the threats posed by religious radicalism and tribal or regional separatism. The economic and political support offered by Turkey may only partially alleviate these problems. However, in cer-tain military and defence spheres Turkey is actively involved in Central Asia. It is supporting the formation of modern, independent armies—that is, independent of Russia—in the Turkic states.

In March 1993 General Doğan Güreş, then Chief of the Turkish Gen-eral Staff, toured Kyrgyzstan, Turkmenistan and Uzbekistan.[12] The Ka-zakh Defence Minister visited Turkey in June 1993.[13] The Turks and Central Asians have exchanged further military delegations. Initially, bi-lateral agreements on military training were concluded. Officers from the Turkic states were enrolled in Turkish war academies as early as 1992. In a speech at the National Defense University in Washington, DC, in February 1998, General Çevik Bir, then Deputy Chief of the Turkish General Staff, noted that around 2300 cadets and officers from Central Asia and the Transcaucasus had graduated from Turkey's war colleges, and another 1700 were continuing their training in Turkey.[14] At that time Turkmenistan had sent over 1000 of its military personnel to study in Turkey.[15] Turkey has been playing a key role in training a new officer corps. Initially, many Russians were officers in the armies of the Turkic states.

The Central Asians were at first sensitive to Russian concerns. In Au-gust 1994 the Kazakh Defence Minister Sagadat Nurmagambetov stated that the agreement he had just signed with Turkey was only a preliminary one dealing primarily with cooperation in arms production. He added that it did not conflict with similar agreements Kazakhstan had concluded with Russia.[16] Two years later Turkey and Kazakhstan signed a military industrial cooperation agreement and a protocol on military training. Turkish officials declared that these agreements were similar to those Turkey had concluded with Israel.[17] Developing links with NATO through the Partnership for Peace (PfP) programme, the Kazakhs by 1996 were eager to promote military ties with NATO members and were less inclined to take Russian anxieties into account.

As of 2000, Turkey is not extensively involved in arms production ventures with the Central Asian Turkic states. Its officials are seeking to expand Turkey's arms industry and are therefore interested in licensed production deals involving third-country sales. Turkey has embarked on a 10-year $31 billion defence procurement programme. In 1998, however, its arms exports totalled only $200 million annually.[18] It does have an industrial base to build ships and produce armoured vehicles, aircraft, electronics, small arms ammunition and rockets. Azerbaijan and Kazakhstan are two of 18 countries it has identified as markets to be penetrated in the short term for defence exports and Turkmenistan is one of 11 countries to be targeted in the medium term.[19] Ironically, Turkey has been procuring Russian armaments on a regular basis since 1993.

Turkey has concluded agreements with the Central Asian Turkic states to cooperate against organized crime, arms smuggling, terrorism and separatism. Turkish officials are especially keen for the Central Asians to clamp down on the activities of elements sympathetic to the Kurdish guerrilla group, the PKK (Kurdish Workers' Party). Visiting Bishkek in April 1998 to sign a Joint Declaration on security issues with the Kyrgyz authorities, the then Turkish Prime Minister Mesut Yılmaz said that he had discussed the Kyrgyz Government's 'soft stance' on the PKK. He noted that in the previous year several pro-PKK meetings had been organized in Kyrgyzstan. The Kyrgyz Prime Minister, Kubanichbeg Cumaliev, assured Yılmaz that such activities would not be allowed in future.[20]

Turkey has not signed military and security agreements with 'non-Turkic' Tajikistan. The then President Demirel only paid his first visit to Tajikistan in September 1995. Turkey played no role in attempting to resolve the civil war in Tajikistan. The conflict ended through a combination of Russian diplomacy and military pressure and Iranian influence on the Islamic opposition groups in Tajikistan.

Officials in Ankara are more apprehensive about the security situation in the Transcaucasus than in Central Asia. But, as noted, the two areas are increasingly interconnected because of heightened interest in possible transport and energy corridors. Turkey has developed extensive military and security cooperation with Azerbaijan and Georgia. By mid-1999 it had allocated $3.5 million to Azerbaijan for the modernization of the Azerbaijani armed forces.[21]

In January 1999 Vefa Gülüzade, then the foreign affairs adviser of President Geidar Aliyev of Azerbaijan, proposed that Turkey, the United States or NATO should establish a military base in Azerbaijan to offset the Russian military presence in Armenia.[22] An anonymous source from the Azerbaijani Government alleged that Azerbaijani and Turkish military experts were studying 'technical issues related to locating a Turkish military base in Azerbaijani territory'.[23] However, in public at least, the Azerbaijani and Turkish authorities were not eager to provoke Russia by following up on Gülüzade's suggestion. The significance of the Declaration on Deepened Strategic Cooperation between Turkey and Azerbaijan, announced when Aliyev visited Ankara in March 1997, remains unclear. Cooperation in the future production of certain weaponry is possible. It has been suggested that according to the terms of this strategic cooperation, which have not been made public, Turkey and Azerbaijan could even work together to protect a possible Baku–Ceyhan oil pipeline.[24]

Apparently, in 1998 Turkey provided Georgia with $5.5 million for defence purposes. In June 1999 it pledged a further $1.7 million for the modernization of the Georgian armed forces.[25]

Speaking in Tokyo in March 1999, Georgian President Eduard Shevardnadze announced that military cooperation with Ankara would not lead to Turkey establishing military bases in Georgia.[26] As with Azerbaijan, though, in future Turkey may cooperate with Georgia to protect pipelines running through Georgian territory. In this context, the possible development of Turkey's relations with the GUUAM (Georgia, Uzbekistan, Ukraine, Azerbaijan and Moldova) grouping will be discussed later. In contrast to its role in Central Asia, Turkey has been involved in efforts for conflict resolution in the Transcaucasus. In June 1999 a conference was organized in Istanbul which discussed possible confidence-building measures with regard to the Georgia–Abkhazia dispute.[27] And in January 2000 President Demirel announced that Turkey would work for the formation of a Caucasus Stability Pact which would supposedly be founded on the norms and values of the Organization for Security and Co-operation in Europe (OSCE).

As in the Transcaucasus, it is extremely unlikely that Turkey will set up bases in Central Asia. Although it may commit itself to defend pipelines in the Transcaucasus, its armed forces will not be able to extend such guarantees to Kazakhstan and Turkmenistan. However, Turkey may conclude further agreements with Kazakhstan and Turkmenistan on military training, arms exports and the joint production of certain weapons. The importance of Turkey in the PfP programme must also be considered here. There are limits to the development of security cooperation between Turkey and Kyrgyzstan given the geographic distance, Bishkek's sensitivity to the interests of neighbouring China, and the fact that Kyrgyzstan does not have extensive energy reserves. As the next section discusses, the formation of GUUAM may lead to further security linkages between the Transcaucasus and Central Asia.

Regional dynamics

This section examines from a security perspective the impact of certain developments in Central Asia on a regional level on Turkish policy towards Central Asia.

As previously noted, the Turkic summits have focused on cultural, economic and social issues. Nevertheless, summit declarations have stressed the importance of cooperation against drugs trafficking, terrorism and separatism. As spin-off from these discussions, in the summer of 1998 the internal security chiefs of Turkey, Azerbaijan, Kazakhstan and Turkmenistan held in Istanbul the first of what are intended to be regular meetings.[28]

In contrast to the first Turkic Summit, which was orchestrated by Turkey, the Central Asians have become involved as agenda-setters in subsequent summits. The third summit at Bishkek in August 1995 praised the regional cooperation efforts of Kazakhstan, Kyrgyzstan and Uzbekistan. Aiming to coordinate their economic activities in particular, these states had launched the Central Asian Union (CAU) which Tajikistan later joined. Significantly, in June 1999 Turkey was only granted observer status to the CAU along with Georgia. The five post-Soviet Central Asian states have also organized summits, to which Turkey has not been invited, to discuss inter alia the ecological problems of the Aral Sea, transport corridors, and oil and gas pipeline routes.

Nor is Turkey a key participant in the regional security schemes envisaged by Uzbekistan's President Karimov and Kazakhstan's President Nazarbayev. In the mid-1990s Karimov had flirted with the idea of establishing in Central Asia an area known as Turkestan which would be under Uzbek leadership and would not include Turkey. Turkish delegates have participated in the two meetings of the Conference on Interaction and Confidence-Building Measures in Asia (CICA) held in Almaty in February 1996 and September 1999. However, at these gatherings, sponsored by Nazarbayev, many states were represented. CICA is unlikely to seriously tackle security issues in Central Asia because of the size of its membership and the range of topics it is attempting to address.

As with Tajikistan, Turkey has not been an active party in the peace talks concerning Afghanistan. Since October 1997, the six neighbouring states of Afghanistan, together with Russia and the United States, have been seeking to resolve the conflict between the warring Afghan factions. Turkey has not been included in spite of its traditional close links with the Uzbek minority in northern Afghanistan and their leader General Abdul Rashid Dostum. Unconfirmed reports alleged that Turkish military officers used to visit Dostum's one-time fiefdom around Mazar-i-Sherif. Certainly, Turkey has dispatched humanitarian relief to Uzbeks fleeing from the advancing Taliban. In August and September 1998 Dostum and former Afghan President Burhanuddin Rabbani visited Ankara and appealed, in vain it seems, for the Turkish authorities to urge Pakistan to stop supporting the Taliban.[29]

In early October 1996 Turkey announced its willingness to host a peace conference on Afghanistan.[30] Instead, a conference was convened in Tehran at the end of the month, to which Turkey sent a delegation. Speaking in Bishkek in September 1998, the Deputy Undersecretary in the Turkish Ministry of Foreign Affairs, Mehmet Ali Irtemcelik, stated that in the face of the Taliban threat Turkey would 'support' the Central Asians. Irtemcelik declared that he was conveying a message from President Demirel which proposed the holding of a summit meeting on Afghanistan in Turkey. In his message Demirel stressed that Turkey could no longer sit on the sidelines.[31] No such summit was held and as of summer 2000 Turkey remains excluded from the peace talks.

In order to have more impact on security issues at the regional level, as opposed to the interstate level, in Central Asia and in the Caspian region in particular, Ankara must improve relations with Uzbekistan. It is an influential state, given its relatively large population, its key strategic location, its energy reserves and the ambitions of its president. It has bolstered its ties with the United States since the landmark first visit of Karimov to Washington in 1996. Significantly, shortly after declaring that Uzbekistan would not renew its membership of the Commonwealth of Independent States (CIS) Collective Security Treaty, in April 1999 in Washington at the fringes of the NATO 50th anniversary celebrations, Uzbek officials signed up to join the pro-Western GUAM (Georgia, Ukraine, Azerbaijan and Moldova) grouping. GUAM thereby became known as GUUAM.

The future significance of GUUAM remains unclear. In April 1999 armed units from Azerbaijan, Georgia and Ukraine conducted their first military exercise which involved guarding the oil pipeline running from Baku to Supsa in Georgia. Could GUUAM become a regional security grouping, perhaps linked with Turkey and NATO? In September 1999 the former US Secretary of State, Zbigniew Brzezinski, referred to GUUAM as a positive initiative. He proposed that it should expand to include Romania, Poland, Turkey and, perhaps surprisingly, Armenia.[32] Turkish officials may become attracted to GUUAM to counter what they perceive to be a developing, and possibly threatening, Russia–Iran–Armenia axis. Kazakhstan and Turkmenistan are unlikely to seek membership of GUUAM, Nazarbayev being concerned not to alarm Russia and suspicious of Karimov's ambitions, and Turkmenistan being committed to neutrality. It seems, though, that Turkish–Uzbek relations will have to improve before a close Turkish association with GUUAM is possible.

The Uzbek authorities had complained about the presence in Turkey of the exiled Uzbek opposition leader Mohammed Salih. The Erk Party leader was forced to leave Turkey in early 1999. However, the Turkish Ambassador was recalled from Tashkent in June 1999 after a further deterioration in Turkish–Uzbek relations. The Uzbek authorities closed 12 Turkish schools in Uzbekistan and recalled 234 Uzbek students who were studying in Turkish universities. This was in reaction to Turkey's delay in handing over two Uzbek citizens who were suspected of involvement in the February 1999 bomb attacks in Tashkent. Evidently, the authorities in Tashkent had several years earlier recalled a large number of Uzbek students studying in Turkey on suspicion that Salih was attempting to recruit these students into an opposition movement. The Turkish Government in summer 1999 also refused to hand over to Tashkent a Turkish citizen who was accused of masterminding the February 1999 explosions in an ostensible attempt to overthrow Karimov. And Uzbek officials complained that Turkish businessmen, together with Erbakan, the former Prime Minister of Turkey, had been encouraging the spread of Islamic radicalism in Uzbekistan.[33]

Apparently the activities of certain rogue elements, possibly acting together with the leadership of the now outlawed Welfare Party, have damaged Turkey's relations with Uzbekistan. Another blow has been struck against the notion or dream of the solidarity and unity of the 'Turkic world'. Significantly, citing ill-health, Karimov refused to attend the Sixth Turkic Summit in Baku in April 2000, and it will be seen that since late 1999 there has been a rapprochement in Uzbek–Russian relations.

Turkey and the strategic scene in Central Asia

This section examines the rivalry and cooperation between Turkey and other states interested in Central Asia, namely China, Iran and Russia. Again, it will be observed that certain security issues concerning Central Asia and the Transcaucasus are interlinked. The limits to Turkish influence in Central Asia with reference to interstate and regional dynamics have been noted. However, Turkey may still have a considerable impact on Central Asia by exploiting its US and NATO connections. These connections have a bearing on how Turkish involvement in Central Asia is perceived by China, Iran and Russia.

Initially, after the break-up of the Soviet Union, Moscow was alarmed at what it believed to be the Turkish Government's Pan-Turkic policy in Central Asia. Commenting on the convening of the second Turkic Summit in Istanbul in October 1994, the spokesman of the Russian Ministry of Foreign Affairs, Mikhail Demurin, noted: 'It is unthinkable that a summit based on the principle of nationality will not disturb Russia'. He added that the first TÜDEV meeting held in Antalya in 1993 was another example of aggressive nationalism.[34] Once aware that Turkey's role in Central Asia was a limited one, however, Russian officials played down the Pan-Turkic threat. In spite of their problems in the Transcaucasus, Turkey and Russia have become important trading partners, as already noted. Turkey remains committed to importing more Russian gas by the Blue Stream project, even though this may damage its ties with Turkmenistan. In Ashgabat in October 1999 President Saparmurad Niyazov publicly upbraided Turkish Energy Minister Cumhur Ersümer for visiting Moscow to discuss speeding up the Blue Stream project. Niyazov even threatened to cancel the Transcaspian gas pipeline project.[35]

Many commentators—and key politicians in the United States—believed that Turkey and Iran would compete for influence in post-Soviet Central Asia. Iran did not attempt to export its form of Islam to predominantly Turkic and Sunni Muslim Central Asia. Nevertheless, Turkey and Iran are rivals. Competition has primarily revolved around securing markets. Iran scored a success of sorts when in May 1996 the Tejen–Sarakhs–Mashad railway link was officially inaugurated, thereby linking Central Asia and the Persian Gulf by rail for the first time. However, in spite of its economic potential, the railway has been underused due to certain 'man-made' causes.[36]

Concerning Caspian energy, Turkey and Iran are both rivals and partners. In spite of US protests, the de facto Turkmenistan–Iran–Turkey gas swap will probably be realized. Iran is lobbying for Azerbaijan, Kazakhstan and Turkmenistan to export oil to Iran via swap arrangements and along what would be new pipelines connecting the Transcaucasus and Central Asia with the Persian Gulf. These projects would jeopardize the prospects for a Baku–Ceyhan pipeline.

Turkey and China have encountered problems concerning Central Asia. The Turkic Uighurs in Xinjiang oppose de facto direct rule from Beijing. The estimated 15,000 Uighurs based in Turkey play on the sympathies of Pan-Turkic groups who still refer to Xinjiang as Eastern Turkestan. Tensions between China and Turkey surfaced in March 1997 following a clampdown in Xinjiang after Uighurs were linked with an explosion in Beijing. China warned Turkey not to interfere in its internal affairs. The Turkish Defence Minister Turhan Tayan told the Turkish Parliament that he had warned the Chinese to 'act prudently' in Xinjiang.[37]

Turkey and China may become competitors in the energy field. Chinese plans to help construct a 250-km oil pipeline to connect Kazakh and eventually Turkmen oilfields with the Persian Gulf may threaten the Baku–Ceyhan pipeline project. More immediately worrying for Turkish officials was China's sale to Armenia of eight Typhoon heavy multiple-rocket-launchers in 1999. These rockets could target a future Baku–Ceyhan pipeline.[38]

However, there has been a warming in ties between China and Turkey. Turkish businessmen in textiles, construction and the food industry are eager to penetrate the huge Chinese market. Seeking international support on Cyprus and the Kurdish question, Turkish politicians have become increasingly aware of China's role as a permanent member of the UN Security Council. And, like their Armenian counterparts, the Turkish armed forces are interested in acquiring relatively cheap Chinese missile technology.[39]

Since the mid-1990s the US Administration has shown a greater interest in Central Asia. The United States and Turkey may operate increasingly in tandem in Central Asia, and this may strengthen Turkey's role in the region. Both their administrations are eager to consolidate the independence of the Turkic states. The increased involvement of NATO, and hence the United States, in Central Asia and the Transcaucasus is bound to affect Turkish policy.

NATO Secretary General Javier Solana toured the Transcaucasus in February 1997 and September–October 1998, and visited Kazakhstan, Kyrgyzstan, Turkmenistan and Uzbekistan in March 1997. In July 2000, Lord Robertson, Solana's successor, was received in Kazakhstan, Kyrgyzstan and Uzbekistan. Except for Tajikistan, all the former Soviet republics in the Transcaucasus and Central Asia are parties to the PfP. Here, NATO offers individually tailored programmes which focus on officer training, joint military exercises, modernization and the inculcation of Western norms with regard to civil–military relations.

Shevardnadze is hoping that a NATO-led force may eventually replace the CIS (i.e., Russian) peacekeeping force separating the Abkhazians and Georgians. Azerbaijani officials anticipate the possible deployment of a NATO peacekeeping force after the conclusion of a peace settlement over Nagorno-Karabakh.[40] In May 1999 a delegation from NATO's Consulting Group on Euro-Atlantic Policy visited Azerbaijan. According to the Azerbaijani Deputy Foreign Minister, Araz Azimov, Baku raised the possibility of NATO units protecting oil pipelines in the Transcaucasus.[41]

Significantly, in June 1998 General Bir announced that Turkey was pressing for the creation of a peacekeeping force in the Transcaucasus. He suggested that it could be formed under the auspices of the PfP.[42] Russia objected strongly and little more was heard of the initiative. Perhaps more feasible is the formation by GUUAM of a permanent peacekeeping force, which may be associated with NATO. Security issues in Central Asia and the Transcaucasus would thereby become more intertwined. Turkish officials have succeeded, however, in creating a Black Sea Cooperation Naval Task Group (BLACKSEAFOR). Here Bulgaria, Georgia, Romania, Russia, Turkey and Ukraine aim inter alia to hold joint naval exercises for humanitarian and search and rescue missions.

In September 1997 the Centrasbat-97 military manoeuvres were held in Kazakhstan. The newly formed Central Asian peacekeeping battalion, composed of Kazakh, Kyrgyz and Uzbek units trained within the framework of the PfP, participated for the first time with US, Russian and Turkish troops in a peacekeeping and humanitarian aid exercise. The Centrasbat-98 exercise held in Kyrgyzstan and Uzbekistan also included units from Azerbaijan and Georgia. The Turkish military are keen to participate in these exercises in order to strengthen ties with the militaries of Central Asia and the Transcaucasus.

In mid-1994 NATO officials delegated to Turkey chief responsibility for promoting NATO's interests and concerns in Central Asia. At that time Turkey was the only NATO member which had military attachés stationed in the region.[43] After Turkish lobbying, NATO opened a PfP Commandership of Education Centre in Ankara in 1998. By mid-1999, 16 courses had been offered at the centre and 313 participants from 28 countries (presumably including the Turkic states) had attended.[44]

China, Iran and Russia are wary of NATO's 'out-of-area' ambitions. In particular, Russia is suspicious of NATO's intentions in Central Asia and the Transcaucasus. Under President Vladimir Putin Russia has become more actively engaged in its 'near abroad'. The Central Asian leaderships, reluctant to heed US advice with regard to democratization and more interested in Russian offers of support in dealing with the threat of Taliban-inspired religious radicalism, have looked more favourably on a Putin-led Russia. The Uzbek regime has increasingly distanced itself from GUUAM. Significantly, instead of welcoming Lord Robertson in Tashkent, Karimov attended as an observer a meeting of the 'Shanghai Five'—a loose cooperative security arrangement consisting of Russia, China, Kazakhstan, Kyrgyzstan and Tajikistan.

In its policy towards Central Asia and the Transcaucasus, after initial efforts to expand its influence by cultivating bilateral and interstate ties, in recent years Turkey has increasingly exploited its close bonds with the United States and its membership of NATO. This may have negative repercussions for its relations with China, Iran and Russia. They may perceive Ankara more as a rival and less as a partner in their relations with Central Asia and the Transcaucasus.

Prospects for the future

The importance of Turkey's relations with Central Asia should not be exaggerated. Ties with the United States and the European Union are more crucial for Turkey. It is not a part of Central Asia. It is not able to play the role of a core state in the region. In spite of the rhetoric of the MHP and Pan-Turkic groups in Turkey, a Turkic Commonwealth will not materialize. Central Asian leaders have preferred to diversify their contacts with the international community.

Nevertheless, Turkey's involvement in Central Asia should not be downplayed. It is a major player in the pipeline politics game. Concerning energy security, though, it is only possible to speculate about the future. The pipeline politics game is a complex, dynamic and ongoing one.

Since the mid-1990s Turkish decision makers have focused more on developments in the Caspian region than on Central Asia as a whole. Turkish officials are likely to continue to concentrate on the geographically less remote Kazakhstan and Turkmenistan, even though these states may not export substantial amounts of energy to it. The future of Turkish–Uzbek relations remains uncertain, especially after Uzbekistan's tilt towards Russia. A stabilization of the internal political situation in Uzbekistan could, however, work to Turkey's advantage. In military and defence matters, Turkey is an invaluable partner for many of the recently formed national armies in Central Asia and the Transcaucasus. Turkey, therefore, is likely to remain an important player in post-Soviet Central Asia and, in particular, in the Caspian region.

Notes

1. *Cumhuriyet*, 24 February 1992.

2. *Turkish Daily News*, 1 May 1992.

3. Mustafa Aydın, 'Turkey and Central Asia: Challenges of Change', *Central Asian Survey*, vol. 15, no. 2 (June 1996), pp. 165–166.

4. *Turkestan Newsletter*, vol. 98, 2-110 (11 June 1998).

5. Roy Allison, 'Central Asia: A Region in the Making', Paper presented for the conference on Central Asia in a New Security Context, organized by the Swedish Institute of International Affairs, Stockholm, 2–3 September 1999, pp. 8–9, referring to British Broadcasting Corporation, *Inside Central Asia*, 8–14 June 1998.

6. *Turkish Daily News*, 31 May 1999.

7. *Radikal*, 2 July 1999.

8. *Turkish Daily News*, 2 July 1999.

9. 'The Turkish Economy in Figures', *DEIK (Foreign Economic Relations Board [of Turkey]) Bulletin* (February 1998).

10. Figures are from the *Foreign Trade Statistics Bulletin*, 5 March 1999, published by the Turkish State Institute of Statistics, <http://www.turkey.org/f-business.htm>.

11. For further details on Caspian energy and Turkey, see Gareth M. Winrow, *Turkey and Caspian Energy* (Abu Dhabi: The Emirates Center for Strategic Studies and Research, 1999).

12. *Cumhuriyet*, 16, 17 and 19 March 1993.

13. *Turkish Daily News*, 19 June 1993.

14. 'Turkey's Role in the New World Order: New Challenges', speech by Gen. Çevik Bir at the Institute for National Strategic Studies, National Defense University, Washington, DC, *Strategic Forum*, no. 135 (February 1998).

15. Glen E. Howard, 'NATO and the Caucasus: The Caspian Axis' in Stephen J. Blank, ed., *NATO after Enlargement: New Challenges, New Missions, New Forces* (Carlisle Barracks, Pa.: Strategic Studies Institute, US Army War College, 1998), p. 173.

16. Radio Free Europe/Radio Liberty (RFE/RL), *Daily Report*, no. 150 (9 August 1994).

17. *Jamestown Monitor*, 10 September 1996.

18. Howard, *op. cit.*, pp. 217–218.

19. Lale Sarıibrahimoğlu, 'Country Briefing: Turkey', *Jane's Defence Weekly*, vol. 30, no. 7 (19 August 1998).

20. *Turkish Daily News*, 15 April 1998.

21. *RFE/RL Newsline*, vol. 3, no. 143, Pt. 1 (26 July 1999).

22. *Turkish Daily News*, 1 February 1999.

23. Sanobar Shermatova, 'Fierce Haggling before CIS Summit', *Moscow News*, 3 March 1999.

24. Howard, *op. cit.*, p. 218; and *Turkish Daily News*, 6 May 1997.

25. *RFE/RL Newsline*, vol. 3, no. 111, Pt. 1 (8 June 1999).

26. *RFE/RL Newsline*, vol. 3, no. 46, Pt. 1 (8 March 1999).

27. *Turkish Daily News*, 10 June 1999.

28. Sanobar Shermatova, 'Why a Turkic Interpol?', *Moscow News*, 4 June 1998.

29. *Turkish Daily News*, 7 and 8 September 1998.

30. *Turkish Daily News*, 3 October 1996.

31. *RFE/RL Newsline*, vol. 2, no. 171, Pt. 1 (4 September 1998).

32. *RFE/RL Newsline*, vol. 3, no. 183, Pt. 1 (20 September 1999).

33. *Radikal*, 6 June and 4 July 1999; and *Milliyet*, 19 June 1999.

34. *Turkish Daily News* and *Hürriyet*, 19 October 1994.

35. *Radikal*, 7 October 1999.

36. Richard Pomfret, *Central Asia Turns South? Trade Relations in Transition* (London: Royal Institute of International Affairs, 1999), p. 8.

37. AFP, 21 March 1997.

38. David C. Isby, 'China Sells Artillery Rockets to Armenia', *Jane's Missiles and Rockets*, vol. 3, no. 9 (1 September 1999).

39. *Aktüel*, 17–23 June 1999.

40. *Jamestown Monitor*, 26 April 1996.

41. *RFE/RL Newsline*, vol. 3, no. 103, Pt. 1 (27 May 1999).

42. Kelly Couterier, *Washington Post*, 17 July 1998.

43. Howard, *op. cit.*, p. 172.

44. Yüksel İnan and İslam Yusuf, 'Partnership for Peace', *Perceptions*, vol. 4, no. 2 (June–August 1999), p. 81.

CHAPTER TEN

Structures and Frameworks for Security Policy Cooperation in Central Asia

ROY ALLISON

Introduction

Deep-rooted tensions in the Central Asian regional complex, which are reflected in competition and conflictual tendencies, have been identified in previous chapters in this book. However, cooperative dynamics have also developed in parallel in the region, resulting in the creation of a variety of interstate structures, frameworks and forums. Some of these have become institutionalized, although others remain loose consultative groupings. The capacity of these various multilateral structures to address the underlying security challenges for Central Asia and the way in which external powers relate to or are involved in such cooperative efforts are crucial for the future of the region.

This chapter assesses the potential of these multilateral structures, in particular the involvement of external powers in creating or sustaining them. The first section considers those frameworks in the region which have been sponsored essentially by the Central Asian states themselves (even if their membership may include regional or external powers). These structures promote Central Asian regional cooperation and reflect an effort to reach consensus on matters of principal concern to the local states. However, local rivalries and imbalances between these states continue to hinder such efforts. Second, the chapter analyses structures and organizations that are sponsored to a greater or lesser extent by regional/external powers: the Commonwealth of Independent States (CIS) (by Russia), the NATO Partnership for Peace (by the United States and to a lesser extent by Turkey), the Shanghai Forum (by Russia and China), and the Turkic States grouping (by Turkey). Finally, the role in Central Asia of two broad international bodies, the Organization for Security and Co-operation in Europe (OSCE) and the United Nations, is examined.

Security structures sponsored by the Central Asian states

The previous assessment of conflictual tendencies among the CIS Central Asian states and of their different regional security interests explains the difficulty they have had in developing any effective joint structures to cooperate over security issues. This also helps account for the difficulty individual Central Asian leaders have had in gaining broad multilateral support in the Eurasian region for their national security initiatives. The need to paper over intra-regional rivalries has undermined the ideal of fostering a regional security identity.

The Central Asian Economic Community

Bilateral treaties and coordination efforts dating back to 1992 between Kazakhstan and Uzbekistan were enlarged in the formation of a trilateral grouping including Kyrgyzstan in February 1994, which resolved to address, among other matters, water management, combatting drug trafficking, and military and security cooperation. The three states formally created a Central Asian Economic Community (CAEC) a few months later. However, as noted in chapter 2, in subsequent years their economies proceeded to develop in directions which were not mutually supportive. One study concluded in 1999 that 'efforts at regional cooperation typically have an official facade, concealing the isolationist ideologies at the top levels of state decision making and, as a result, growing disintegration'. A key problem has been that 'economic leverage is a popular tool officials wield to alter the policies of neighbouring countries, and economic disputes and rivalries are on the rise'.[1]

This did not augur well for cooperation in the security field. In December 1995 the CAEC resolved to form a joint Council of Defence Ministers, tasked with the consideration of regional security and defence coordination, including the coordination of military exercises, air defence and defence supplies, and a decision was taken to create the tripartite peacekeeping battalion, Centrasbat. In fact, a lack of economic resources and political will, which reflected intra-regional disputes, meant that such regional security and defence coordination was stillborn.[2] Centrasbat was created, but it has acted only as a showpiece military formation. The interest in the battalion displayed by the key state of Uzbekistan has waned, and only relatively small units from Uzbekistan and Kyrgyzstan took part in the Centrasbat-2000 exercise, hosted by Kazakhstan in September 2000. Tajikistan joined the CAEC in 1998 (and Turkey and Georgia were granted observer status in 1999), but a company of Russian troops based in Tajikistan, rather than Tajik troops, were present at this exercise.[3]

The tensions between Uzbekistan and Tajikistan, which have at times erupted into bitter mutual recriminations between them, show that Tajikistan's inclusion in the CAEC further weakened the ability of this body to reach consensus and cohesion, even if it broadened its Central Asian membership and left only Turkmenistan outside the group.

Uzbekistan has been the CAEC state which has argued most strongly for independent efforts by the Central Asian states at bolstering their security. Speaking in autumn 2000, President Islam Karimov argued that 'if we are not able to provide security for our populations and the countries of the region ourselves, no one will help us from the outside. We must look to our own resources', especially through 'reinforcing the armed forces and border guards'.[4] But whatever steps Tashkent might take to strengthen its own defences, in reality it would take a strong perception of mutual and commonly defined threat or threats for the CAEC to overcome the schisms between its members and to develop substantive interstate cooperation on security issues.

On the one hand, one might expect that the challenge posed by Islamist insurgents in summer and autumn 1999 and again a year later, as well as associated threats from Afghanistan, could generate this kind of common reaction. For example, in August 1999 the foreign and defence ministers and heads of national security of the CAEC member states issued a joint declaration on the activity of militant groups in the south of Kyrgyzstan, which confirmed their perception that terrorism and extremism were becoming international and represented a threat to all states in the region.[5]

However, the likelihood of insurgency in Central Asia leading to common security responses among the CAEC states has to be set against the

effect of the Islamist challenge in generating recriminations between the
states most immediately affected by insurgency in the region of the Ferghana Valley. Kyrgyzstan has incurred criticism for its military failures
in dealing with the insurgents during 1999. Uzbekistan has received complaints for ignoring its neighbour's borders in its own more robust military response to the threat.[6] Tajikistan in turn has been criticized for
allowing the militants refuge or unhindered passage across its territory.
At a meeting of the presidents of the CAEC states in April 2000 it was
heavily criticized for tolerating the presence of Uzbek Islamists on its territory the previous year.

Despite such differences, the four leaders signed a significant agreement at this meeting on cooperation in fighting terrorism, extremism and
trans-border organized crime. This collaboration was intended to range
from intelligence-sharing and covert operations to the use of armed
forces.[7] President Nazarbayev of Kazakhstan even called the agreement
'a defence union because this document determines our joint method of
fighting against any threat'. The cooperative impulse was reinforced by
a bilateral statement signed by the Kazakh and Uzbek presidents that the
two countries 'will perceive any actions directed against one of the states
as a common threat and will take all measures to counter them' and 'if
necessary, joint and coordinated measures will be carried out'.[8] This represents a mutual security pledge forged out of the perceived need for the
two states to tackle the Islamist threat jointly. But it is unlikely to alter
the deep-seated rivalry between them.

The incursion of armed Islamist groups into Kyrgyzstan and Uzbekistan during summer 2000 tested these cooperation pledges by the leaders of the four CAEC states. A coordinating centre for the defence,
interior and security agencies of Kyrgyzstan, Uzbekistan and Tajikistan
was formed in Khujand in Tajikistan. But the Kyrgyz proposal to establish a joint task force of the three states to destroy the bases of the insurgents in Tajikistan was not accepted. Kazakhstan meanwhile unilaterally
redeployed forces to its Southern Military District. Crucially, at a summit meeting in Bishkek in August 2000 the four presidents called on Russia to join the anti-terrorism agreement they had signed four months
previously and appealed to the CIS Collective Security Council to map
out action to counter the terrorist threat.[9]

This indicated that the Islamist security challenge is more likely to rally
the CAEC states behind Russian/CIS security structures, as discussed
below, rather than to consolidate a separate CAEC military/security iden-

tity. Nonetheless, the CAEC states (except for Tajikistan, which is locked into a tight military security relationship with Russia) may be ready to develop a more pragmatic relationship with the dominant Taliban leadership of Afghanistan than Russia is prepared to do. This would reflect a perception on the part of the Central Asian states of their distinct interests based on their geographic proximity to Afghanistan, as well as the possibility of new trade routes being developed in the future to their south.

Further structures sponsored by Central Asian states

The difficulty in agreeing on effective security cooperation confined to the four CAEC states has encouraged Kazakhstan and Uzbekistan to promote broader structures for regional cooperation, which encompass the CAEC states and a variety of other countries. However, these structures have had functionally diverse agendas and the very fact of their wide membership has introduced additional state rivalries and non-complementary security interests under the framework concerned.

Since March 1994 President Nazarbayev has promoted the concept of a Eurasian Union. This project includes a section on defence which envisages joint measures to strengthen the armed forces of Union states and the creation of a 'common defence space' to coordinate defence activities. The Union would include Russia, but a strong emphasis on the parity of the members would make it difficult for Russia to dominate its proceedings. Russian support for the project has anyway been lukewarm, since it has interpreted the Union as an attempt to shift the initiative and terms for integration from Moscow to Almaty (as well as to enlarge its scope to cover non-CIS Asian countries). Uzbekistan in turn has viewed the Union as an instrument to raise the standing of Kazakhstan in Central Asia and has rejected it decisively.

Nazarbayev has had more success in initiating an even broader forum for regional cooperation, the Conference on Interaction and Confidence-Building Measures in Asia (CICA), modelled on the OSCE. The CICA was first proposed by Nazarbayev in the United Nations in 1992 and subsequently has held periodic summit meetings. But its broad membership, including not only Russia and states from Central Asia, but also China, Turkey, India, Pakistan and other Asian states, results in rather bland resolutions on strengthening peace, stability and cooperation in Asia. This is reflected in a declaration on principles guiding relations among the CICA states signed in Almaty by 15 Asian states in September 1999. The CICA therefore has little operational value in coordinating the security policies of the CIS Central Asian states, and Turkmenistan anyway remains outside this grouping. But the process of reaffirming broad international norms alongside other non-CIS Asian states may contribute to the ongoing effort of the CAEC countries to construct national identities which are not tied to the Soviet past.

A more functional form of regional cooperation is represented by the dialogue to form a Central Asian Nuclear Weapons Free Zone (CANWFZ). This idea was first proposed by Uzbekistan and Kyrgyzstan at the 48th session of the UN General Assembly in 1993, and was promoted further by Uzbekistan at the Lisbon summit of the OSCE in 1996. However, the debate on the issue only began seriously with the February 1997 Almaty Declaration of the five regional heads of state and a statement of their foreign ministers after a conference in Tashkent later that year.

This zone would comprise all five CIS Central Asian states, despite Turkmenistan's reluctance to engage in other regional cooperation agreements. It would involve commitments by these five states, as well as some sort of security assurances by the nuclear-weapon states, especially neighbouring Russia and China. The latter states have been involved in the discussion process in a more informal manner, and they may enter the talks more seriously once the five states of the zone have agreed on a common position on all articles of the draft treaty.[10] Meetings in 1999 and 2000 of the 'Shanghai Five' group, which includes Russia and China and three Central Asian states (see below) specifically have backed efforts by the Central Asian countries to set up a nuclear weapon-free zone.

However, the most contentious aspect of the discussions, on which no common ground has been found, is the relation of the proposed treaty to Russia's security cooperation with the five Central Asian states. The 1992 Tashkent Collective Security Treaty (CST) and certain other bilateral agreements between Russia and these states are a stumbling block since in theory they offer these states a Russian nuclear umbrella. There is no consensus among the five Central Asian states on how to approach this problem.[11] Turkmenistan, which never signed the CST (and perhaps Uzbekistan which has left the treaty) may be ready to dispense with this theoretical Russian nuclear guarantee. However, Kazakhstan, and perhaps Kyrgyzstan and Tajikistan, may not be ready to do so, since Russian tactical nuclear weapons might be viewed as a positive security assurance in the event of any major threat in the future from other regional powers, particularly from China.

If a nuclear weapon-free zone for Central Asia is eventually formally agreed it will have some effect in building interstate trust and it would certainly be an effective preventive measure with regard to the challenge of nuclear non-proliferation. Agreement between the states involved has already been achieved on certain issues which would form part of the treaty on the zone, related to the peaceful use of nuclear technology, the physical protection of nuclear facilities and the transit of nuclear weapons. The very process of joint discussions on this security issue by all five CIS Central Asian states encourages thinking in terms of a regional security agenda.

Another framework for Central Asian regional cooperation on a functional issue is the '6 + 2' group of 'neighbours and friends' of Afghanistan. This arose from a proposal presented by Uzbekistan in August 1997 to establish a contact group under the aegis of the UN with the participation of the six countries bordering Afghanistan—Iran, China, Pakistan, Tajikistan, Turkmenistan and Uzbekistan—as well as the United States and Russia. The 6 + 2 group became the most prominent international mechanism for the settlement of the conflict in Afghanistan, which is a vital security policy objective of all the CIS Central Asian states. The group tried to create favourable external conditions to involve the warring parties in Afghanistan in the negotiation process. It held two meetings in New York and an important conference in Tashkent in July 1999.[12]

The Tashkent conference issued a declaration on the fundamental principles for a peaceful settlement of the conflict in Afghanistan, signed by all countries of the group except Turkmenistan. Among other provisions this included a declaration of intent 'not to provide military support to any Afghan party and to prevent the use of our territories for such purposes'. However, this declaration does not seem to have been adhered to and direct negotiations between the warring parties in Afghanistan, as promoted by the delegates in Tashkent, had not been achieved a year later. A meeting of the 6 + 2 group in September 2000 approved a Regional Action Plan, but this was limited to specifying measures to stem the flow of drugs from Afghanistan.[13]

Despite this outcome, the 6 + 2 multilateral framework offers an interesting model for confidence building and regional negotiations, one which enables the Central Asian states concerned with a particular security issue to engage in talks with other interested regional states. The ambitions of major powers are balanced in this framework by the presence of both Russia and the United States, while the imprimatur of the United

Nations provides international legitimacy and offers the best assurance of impartiality for any agreements reached.

Overall, the capacity of the Central Asian states to cooperate on traditional military–security issues on a regional basis has been severely limited by their continued emphasis on the process of state-building, which has inflated their intra-regional perceptions of insecurity and differences over border demarcation, water distribution and so on. The military preponderance of Uzbekistan among the five Central Asian states has also created a reluctance among its weaker neighbours to forgo their membership in CIS and other security structures (as examined below) for a more exclusive form of Central Asian regional security cooperation. Nevertheless, some coordination in countering growing low-intensity and non-traditional threats has developed and is likely to continue. The Central Asian states have also had some success in promoting broad structures to coordinate their position on functional security concerns—such as nuclear weapons and Afghanistan.

Security structures sponsored by regional/external powers

For at least the first half of the 1990s the possibility of regional powers such as Turkey or Iran, let alone the United States, developing security structures to incorporate the new Central Asian states appeared improbable and was anathema to Russia, which viewed all CIS states as falling within its 'near abroad'. The security policy engagement of powers besides Russia in Central Asia has been a phenomenon essentially since the late 1990s, as Russia has found it more difficult to credibly represent itself as the security manager or dominant security policy patron for the region.

The Commonwealth of Independent States

The overarching structure for Central Asia which has generated the most rhetoric and paper agreements is the CIS organization. In security terms the core agreement of the CIS has been the 1992 CST and various institutional offshoots of the treaty.[14] By 2000, however, the CIS organization had essentially been displaced by Russia's focus on bilateral relationships with CIS member states. This was evident from the first CIS summit attended by Russian President Vladimir Putin in January 2000, where formal multilateralism papered over the substance of discussions undertaken mostly on a bilateral basis between Russia and the other states. This is likely to remain the case despite Russian efforts to revive CIS multilateralism on certain aspects of security policy, as noted below.

In the economic field a grandly entitled Eurasian Economic Community (EAEC) was proclaimed in October 2000, the successor to the failed Customs Union of Russia, Belarus, Kazakhstan, Kyrgyzstan and Tajikistan. The new treaty signed by these five countries envisaged *inter alia* 'ensuring economic security on the outer border of the community' and 'forming a common energy market'.[15] However, the divisions between these states, which founded the Customs Union, make it unlikely that the EAEC will constitute a meaningful step towards the creation of a union of Eurasian states, as some of the EAEC members may hope. Its divisive effect in Central Asia was apparent from a declaration by Islam Karimov, the President of Uzbekistan (which remains outside the EAEC), that 'this is an organization which has been built on some illusory schemes and constructions'.[16]

The idea of developing security or foreign policies under the aegis of the CIS still confronts a core problem: whereas Russia in principle can identify common interests in its policy towards the CIS states in Central Asia and beyond, these states themselves have had in common only their relative proximity to Russia (and other non-CIS states are often closer) and their Soviet legacy. The variations in the geographical locations and resources of the CIS Central Asian states—a variation com pounded greatly when other CIS states are taken into account—has led them generally to resist Russian efforts to pool their interests and aspects of their sovereign decision making in the realization of 'CIS integration'. In brief, talk of integration 'has been the means by which the other CIS states try to get Russia to pay for actions, policies or programs that they desire, but can not afford themselves, while Russia uses such discussions to try to secure control of infrastructure and other assets that now belong to other states'.[17]

A multilateral CIS approach to problems of Central Asian security only has real prospects if it addresses a genuine joint security concern of the Central Asian states, and is used as a means to gain a Russian guarantee or credible and limited military/security resource commitment which directly addresses this security concern. Even in this case, the relevance of multilateral coordination or discussion of the issue concerned with CIS states outside Central Asia, besides Russia (Belarus, for example), is open to serious doubt. Moreover, there is a distinction between those commitments under the CIS aegis which are developed and intended to bolster the capabilities of the Central Asian states to meet military/security challenges and those which are promoted more explicitly as part of a broader Russian agenda of creating a Russian-dominated security structure or coalition. These considerations have been reflected, for example, in the responses of Central Asian states to Russian efforts to rally them in an anti-terrorist alliance.

The incursion of armed Islamist groups into Kyrgyzstan over summer 1999 was the catalyst which encouraged four states—Russia, Kyrgyzstan, Tajikistan and Uzbekistan—to offer units for the joint command-and-staff exercise CIS Southern Shield-99 in October–November 1999. The subsequent CIS Southern Shield 2000 exercise, which ended in April 2000, may have been the largest held in Central Asia since the Soviet Union collapsed and also included Uzbek forces, though their role was confined to Uzbek territory.[18] This exercise, which was aimed against an incursion by extremists from the direction of Afghanistan, involved combat training and interaction not only of armed forces but also of security services, border troops and interior troops. In April 2000 Russia, Kazakhstan, Kyrgyzstan and Tajikistan agreed to create a CIS Anti-Terrorist Centre, supported by the Russian Federal Security Service. In discussing this idea with other CIS states Russia initially tried to persuade them of the need for a multilateral operational structure under its own command. However, it seems that this centre will operate primarily as a data bank, and offer recommendations but not engage in operations.[19]

These military exercises and the limited version of the anti-terrorist centre could be viewed as measures to develop coordination against a perceived common and immediate threat and as a result were supported by Central Asian states. (Turkmenistan remained an exception since it did not characterize Afghanistan or Islamist groups as a threat.)

In contrast it is notable that a Russian proposal of autumn 1999, which was formally presented at the January 2000 CIS summit, to create 'joint rapid-deployment anti-terrorist forces' under the CIS Collective Security Treaty was turned down. This idea was similar to Russian proposals in the early 1990s and implied an essentially Russian force under Russian command, which could be projected at short notice onto the territory of other CIS states. This Russian démarche could reasonably be interpreted by Central Asian states as part of an attempt to reactivate Russia's integration agenda, with all the implications for national sovereignty associated with that policy. It is for this reason also that continued Russian efforts to establish ostensibly multilateral CIS peacekeeping mechanisms to manage local conflicts in CIS member states are unlikely to develop any further than they did in the 1990s. A CIS Commission on Peacekeeping was created in 1999 and includes Kazakhstan, Kyrgyzstan and Tajikistan among the Central Asian states, but this body will probably be consultative rather than operational, let alone result in joint peacekeeping units.[20]

Despite these considerations, Russia remains committed in principle to the objective, revived at various times in the 1990s, of creating CIS 'regional groups of forces'. In June 2000 a meeting of the CIS Collective Security Council, and of defence ministers of member states of the CST, reportedly approved Russian proposals to create such a force. They would include a Central Asia group of Russia, Kazakhstan, Kyrgyzstan and Tajikistan. Four months later the CST member states openly proclaimed the goal of forming joint regional security forces.[21]

An important limitation is that this scheme stipulates that the regional groups would still consist of national units, stationed on the respective national territories and subordinated to the national political and military leaderships. Subunits apparently could be earmarked for joint training and joint actions in crises, and these rapid-response forces could be under joint command.[22] But Moscow is unlikely to gain the acquiescence of these countries to the formation of some supranational military structure, despite its plans to form a joint staff, common programmes for military procurement and regular joint exercises for units of the 'regional groups'. Moreover, a crucial handicap to the plans under consideration is that even if the other Central Asian states were to accept the idea of a 'coalition military force' with Russia in Central Asia, Uzbekistan and Turkmenistan would operate outside such a regional security system.[23] President Karimov has said explicitly that he is opposed to collective regional armed forces and that no such forces will be deployed in Uzbekistan, even to resist aggression from Afghanistan.[24] Perhaps the main reason why Kazakhstan and Kyrgyzstan at least accede in principle or pay lip service to Russian designs for regional military forces is that the CST states are offered Russian arms and other equipment at Russian domestic prices rather than 'export' prices.[25]

This leaves cooperation or coordination on security-relevant issues through actual or notional CIS structures which bring together Russian and Central Asian border guard troops, ministries of the interior, and internal security services. General cooperation on counter-terrorism is likely to increase interactions on these levels. The Russian involvement in cooperation under these structures may serve to reduce or de-escalate tensions between the Central Asian states which arise from internecine disputes of various kinds. On the other hand the Russian role may deepen divisions and friction between the states in the region, for example, if it tries to use these security bodies in a manner that favours the regional policies of one of these states over those of its neighbours.

The Council of CIS Border Troops Commanders is anyway virtually defunct as a body, even if Russian officials claimed that it played a role in the CIS Southern Shield 2000 exercise, and in fact cooperation on border protection between Central Asian states and Russia is likely to occur only on a limited (except in Tajikistan) and bilateral basis.[26] The Council of CIS Ministers of the Interior (which also has a Bureau for Counteracting Organised Crime attached to it) may have a certain role in the new conditions of insecurity in Central Asia in pooling efforts to combat drug trafficking and organized crime, as well as to coordinate attempts to counter what is described as international terrorism. This is indicated by a package of agreements in this area agreed at a meeting of CIS interior ministers in September 2000.[27]

The Council of CIS Heads of Security Services (chaired by the Russian Colonel-General Nikolai Patrushev) is a body which Russia under Putin may seek actively to revive for Central Asia, in an effort to resurrect a multilateral intelligence network in association with the CIS Anti-Terrorist Centre. On the other hand Moscow may not wish to use a body like this for intelligence information exchanges with Central Asian states since their intelligence-gathering capabilities are much weaker than those of Russia. In that case Russian intelligence information would continue essentially to be part of the agenda of broader bilateral discussion with Central Asian states.

If Central Asian leaders become more reliant on Russian intelligence in countering perceived terrorism and extremism it may be that only Central Asian intelligence chiefs 'who can balance the relationship between Moscow and the Central Asian capitals while maintaining stability at home will retain their positions'.[28] This may suit Russia's integration agenda, but it is far from clear that coordination of this kind and consequent Russian influence will actually assist the resolution of the internal security challenges which confront Central Asia any more than Russia has resolved its own internal security problems in the North Caucasus. An awareness of this quandary would encourage the Central Asian leaderships to explore the potential of alternative structures to the CIS, sponsored by other powers, to address their security concerns.

The NATO Partnership for Peace programme

In principle the NATO Partnership for Peace (PfP) programme (which includes all the CIS Central Asian states except Tajikistan and is open to all OSCE nations) could be viewed as such a potential alternative framework to the CIS for military and security cooperation in Central Asia, as in other parts of the former Soviet Union. An underlying goal of PfP activities, as noted in chapter 6, might then be to prevent Russia from acting as the only mediator in conflict resolution in the region—its main means of asserting its power there. This would be consistent with the broad goals of the United States, which could be characterized as the principal sponsor of the PfP structure in Central Asia, with Turkey as a second-level sponsor.

However, as noted in the introduction to this volume, PfP membership cannot provide a security guarantee (unlike NATO membership) and therefore cannot be expected to address significant external challenges to the security of Central Asian states. It may stimulate measures for confidence building and preventive diplomacy and even prompt coordination against certain non-traditional security threats. It also tries to achieve interoperability in peacekeeping or search and rescue between NATO and the local states. But it makes no efforts to shape basic decisions about doctrines or forces for more serious operations and has no mechanisms for responding to violent conflicts. Nor is it likely that the PfP will oversee large-scale peacekeeping or peace enforcement operations in Central Asia. It is true that NATO encouraged the creation of the joint Central Asian battalion (Centrasbat). But the functions of this unit are uncertain. It has seen no real military action, although it enables annual well-publicized 'regional' exercises with a variety of PfP partner states, including Turkey, Russia, Georgia and Azerbaijan.

Despite these limitations, collaborative PfP military exercises in the Central Asian region, such as the annual Centrasbat exercises since 1997, could be expected to have the overall effect of modifying the security policy conduct and expectations of partner states to some extent, as well as of displacing or diluting training and exercise regimes developed under Russian or Soviet military programmes. The latter is not a formally acknowledged objective of NATO, however, and Russian troops have been involved in the Centrasbat exercises, including a company of Russia's

201st Motor Rifle Division based in Tajikistan in the Centrasbat-2000 exercise. But it is clear that to the extent that PfP activities enhance local military capabilities for self-defence they weaken the military reliance of Central Asian states on Russia and promote the diversification of their security policies.

Furthermore, PfP exercises are linked to US bilateral support programmes and plans, which have a broader strategic remit. This is indicated by the decision to place Central Asia under the responsibility of CENTCOM, the United States Central Command, which, as noted in chapter 6, represents a significant step in US contingency planning. At the signing ceremony of a bilateral Kazakh–American Defence Cooperation Agreement in November 1997, the US Secretary of Defence noted directly that the two parties were working bilaterally and through the PfP 'to build new structures for regional stability in Central Asia'.[29] The interaction of the PfP with US planning is also suggested by the existence of the US State Partnership Programme, which exists as a subset of its PfP activities and is operated by the US National Guard. Indeed, in many instances national assistance to partner countries has been wrapped in the guise of a PfP activity, and been labelled by NATO as 'in the spirit of PfP', when in fact it has nothing to do with the programme.[30]

A potentially important function of PfP activities in Central Asia has been the encouragement of nascent regional security processes under the Central Asian Economic Community by offering a framework for joint exercises, particularly for the regional rivals Kazakhstan and Uzbekistan, and by providing technical support for the formation of Centrasbat. In this sense the PfP has been working to overcome the lines of division in the region and to build habits of regional military cooperation, even if enthusiasm for Centrasbat has declined in Central Asian capitals since the late 1990s, and Central Asian military officials may have reached the conclusion that bilateral agreements with the USA and Turkey offer more political and operational benefits than do PfP programmes.[31]

It remains uncertain how far the PfP programme or other NATO instruments can offer the Central Asian states the kind of practical assistance against low-intensity threats that they have sought more urgently since summer 1999 and which Russia is prepared to provide through supposed CIS structures or bilaterally. The USA and Turkey may continue to offer small security assistance packages on a bilateral basis. For example, in autumn 2000 the USA pledged $3 million-worth of border surveillance equipment for troops in southern Kazakhstan. But for multilateral NATO security assistance to be effective it would clearly need to go further than encouragement for the show-case and ineffectual Centrasbat.

It would also be necessary for NATO to justify further engagement in Central Asia in terms of NATO's overall objectives and remit. This would need to be done in conditions where alliance members view Central Asia as peripheral or marginal to their core security interests and where most member states tend to see threats in Central Asia and the wider Caspian region in non-military terms and would prefer to emphasize economic, political and diplomatic engagement.[32] However, it seems that the required justification is being developed in current NATO thinking. During a visit to Kazakhstan in July 2000, NATO Secretary General Lord Robertson noted explicitly that terrorism, the trafficking of narcotics and extremism are threats which have direct and far-reaching consequences also for Europe and that 'a crisis in the Central Asian region could put under threat the security and stability in the whole Euro-Atlantic region'. This followed his reported declaration in May that Moscow should team up with NATO, which has experience in this field, to tackle terrorism and extremism and his warning that on its own Russia could not boost security in Central Asia.[33]

NATO assistance for counter-terrorism in Central Asia could take place in the context of the PfP programme and in principle could be co-ordinated with Russia, which remains a (largely inactive) PfP member state. However, this option does not appear promising since Russia has strongly condemned PfP activities in Eurasia as part of a Western strategy of advancing 'geopolitical pluralism' and Western interests in the 'post-Soviet space'. Joint NATO–Russia cooperation in this new field may therefore be better considered under the agenda of the Euro-Atlantic Partnership Council (EAPC) or the NATO–Russia Permanent Joint Council (PJC), even if the PJC agenda to date has not included discussions on how to manage conflicts or respond to security challenges in the CIS region. It is feasible in principle that a new subject for dialogue in the PJC 'could be the security situation in Central Asia and Afghanistan provided that NATO can calm Russian fears that it seeks to supplant Moscow as the security patron of the region'.[34] Such a dialogue may be encouraged by the beginning of a US–Russian dialogue in a new joint working group on Afghanistan, which met for the first time in August 2000. But it is unlikely that Russia would be ready to use the PJC to expedite a significant expansion of NATO security assistance programmes to the Central Asian states.

The Shanghai Forum

Moscow may anyway prefer to rely on expanding its security cooperation in Central Asia with China, a preferred partner in the Russian foreign policy view of a multipolar world. The vehicle for this effort would be the Shanghai Forum. The formation of this group, known informally until it was renamed at the July 2000 Dushanbe summit as the 'Shanghai Five', and its early activities are discussed in chapter 7. The group has expanded its remit beyond its initial objectives of involving China in strategic cooperation and confidence-building measures in Central Asia on matters related to China's border regions. It has become a means for Russia, China, Kazakhstan, Kyrgyzstan and Tajikistan to discuss broad proposals for Central Asian security and to coordinate on more detailed needs in the unstable border regions adjoining China and the other states. As noted in chapter 5, it has also been used by Russia since 1999 as a vehicle in efforts to rally the Central Asian states with China on a broad anti-Western front, even if Kazakhstan and Kyrgyzstan have not been comfortable with this effort.

However, until Uzbekistan was invited in spring 2000 to send an observer to future summits of the five, its exclusion from the group risked deepening divisions between Tashkent and Almaty and undermining efforts of the five to address Central Asian security issues beyond those related to the Chinese border regions. It is notable that a summit of the five in July 1998, dedicated to problems of regional security, endorsed the idea of a Central Asian nuclear-free zone, which had previously been proposed by Uzbek President Karimov outside the context of the five. This appears to have been intended consciously to balance the support offered by the five for separate security initiatives sponsored by Kazakhstan.[35]

A summit meeting of the five in Bishkek in August 1999 resulted in a shift in the emphasis of the group. It placed on the agenda the need for collective efforts to combat religious and separatist extremism and the international flow of drugs, as well for mutual assistance to protect problematic parts of their joint borders. The so-called Bishkek group was set up, comprising the chiefs of law-enforcement agencies and special services, which would meet at least annually to discuss urgent issues and coordinate activities.[36] The themes of the Bishkek summit were reaffirmed at a meeting of defence ministers of the five in Astana in March 2000.[37]

The five declared that they would 'resolutely oppose any activities directed against other countries' carried out within their own territory by the forces of 'national ethnic separatism, religious extremism and terrorism'.[38]

These goals offer a basis for broader cooperation, some of which could be intended, at least in the eyes of Russia and China, to supplant NATO PfP activities in Central Asia. At the Astana meeting the ministers determined that they would study how to 'exchange experience in peacekeeping and cooperate in peacekeeping action'. At the same time they warned that their intention of maintaining long-term peaceful cooperation in Central Asia 'should not be undermined by the intervention of forces outside the region' and that for this purpose they would strengthen consultations and cooperation between their defence departments.[39]

The next summit of the five in July 2000 in Dushanbe was attended by President Karimov as an observer. At this meeting the five states agreed to draw up a multilateral programme and conduct regular meetings of their law-enforcement and security services, and even to hold 'exercises on combating acts of terrorism and violence'. The participants accepted a Kyrgyz proposal to form, within the Shanghai Forum framework, a regional anti-terrorist centre based in Bishkek. Karimov declared that Tashkent's security interests on a variety of low-intensity threats coincided with those of the Shanghai Forum and expressed a wish for Uzbekistan either to join the group or to establish cooperation with it on a permanent basis.[40] This option raised the standing of the Forum and the Kazakh Foreign Minister, Yerlan Idrisov, declared that it was becoming a 'serious integrational regional union'.[41]

The Shanghai Five grouping originally arose out of a real functional need to address unresolved traditional security issues in the Chinese border regions rather than on any assumptions about a common heritage or outlook. Its focus has shifted to address common concerns about separatism, terrorism, drugs trafficking and so forth, which are taken very seriously by the Chinese out of concern about growing instability in Xinjiang and its neighbourhood. The Dushanbe summit also placed a new emphasis on economic cooperation as a key aspect of strengthening regional security and stability (Kazakhstan even proposed holding regular meetings of heads of government of the five on deepening trade and economic cooperation).[42] This framework of issues offers real possibilities for coordination and the Chinese presence dilutes any Russian efforts to impose unwanted aspects of its integration agenda on the Central

Asian states. Equally, the Russian presence reassures the Central Asian states about Chinese policies.

The Dushanbe summit decided to form a Council of National Coordinators of the Shanghai Forum and to regularize meetings of the five heads of government, ministers of foreign affairs and ministers of defence.[43] However, the previous summit had already indicated that the two main powers involved, Russia and China, had a larger international agenda on strategic issues to which most Central Asian states did not wish to subscribe and which they do not consider a priority in the context of this group.[44] Moreover, there are a variety of intra-Central Asia disputes in which the Central Asian states would not want Chinese involvement, and the remit of the Forum is limited by Turkmenistan's absence from its meetings.

The Turkic States grouping

The Turkic States grouping offers a contrasting model of cooperation between a regional power and the Central Asian states. In this case the forum did not arise out of a pressing need to resolve security dilemmas of any kind but, as noted in chapter 9, out of the interest of the regional power, Turkey, to promote a broader agenda based on cultural commonality. This forum has backed the formation and operation of a Eurasian transport corridor and a decision in principle has been taken to set up a secretariat, which would have a coordinating function between the Turkic-speaking states. A declaration adopted at the sixth summit of the grouping in Baku in April 2000 also condemned the militarization of the region's conflicts and resolved 'to implement coordinated actions in the fight against the drugs trade, international terrorism, religious extremism and separatism'.[45]

Nevertheless, the Turkic States grouping is unlikely to develop a military security aspect or a clear international agenda, partly as a result of the sensitivity of the Central Asian states to any perceived efforts by Turkey to dominate or patronize its members and because of strains in Uzbek–Turkish relations. Karimov has argued that politicizing the Turkic States grouping would bring about confrontation. Its Central Asian membership anyway excludes Tajikistan, which further reduces its relevance for the most pressing security issues in Central Asia. Russia, Iran and China would all strenuously resist the improbable development of any 'Turkic commonwealth' in the future, especially if it were to have any politico-security dimension.[46] As indicated in chapter 8, differences between Turkey, Iran and Pakistan will also continue to prevent the Economic Cooperation Organisation (ECO) from expanding its remit from economic, technical and cultural cooperation to security affairs.[47]

In many respects the involvement of external powers in security arrangements in Central Asia reflects the strengths and weaknesses that derive from their broader strategic engagement and competition in the region. This strategic rivalry may deepen and be reflected in alternative and increasingly exclusive security assistance programmes to unstable states. However, alternatively it can be argued that an agenda of security interests and priorities in Central Asia is developing to which the three main powers involved, Russia, the United States and China, can all subscribe. Despite their distinct national interests, they may all be able to contribute in different ways to help overcome shared security concerns in a region of great potential instability. This would also create the permissive environment for these powers to benefit mutually from their economic and energy investments in the region.

The role of the United Nations and the OSCE in promoting security in Central Asia

Questions about legitimacy and impartiality are particularly relevant in considering security structures in Central Asia sponsored by external or regional powers, which are likely to seek to project their interests into the region even if they may share the objective of promoting regional stability with the Central Asian states. In turn, the security structures in Central Asia sponsored by the Central Asian states themselves are liable to suffer from ineffectiveness as a result of differences and rivalries between these states, of pressures from powerful regional states and of inadequate material resources and military capacity.

In these circumstances the engagement of broader international organizations, such as the UN and the OSCE, which includes the new Central Asian states as members, may be viewed as desirable for the management of security in Central Asia. In the case of the 6 + 2 group only the UN could offer the overall authority to bring together the diverse group of states involved (several of which are outside the OSCE space). However, if the security issue concerned is confined to the OSCE space (effectively the Eurasian region) then the OSCE, which provides an important link between Eurasian and global security, could be the appropriate framework for security dialogue and the management of post-conflict security challenges.

In Tajikistan OSCE and UN missions began to operate in February and December 1994, respectively. The practical role of the OSCE was confined to such matters as commenting on the draft Tajik constitution and monitoring human rights practices, although it has sought more generally to assist in the restoration of peace and stability.[48] But the role of the UN Mission in Tajikistan (UNMOT) in chairing the Joint Commission, which oversaw the ceasefire between the parties to the civil war in Tajikistan, and in overseeing the June 1997 peace settlement, has been very significant. The experience of UNMOT is interesting as an indication of the way in which international organizations may be able to operate in a region where Russian military influence and geopolitical concerns remain strong.

UNMOT was mandated to maintain close liaison with the so-called collective peacekeeping forces of the CIS in Tajikistan (whose mission as a 'CIS force' was finally terminated in June 2000) and with the border forces, but not explicitly to act as a monitoring mission. However, the role of the OSCE and UN in mediation and/or monitoring for conflicts in the Caucasus states and Moldova suggests that a broader UN or OSCE role is possible in possible future conflicts in Central Asia and that Russia may not be opposed to such involvement by these bodies. The UN mission in Abkhazia (UNOMIG) was explicitly tasked with observing operations conducted by the CIS peacekeeping troops (effectively the Russian troops) deployed there. The mandate of the OSCE mission in Georgia in turn has included the conduct of negotiations with both sides, cooperation with local military forces in support of the ceasefire and cooperation in the creation of the political basis for the achievement of lasting peace.[49]

Regardless of the specific mandate of possible future UN or OSCE missions for Central Asian conflict zones, the presence of these organizations ensures that regional security issues related to potential conflicts can be aired in these prominent international forums and the norm of the peaceful resolution of conflicts is likely to be taken more seriously, at least with respect to interstate tensions. If there are regional efforts to establish peacekeeping forces in response to instability, the UN and OSCE are bound to emphasize the significance of internationally recognized, if increasingly fluid, norms of peacekeeping, even if the UN Security Council fails to actually authorize the use of military forces or the establishment of the peacekeeping force in the region concerned.

The case of UNMOT indicates anyway that a limited UN local presence can ensure greater transparency around any Russian military role in such conflicts and thereby influence Russian conduct. Attention should be given to this kind of limited UN or OSCE involvement since the latter lacks the military potential and the former appears to lack the political will to become heavily involved in a situation of violent conflict in Central Asia. The Centrasbat 2000 military exercise in Kazakhstan apparently was based on a scenario in which UN peacekeepers in the form of airborne units were sent to restore peace between two states. In this scenario, the two states had been fighting each other for some years, had recently concluded a peace agreement, but had resumed combat as a result of a conflict provoked by international terrorists. In reality, however, a substantial peacekeeping force in Central Asia under OSCE or UN aegis is not likely in the near future, especially in conditions of wide-scale insurgency or before a ceasefire is established between identifiable parties. The possibility of some peacekeeping presence, delegated by the UN to regional organizations or groups of states, should not be ruled out. But it is clear that neither international organization is in a position to provide explicit security guarantees for Central Asian states.

Despite this the Central Asian leaders are interested in a greater UN and OSCE involvement in regional stabilization efforts, especially in relation to Afghanistan. President Karimov of Uzbekistan has explicitly urged the OSCE to be more active in forming the regional security system in Central Asia, especially with respect to conflict prevention. He has appealed for the creation of an OSCE centre to combat international terrorism (he has also called on the UN to set up a similar centre under its aegis—a proposal supported by Kyrgyzstan).[50] But other Central Asian states have also urged the OSCE to increase its awareness of security risks originating outside its area—for example, drug trafficking and terrorism.[51] At a CAEC summit in Dushanbe in June 2000 Central Asian presidents jointly appealed to the UN, the OSCE and other international bodies for greater efforts to resolve the crisis in Afghanistan which created a serious security threat to their countries.[52]

In fact, in addition to overseeing the 6 + 2 group, the UN has placed under its auspices several rounds of negotiations on Afghanistan hosted by Turkmenistan.[53] The UN is likely to continue to explore channels for addressing this primary security concern of the CAEC states. The OSCE's mandate limits its ability to respond directly to any regional threat posed by Afghanistan. But OSCE officials accept that the Taliban has to be taken into account in the formulation of policies to foster regional stability in Central Asia, and they have held direct discussions with Central Asian leaders about the possibilities for the OSCE to combat terrorism, organized crime and the drugs trade in the region.[54] The OSCE has been developing a concept of comprehensive security in Central Asia which concerns a variety of non-traditional security threats that are undermining this fragile part of the OSCE region.

Prospects for the future

This chapter has analysed a wide variety of structures, frameworks and forums for consultation on security issues in Central Asia. It is clear that the relevance of these various arrangements depends on a number of factors, which include the kind of security challenge involved; the foreign policy orientations and priorities, as well as the indigenous military capacities of the Central Asian states and subsets of these states; and the nature of the interests of the regional and external powers on local, regional and strategic levels.

The diversity of structures and groupings which have emerged reflects the failure of the Central Asian states to develop effective and regulated cooperation on security matters among themselves on a subregional level, even among just the four states of the CAEC, in a form which does not rely on the resources or influence of major regional and external powers. This partly reflects the traditional ties of these states to Russia, the historically preponderant power in the region. It is partly determined by the underlying regional rivalry between Kazakhstan and Uzbekistan, as well as a number of other axes of tension between the five Central Asian states. It is also a product of the continued weakness of these states in their capacity to respond to low-intensity but serious threats arising from internal conflicts or emanating from Afghanistan. The Central Asian states bordering China also remain uneasy about how to manage relations with this growing regional power.

As a result the Central Asian states have not been prepared to dispense altogether with bilateral military–security ties with Russia, although these links are still sometimes cloaked in a CIS mantle, nor to renounce wholesale the CIS organization as a means to engage Russian security assistance even if this may come at a political price. Similarly, bilateral security assistance from the United States or that obtained from individual PfP state programmes with NATO are more valued by the Central Asian states than the multilateralism represented by regional PfP exercises.

One paradox of subregional security cooperation in Central Asia, as elsewhere in the CIS region, is that the greater or more serious the regional security concerns are the more unlikely the local states are to engage in significant defence and security cooperation with each other rather than to build bridges to powerful regional or external states. Furthermore, as issues of domestic and internal security become paramount concerns for Central Asian states (and the external threat of Afghanistan is linked to these) then antagonisms arise between these very states from a variety of unresolved internecine disputes—a key obstacle to regional cooperation which is re-examined in the concluding chapter of this volume.

The Central Asian states are still engaged in a protracted effort to establish their statehood and national identities. An important part of this struggle is to develop well-equipped, trained and disciplined national military forces—an objective that can be assisted by their national PfP programmes but will take years more to accomplish. It is hardly surprising, therefore, that Central Asian leaders continue to emphasize the importance of developing their own military forces, despite the economic constraints they labour under, and are reluctant to place too much reliance for their security on groupings, structures or purely consultative forums which are still poorly institutionalized and can easily collapse.

An important role remains for confidence building measures in Central Asia, which can erode suspicions and raise the threshold for security policy cooperation. This was successfully achieved through the Shanghai Five group, which originated from the need to resolve a serious legacy of military confrontation on the Chinese border with Central Asian states and Russia and from the need to demarcate that border, but has shifted its focus to new low-intensity threats which may destabilize the region. The CICA grouping in contrast, which has confidence building as its *raison d'être*, may be too broad and amorphous in its Asian composition to tackle the security challenges within Central Asia, though it may be helpful in familiarizing the Central Asian states with evolving security perspectives in south-west Asia (such as Iran and Pakistan) and Asia at large.

It would be particularly significant if an effective framework for Russia–NATO cooperation could be created over shared threats from terrorism (if this can be defined) and drugs trafficking in Central Asia, and on the basis of the acceptance of joint and compatible interests between Russia and NATO states in this fragile region. This would benefit the local states, and offer a more efficient coordination of resources towards the common end of conflict prevention and stabilization of the region, as well as help avert the risk of an acrimonious collision between Russian and NATO policies in Central Asia.

The security policy horizons of the Central Asian states were enlarged by their entry into the OSCE and the United Nations. At the same time these international bodies have developed responsibilities for this Eurasian 'Heartland', even if their resources are heavily committed in other parts of the world. The growing engagement of competing regional powers in Central Asia, threats arising from Afghanistan and their broad international implications, and the risks of the escalation of local conflicts within and between the Central Asian countries, all suggest that more coordinated international efforts are required for the purposes of international confidence building, conflict prevention and post-conflict rehabilitation (in Tajikistan). The UN and the OSCE are in the best position to encourage cooperation between states and regional groupings located or engaged in Central Asia towards this end.

Notes

1. Anara Tabyshalieva, *The Challenge of Regional Cooperation in Central Asia: Preventing Conflict in the Ferghana Valley*, Peaceworks no. 28 (Washington, DC: United States Institute of Peace, June 1999), p. 32. For the economic problems besetting the CAEC at its inception, see Heribert Dieter, 'Regional Integration in Central Asia: Current Economic Position and Prospects', *Central Asian Survey*, vol. 15, no. 3/4 (December 1996).

2. The effects of these differences on the plans for CAEC defence cooperation are described trenchantly by the Russian analysts K. Zatulin, A. Grozin and V. Khlyupin, *Natsional'naya bezopasnost' Kazakhstana: Problemy i perspektivy* (Moscow: Institut Diaspory i Integratsii, 1998), pp. 26–29.

3. *Jamestown Monitor*, vol. vi, issue 171 (15 September 2000).

4. Interfax (Moscow), 27 September 2000, in British Broadcasting Corporation, *Summary of World Broadcasts: Former USSR* (henceforth SU), SU/3958 G1, 29 September 2000.

5. ITAR-TASS (Moscow), 28 August 1999, report of meeting in Bishkek, in SU 3626 G/1, 30 August 2000.

6. Orozbek Moldaliev, 'An Incongruous War in the Valley of Poison: The Religious Conflict in Southern Kyrgyzstan', *Central Asia and the Caucasus*, no. 1 (2000), p. 19.

7. *Jamestown Monitor*, vol. vi, issue 81 (26 April 2000); and vol. vi, issue 88 (4 May 2000).

8. *Inside Central Asia*, issue 321 (17–23 April 2000); and *Times of Central Asia*, 26 April 2000. The text of the bilateral statement is in SU/3822 G/3-4, 24 April 2000.

9. *Inside Central Asia*, issue 338 (14–20 August 2000); and issue 339 (21–27 August 2000).

10. For the discussions on the zone concept at the 1997 Tashkent conference, the attitudes of the main nuclear-weapon states towards the idea, an analysis of the possible mechanisms of a Central Asian nuclear weapon-free zone, and the particular problems for this zone raised by the status of the Caspian Sea, see *Problema sozdaniya v Tsentral'noi Azii zony, svobodnoi ot yadernogo oruzhiya* (Almaty: Kazakhstan Association for the Study of Problems of Non-Proliferation, November 1998). See also Oumirserik Kasenov, 'On the Creation of a Nuclear-Weapons-Free Zone in Central Asia', *Nonproliferation Review*, fall 1998, pp. 144–47; and A. Dzhekshenkulov, 'O bezyadernoi zone v Tsentral'noi Azii', *Mezhdunarodnaya zhizn'*, no. 6 (1999), pp. 92–96.

11. Conrad Burkhard, *Regional (Non-)Proliferation: The Case of Central Asia* (Sandhurst: Conflict Studies Research Centre, Royal Military Academy, April 2000), pp. 4–5. See also I. Safranchuk, 'Rossiiskaya Pozitsiya po Voprosi Sozdaniya v Tsentral'noi Azii, Zony Svobodno ot Yadernogo Oruzhiya' in *Problema sozdaniya* (note 10), pp. 24–39.

12. *Report of the Tashkent Meeting of the '6+2' Group on Afghanistan under the Auspices of the UN* (Tashkent: Ministry of Foreign Affairs, Information Agency, 1999); 'The 6 + 2 Meeting in Tashkent', *Amur Darya: The Iranian Journal of Central Asian Affairs*, vol. 4, no. 3 (fall 1999), pp. 401–15; A. Dubnov, 'Tashkent Peace Talks', *Moscow News*, no. 27 (21–27 July 1999); and *Nezavisimaya gazeta*, 21 July 1999.

13. Todd Diamond, 'The Six-Plus-Two Group Unveils Anti-Trafficking Action Plan for Afghanistan', *Eurasia Insight*, 15 September 2000.

14. As one Russian analyst argued succinctly, the CIS Collective Security Treaty failed to specify any common adversaries and none were clearly and jointly identified by the treaty member states in the 1990s, except Afghanistan to some extent. It became apparent that for these states 'the only serious threats are posed by the ethnic and religious conflicts among themselves and in internal armed conflicts', that Russia lacked the means to develop an alliance or even to adopt the role of an effective security manager for Central Asia, and that serious efforts in this direction would only threaten to embroil Russia. Andrei Mikhailov, *Nezavisimoe voennoe obozrenie*, no. 24 (7–13 July 2000), pp. 1–2. See also Andrei Zagorski, 'CIS Regional Security Policy Structures' in Roy Allison and Christoph Bluth, eds, *Security Dilemmas in Russia and Eurasia* (London: Royal Institute for International Affairs, 1998), pp. 281–300.

15. Text of statement setting up the Eurasian Economic Community, ITAR-TASS (Moscow), 10 October 2000, in SU/3698 A/1-2, 11 October 2000. See also *Inside Central Asia*, issue 346 (9–15 October 2000); *Jamestown Monitor*, vol. vi, issue 189 (11 October 2000); and Sanobar Shermatova, 'Putin Builds Up Integration with Kazakhstan, Kirgizia', *Moscow News*, no. 41 (18–24 October 2000), p. 3.

16. Uzbek Television, Tashkent, 13 October 2000, in SU/3973 G1/-2, 17 October 2000.

17. Martha Brill Olcott, Anders Åslund and Sherman Garnett, *Getting It Wrong: Regional Cooperation and the Commonwealth of Independent States* (Washington, DC: Carnegie Endowment for International Peace, 1999), p. 95, and see pp. 77–102. See also Allison and Bluth, *op. cit.*, pp. 13–16; and Mark

Webber, *CIS Integration Trends: Russia and the Former Soviet South* (London: Royal Institute of International Affairs, 1997), pp. 34–44. For a broad Russian analysis which includes chapters on each of the Central Asian states, see Ye. Moiseev, *Mezhdunarodno-pravovie osnovi sotrudnichestva stran SNG* (Moscow: Yurist', 1997).

18. *Inside Central Asia*, issue 319 (3–9 April 2000); and Interview of Lt-Gen. Leonid Maltsev, Senior Deputy Chief of the Staff for Coordination of CIS Military Cooperation, *Krasnaya zvezda*, 29 March 2000.

19. *Inside Central Asia*, issue 309 (24–30 January 2000); Alexander Igorev and Oleg Kutasov in *Kommersant daily*, 22 June 2000; and *Jamestown Monitor*, vol. vi, issue 169 (13 September 2000).

20. *Jamestown Monitor*, vol. iv, no. 84 (28 April 2000); and vol. vi, no. 129 (3 July 2000). The decision to disband the so-called collective peacekeeping forces in Tajikistan was finally made at a meeting of foreign ministers of CIS states in June 2000.

21. *Inside Central Asia*, issue 346 (9–15 October 2000); and issue 348 (23–29 October 2000).

22. Statement by Secretary-General of the CIS Collective Security Council Valerii Nikolayenko, as reported on Tajik Radio (Dushanbe), 21 September 2000, in SU/3953 G/1, 23 September 2000; and statement by Kazakh Foreign Minister Yerlan Idrisov, Interfax Kazakhstan (Almaty), 11 October 2000, in SU/3970 A/3, 13 October 2000. See also *Jamestown Monitor*, vol. vi, issue 192 (16 October 2000).

23. Vladimir Mukhin, *Nezavisimaya gazeta*, 30 September 2000.

24. *Inside Central Asia*, issue 343 (18–24 September 2000).

25. *Jamestown Monitor*, vol. vi, no. 130 (5 July 2000); and Mikhail Kozyrev, *Kommersant*, 28 June 2000.

26. Roy Allison, 'The Military and Political Security Landscape in Russia and the South' in Fedorov *et al.*, eds, *Russia the Caucasus and Central Asia: the 21st Century Security Environment* (Armonk, N.Y.: M. E. Sharpe, 1999), pp. 53–55; Olcott *et al.*, *op. cit.*, pp. 88–89; and Webber, *op. cit.*, p. 42.

27. *Inside Central Asia*, issue 341 (4–10 September 2000).

28. Theodore Karasik, 'Rising Russian Intelligence and Security Objectives in Central Asia', *Cacianalyst*, 12 April 2000, p. 2.

29. Cited in Mikhail Alexandrov, 'Military Relations between Russia and Kazakhstan in the Post-Soviet Era (1992–1997)', *Central Asian Monitor*, no. 3 (1998), p. 24.

30. Robin Bhatty and Rachel Bronson, 'NATO's Mixed Signals in the Caucasus and Central Asia', *Survival*, vol. 42, no. 3 (autumn 2000), p. 132.

31. *Ibid.*, p. 133.

32. Richard Sokolsky and Tanya Charlick-Paley, 'Look Before NATO Leaps into the Caspian', *Orbis*, vol. 43, no. 2 (spring 1999), p. 297.

33. Agence France-Presse, 24 May and 4 July 2000; and *Inside Central Asia*, 3–9 July 2000.

34. Dimitri Trenin, 'Russia–NATO Relations: Time to Pick up the Pieces', *NATO Review*, vol. 48 (spring/summer 2000); and Lena Jonson, 'Russia and NATO on Former Soviet Territory: at a Crossroads or up a Blind Alley', unpub-

lished paper presented at the seminar on Russia and NATO, Stockholm, 19 May 2000.

35. Particularly for the CICA. See *Inside Central Asia*, issue 230 (29 June–5 July 1998); and *Russkii Telegraf*, 4 July 1998.

36. For the joint declaration on security signed at the summit, see ITAR-TASS (Moscow), 25 August 1999, in SU/3623 G/1, 26 August 1999.

37. Col-Gen. Leonid Ivashov in *Krasnaya zvezda*, 13 April 2000; and *Inside Central Asia*, issue 318 (27 March–2 April 2000). At this meeting the decision was taken also to invite the Uzbek defence minister to future summits.

38. 'Joint Communiqué of Defence Ministers of the Shanghai Five Countries', Xinhua (Beijing), 30 March 2000, in SU/3805 B/12-14, 3 April 2000.

39. *Ibid.*

40. *Inside Central Asia*, issue 332 (3–9 July 2000).

41. Interfax Kazakhstan (Almaty), 1 April 2000, in SU/3805 G/3, 3 April 2000.

42. Joint communiqué of foreign ministers of Shanghai Five, as reported by ITAR-TASS (Moscow), 4 July 2000, in SU/3885 G/1, 6 July 2000. Kazakh proposal as reported by ITAR-TASS (Moscow), 2 July 2000, in SU/3883 B/8, 4 July 2000.

43. Marat Mamadshoyev, 'The Shanghai G-5 Becomes the Shanghai Forum', *Eurasia Insight*, 7 July 2000.

44. *Segodnya*, 6 July 2000; and David Bachman, 'China and the G-5 Summit', *Eurasia Insight*, 5 July 2000.

45. Text of declaration from Turan news agency (Baku), 8 April 2000, in SU/3811 F/4, 10 April 2000. See also *Nezavisimaya gazeta*, 11 April 2000.

46. For example, the Russian Foreign Ministry strongly criticized a Turkish minister's proposal in January 2000 to establish such a commonwealth. *Inside Central Asia*, issue 309 (24–30 January 2000).

47. The members of the ECO are these three regional powers, Afghanistan, the five post-Soviet Central Asian states and Azerbaijan. From 2003 the ECO secretary-general will be a representative from Kazakhstan.

48. Megumi Nishimura, 'The OSCE and Ethnic Conflicts in Estonia, Georgia, and Tajikistan: A Search for Sustainable Peace and Its Limits', *European Security*, vol. 8, no. 1 (spring 1999), pp. 36–37.

49. Lena Jonson, *Keeping the Peace in the CIS: The Evolution of Russian Policy*, Discussion Paper 81 (London: Royal Institute of International Affairs, 1999), pp. 32–33; and S. Neil MacFarlane, 'On the Front Lines in the Near Abroad: The CIS and the OSCE in Georgia's Civil Wars', *Third World Quarterly*, vol. 18, no. 3 (1997), p. 515.

50. Statement by Karimov at OSCE summit in Istanbul, Uzbek TV, 18 November 1999, in SU/3697 S2/4-5, 20 November 2000; and *Inside Central Asia*, issue 344 (25 September–1 October 2000).

51. 'Personal Representative of the Chairman-in-Office Ensures Central Asian Views Are Taken into Account', *OSCE Newsletter*, vol. 6, no. 6 (1999), pp. 5–6; and 'Chairman-in-Office Visits Each of the OSCE Central Asian Participating States', *OSCE Newsletter*, vol. 7, no. 6 (2000), pp. 3–4.

52. *Inside Central Asia*, issue 329 (12–18 June 2000).

53. Ertan Efegil, Ayse Olcay and Huseyin Kydky, 'Cooperation between Turkmenistan and International and Regional Organizations', *Central Asia and the Caucasus*, no. 3 (2000), p. 91.

54. 'OSCE Secretary-General Expresses Concern about Afghanistan's Destabilizing Role in Central Asia', *Eurasianet Recaps*, 4 May 2000; and 'Meeting between OSCE Secretary-General Jan Kubis and President Nazarbayev', ITAR-TASS, 14 March 2000, in SU/3791 G/2-3, 17 March 2000.

CHAPTER ELEVEN

Conclusion: Central Asian Security in the Regional and International Context

ROY ALLISON

Introduction

The main purpose of this volume is to analyse the security policy consequences of the growing engagement of regional powers in Central Asia.
Regional powers are defined as those powers that have a significant impact on the region, including the United States. The intention is not to
identify and assess all the multifarious factors which shape the security
of the Central Asian states, nor to analyse in any detail the security policy perceptions of policy makers or elites in these states, which would require a far deeper examination of internal processes in these states than
is offered or possible in chapters 2–4. These chapters highlight instead
key factors of instability, 'internal dynamics', which in certain circumstances could threaten interstate conflict and wider regional security. A
premise of the volume is that the impact of the external engagement by
states in the region depends on how this involvement interacts with these
internal dynamics, which may be constructive or destructive in character. Therefore the fact that much of the foregoing analysis takes the form
of 'looking into' Central Asia through the images and perspectives of
other states and their security concerns (chapters 5–9) reflects the meth-
odology and goals of the volume.

This concluding chapter seeks to identify trends in the interplay between the policies of regional powers and the security dynamics of Central Asia.

In the introduction to this volume the development of the regional system in Central Asia was presented as the result of the interaction of dynamics on the local and international level in the region. Four possible
options were drawn up for the development of security aspects of the regional system (which are developed below). These depended on trends in
cooperative and conflictual dynamics firstly of internal factors on the
local level, and secondly of external factors on the international level.

It was also suggested that the dynamics at the local level would be predominant in the sense that external states usually fall in line with lines of
division within the region. In the case of Central Asia it is clear that a
significant degree of deep-rooted rivalry and suspicion exists between the
two largest states, Kazakhstan and Uzbekistan. Nevertheless, as noted in
chapter 10, these states cooperate in a variety of regional and international forums and their competition has not generated a division of Central Asia into sub-groups of states linked with specific external powers.
In fact Russia and the United States have sought to develop their relations with the same group of states, although Uzbekistan veered closer to
Washington in the late 1990s and Tajikistan, exceptionally, has remained in a close military alignment with Russia.

It is true that Russia was able to maintain a close military–security relationship with most of these states in the first half of the 1990s, which
was underpinned by bilateral and CIS (Commonwealth of Independent
States) agreements on military coordination. But this was achieved
through forging ties in parallel with the Kazakh and Uzbek leaderships
and by avoiding close support for specific security policy initiatives of
one or the other, such as the Eurasian Union sponsored by President
Nazarbayev. As noted in chapter 5 and below, however, Russian policy
under President Vladimir Putin may be becoming less even-handed,
which may increase regional lines of division in Central Asia and set back
achievements in Central Asian regional cooperation on security.

The stakes, interests and policies of regional powers

Russia and the United States are the only powers that wish or are able to
develop policy towards Central Asia from a broad strategic perspective,
which as noted below carries the risk of generating alternative regional

alignments. Russia identifies core security interests in the region and continues to view it as a buffer zone or forward security zone against instabilities from further south. In engaging with Central Asia Moscow has
an advantage in its geographical proximity, although the huge 'hinterland' of Kazakhstan separates it from the land borders of the other Central Asian states. Moreover, various non-traditional security threats are
seen as potentially impacting on Russia precisely because of its Eurasian
geography and the absence to date of any effective Russian–Kazakh border regime. This creates a sense of both opportunity and vulnerability, of
unavoidable entanglement in the region. But for a 'positive-sum' engagement in the region Russia has progressively been disadvantaged by the
unavailability of resources to invest in the states of the region (including
even military resources, which were greatly overstretched by the late
1990s) and by declining levels of trade with Central Asian partners.

The United States is far less affected by non-traditional sources of
threat in Central Asia, but equally it lacks the various connections between Moscow and the Central Asian republics that derive from the Soviet period, including continued infrastructural and cultural links. In
common with its policy in other parts of the world, Washington formally
promotes a broad agenda of democratization, market economic development and human rights in Central Asia. On the other hand it has been
difficult for US policy makers to identify core security interests in common with Central Asian leaders, although they have won favour by supporting Central Asian efforts at diversification in trade, energy and
security policies away from structures focused on Moscow. It is true that
drugs and arms trafficking, arms proliferation and terrorism increasingly
feature in bilateral discussions between US and Central Asian officials.
However, the interests of the United States in Central Asia are defined
more by energy and trade, and by its policy towards regional powers
such as Iran and Russia, than by efforts to rally the Central Asian states
behind a common agenda of security concerns.

Turkey, Iran and China have more regionally and culturally defined
interests in post-Soviet Central Asia. They have either had no interest in
promoting a broad strategic vision for the region or been unable to raise
significant local support for such a vision. In the early 1990s Turkish politicians were attracted to the romantic image of a Pan-Turkic commonwealth of nations, an embracing of the 'Turkic' peoples of Central Asia.
But in practice, and despite continued meetings of the Turkic Union, Turkey lacked the economic resources to prove a pole of attraction for Cen-

tral Asian leaders. Its links have been closer with Turkmenistan and Kazakhstan in the western part of the region, driven by economic and energy links, and have been less developed with Uzbekistan, which has resisted Turkish patronage.

For Iran relations with the only Central Asian country with which it shares a border, Turkmenistan, have had direct security relevance. Iran's cultural links with Tajikistan account for its interest in helping broker a peace agreement to the conflict in that country. Iran is antagonized by the characterization of Islam by Uzbekistan, but it shares the security concern of most Central Asian states about the destabilizing nature of Afghanistan under the domination of the Taliban leadership. Iran has cultivated trade, economic and energy relations with its northern neighbours and has projected the image of itself as an influential Caspian state. At the same time it has been careful not to reveal any threatening political ambitions in the region.

China may develop broader strategic concerns in Central Asia, which are influenced by its relations with Russia or Iran. To date, however, China has direct security concerns in the states of the region which it borders—Kazakhstan, Kyrgyzstan and Tajikistan—which can be addressed through the Shanghai Forum as well as bilaterally (although Russia's presence in Tajikistan has dissuaded China from trying to develop a direct and active security policy dialogue with this troubled country). Chinese trade and energy policy in the region has focused on Kazakhstan and Kyrgyzstan, which are developing significant cross-border ties with the economy of Xinjiang. Chinese anxiety about the growth of a Uighur secession movement or of Islamic resistance in Xinjiang could draw it eventually into a closer political and security relationship with its Central Asian neighbour states. This process has been inhibited so far by the larger strategic relationship between Russia and China, in which China still perceives Central Asia as a Russian zone of influence.

Overall, as observed in the introduction to this volume, despite the different priorities of the regional powers, their growing engagement in Central Asia since the mid-1990s has led to a dynamic of strategic competition and this has been reinforced, though not determined, by rivalry over access to Caspian Sea energy resources. Behind various forms of official rhetoric Russia and the United States have tended to view Central Asia as an arena for free competition and the promotion of their national interests, despite their formal support for multilateral cooperation in the region through regional and international organizations.

American leaders have been careful publicly to accept that Russia has legitimate security interests of various kinds in Central Asia, even if the instruments chosen to support those interests have been questioned or challenged. Russian leaders in contrast have been reluctant to acknowledge the existence of legitimate US interests so far from US shores, arguing that the United States is for Central Asia an extra-regional power and that the resolution of security problems should be left to the countries within or adjacent to Central Asia.

This view of the US presence is also supported by Iran, although the competitive aspect to Iranian policy in the region has been limited and has focused on Caspian energy issues. Iran is not only critical of the growing US regional role in general but also appears to be concerned about the dynamic of strategic rivalry in its neighbourhood. One analysis noted that because of their military weaknesses the Central Asian states turned to 'two different powerful foreign alliances', and that Russia would not accept 'the presence of any opponent' in Central Asia while 'the USA is trying to set up its own base in Central Asia and wants to outdo Russia in this'. Iranian experts noted that bringing the military forces of Russia and the USA into the region in the long term would 'cause a dangerous crisis, a conflict between superpowers'.[1]

China for its part may assume a more competitive role in Central Asia in the period 2000–2005 if the Russian presence weakens further. China is the only proximate power which has the capacity eventually to counterbalance Russia geo-economically in the region and is likely to advance its economic, trade and energy interests. But in relation to security policy Beijing may calculate that its priority objective of reinforcing stability in Xinjiang may best be served through an emphasis on cooperative regional discussions which include Russia.

This kind of competition in Central Asia between external powers has led to efforts to form alignments with states and to deny or limit other powers access to favoured states. It is true that subregional cooperation has also been selectively encouraged by the powers involved in the region. But, as indicated in chapter 10, this has tended to be done by these powers to the extent that it supports their overall interests and patterns of alignment. In broad terms, therefore, the United States and Turkey (as well as the European Union) support an east–west axis of subregional cooperation, which conforms with their strategy for Caspian energy development, trade diversification and NATO-oriented security programmes. In contrast Russia and to some extent Iran favour an alternative north–south axis for subregional interactions, which fits their plans for trade routes, oil and gas transport and military security links. For Russia this axis also reinforces traditional political relationships and dependencies in the region.

In a wider context the evolution of the Central Asian region cannot be dissociated from the political and strategic relationship between Russia and the United States. The deterioration of Russian–US relations in the late 1990s was expressed in Russian reactions to the crisis over Kosovo and the NATO air campaign against Serbia, and in the associated rise of anti-Western and particularly anti-American currents in Russian public opinion. It is also evident in Russian campaigns against US attempts to construct a 'unipolar' world and against Washington's interests in a national ballistic missile defence system. This strategic context leads Russian decision makers under President Putin to conclude that the United States and NATO are seeking unilateral and exclusive advantage from their policy in Central Asia and the Caspian region, despite all the talk by Western officials of their interest in 'positive-sum' outcomes in the region. It also encourages zero-sum approaches in Russian policy itself. There is some chance, however, that Russian, US and NATO cooperation over the common perception of dangers emanating from Afghanistan might qualify these tendencies, and US policy might anyway become less engaged in Central Asia under the presidency of George W. Bush.

Since the mid-1990s it has become clear that, among the powers engaged in Central Asia, Russia and the United States are the two that can most easily attract or offer dependent/client relationships in the region. At the same time no formal agreements or tacit norms to regulate the competition of these two states in Central Asia and the Caspian region have been developed.[2] As long as Moscow and Washington are committed to pursuing their interests in Central Asia there remain pressures for bloc building between the local states and one or other of these powers.

This counteracts or inhibits the development of a more diverse pattern of security relations in Central Asia, which would lay greater emphasis on interactions with immediate neighbour states or even, as in the case of Turkmenistan, on a form of neutrality. Such diversity may be considered desirable for those opposed to great-power intrusion in Central Asian regional developments (although Russia of course borders the north of the region). But it would not necessarily deliver greater stability, since the chapters in this volume show that internal local developments within these countries and the interstate relations between them exhibit pronounced conflictual as well as cooperative tendencies, irrespective of their ties with Moscow or Washington. The continued engagement of Russia and the United States in the region could reinforce either tendency.

In brief, rivalry between Russia and the United States/NATO has prevailed over cooperative approaches to security policy in Central Asia, although so far China has managed to cooperate with Russia. This dynamic is unlikely to change so long as Russian political elites continue to view the erstwhile southern Soviet republics as in a natural Russian sphere of influence and use the advantages offered by Russia's Eurasian geographical location to develop policy based on that assumption. However, Russian resource constraints limit its ability to manage or manipulate security processes or threats in the region. For this reason the United States, NATO, China and even Turkey, depending on how they define their own political and security interests in the region, may all assume a greater role in security assistance to the states of the region or in conflict prevention efforts. At the same time the dangers of serious destabilization in Central Asia in the future from non-traditional threats, which could spread to Russia, could persuade Russia to approve and work collaboratively with such assistance programmes.

The potential for conflict and cooperation within Central Asia

Overall, there is a growing potential for conflict from within Central Asia, which may deepen lines of division and the fragmentation of the region. But this coexists with a variety of initiatives aimed at cooperation on regional security, as analysed in chapter 10, and with a historical and infrastructural legacy which provide important commonalities. This section highlights some of the more important pressures for the fragmentation of the Central Asian region arising from the national policies of states, as previously discussed in chapter 2, to indicate how this continues to impede the development of a regional approach to security in Central Asia.

In chapters 2, 3 and 4 this study has identified the volatile nature of the complicated ethnic matrix the Central Asian countries inherited with the borders of the former union republics, the competing national strategies of the Central Asian states in the economic and foreign policy fields, the danger of destabilization linked to national and interstate responses to Islamist opposition groups, and the likelihood of conflict over scarce and unevenly distributed water resources. These non-traditional security challenges pose the greatest danger to regional stability. They risk conflict within states with implications for interstate relations and the further danger of violent conflict between states, which may escalate to involve neighbour states or patron states further afield.[3]

Fortunately these threats gave rise to remarkably little violent conflict in the 1990s, except for the protracted civil war in Tajikistan, and this war did not draw other Central Asian states into direct interstate military conflict. However, despite the peace process in Tajikistan, the overall security situation in Central Asia has been deteriorating in various respects since the end of the decade.

At the same time the risk factors outlined above are an incentive for interstate multilateral dialogue and a search for collaborative solutions. Initiatives at the subregional level confined to the CIS Central Asian states (such as the Central Asian Economic Community, the CAEC) or together with regional powers (such as CIS initiatives or the 'Shanghai Five', now the Shanghai Forum) have sought to address tensions related to trade, water and the violation of borders by opposition groups. But the constraints on these cooperative efforts are indicated in chapter 10. It is not clear that the impulse to cooperate through such initiatives is stronger than the pressures among the Central Asian states for fragmentation and for imposing national solutions which may be viewed as threatening by neighbour states or provide opportunities for regional powers to intervene to promote their own strategic interests.

A key problem arises from the processes of nation and state building in Central Asia. These slow and complicated processes do not harmonize well with the development of Central Asian subregional cooperation on functional security issues. Such cooperation is more likely to be attractive to states which are more internally secure with more clearly established identities. Even after 10 years of nation-building efforts the stronger Central Asian states, Kazakhstan and Uzbekistan, are sensitive to any plans which might provide for pooling their sovereignty with states around them, especially if the result could shift their relative influence on local developments.

The sensitivity of most of the Central Asian states to their sovereignty and the way this hampers cooperative efforts to address security-related problems in Central Asia can be illustrated by analysing their approaches to the interrelated tasks of building armed forces and securing borders. These tasks are basic traditional security responsibilities of states. In Central Asia, however, they have been increasingly related to the core challenge of maintaining internal security.

None of these states has effective, well-functioning armed forces and they have been very slow in clarifying the purposes and doctrines of their incipient armies. This reflects a reluctance or inability to specify regional threats and impedes military organizational development. The two key states of Kazakhstan and Uzbekistan are only beginning to address these deficiencies.

Kazakhstan was ambivalent for many years as to whether its forces in principle should be held in some central reserve for rapid deployment against military contingencies on any threatened axis (potentially including the north if tensions were to arise with Russia), or whether they should be deployed with an emphasis on a particular southern/southeastern axis. In 1999 Kazakhstan decided finally to create four military districts: southern, eastern, western and central. But priority was given to setting up the southern district, which was established by summer 2000 and reflected concerns about possible incursions of extremists from the south. A new Kazakh National Security Strategy for 1999–2005 and a new military doctrine adopted in February 2000 apparently will develop military policy and organization in response to 'existing and potential sources of armed conflict in close proximity to the border of the state, possible infiltration of the territory of the country by armed formations of extremists and international terrorists, and the appearance of new nuclear powers in the region'.[4]

Uzbekistan has the largest military budget among the CIS Central Asian states and the largest military manpower pool, but throughout the 1990s the impulse behind this military effort was uncertain. It adopted a new military doctrine early in 2000 which appears to emphasize border and internal troops and the creation of mobile and self-sufficient units. The doctrine identifies terrorism related to drug trafficking and religious extremism as two of the most serious threats to national security. But it is not clear under what scenarios Uzbek regular forces may be deployed in action. Uzbekistan plans to create five military districts and to deploy one new battalion in each of these. By 2000 two such battalions were already formed and stationed near the Afghan border.[5] However, only a minority of the Uzbek armed forces have the training in low-intensity operations required if their main function is to tackle the cross-border intrusion of armed militants.

Kazakhstan and Uzbekistan have provided the largest contingents for the joint Central Asian peacekeeping battalion (Centrasbat), which also includes Kyrgyz forces. But this battalion, the only joint Central Asian military formation, was not used for the politically sensitive task of peace-keeping during and after the civil war in Tajikistan, nor was it called on to combat the incursion of Islamic militants in summer 1999 and 2000. Centrasbat has been involved in various NATO Partnership for Peace exercises, but it has been difficult to find a definite operational role for this symbol of Central Asian military cooperation. National sensitivities have overridden the ability of the Central Asian states to invigorate such cooperation.

Like the creation of national armed forces, the issue of border protection has been particularly sensitive for the Central Asian states, since it has been a defining feature of national sovereignty. Central Asian leaders have devoted most attention to the so-called outer 'CIS borders' with China, Afghanistan and Iran, since the new Central Asian states inherited the border regimes of the former Soviet Union and for many years Russia was insistent in its efforts to maintain these outer defences, preferably with the use of Russian border guard contingents. By the end of the 1990s, however, the picture in Central Asia had altered greatly. Russian border forces under Russian authority remained only in Tajikistan and assistance for the border protection function in Kyrgyzstan was arriving from Turkey and the United States as well as Russia. The concept of a 'CIS border' instead of a national border had lost its force.

The fact that Kazakhstan, Kyrgyzstan and Tajikistan share a border with China may sustain a sense of dependence by these Central Asian states on Russia out of anxiety about China. But this concern has significantly declined since meetings of the Shanghai Forum have led to the demarcation of Chinese borders with Central Asian states (except for part of the Tajik–Chinese border), confidence-building measures for the border regions and a venue for consultations.

An alternative source of dependence on Russia could be the border Afghanistan shares with Tajikistan, Uzbekistan and Turkmenistan. Since Taliban forces approached the Tajik border in northern Afghanistan in summer 1998 this has become a focus of Russian efforts to rally the Central Asian states behind CIS collective military efforts. This is serving to justify its continuing to use Tajikistan as a Russian military outpost; in addition to the Russian border troops in Afghanistan, the role of the Russian 201st Division, down-sized and transformed into a military base, is essentially that of an anti-Taliban force. But the Afghan border is also a source of division between Central Asian states, since Turkmenistan does not share the perception of the Taliban as a threat and Uzbekistan has criticized the Russian–Tajik agreement on forming a Russian base with a long-term lease in Tajikistan.

In contrast to the attention paid to their borders with non-CIS states, Central Asian officials have devoted far less attention in public to their joint borders. These are mostly poorly demarcated or disputed and make little sense in terms of the transport infrastructure of the new independent states. Crucially the borders are configured on the basis of the former Soviet administrative borders and cut tortuous lines through distinct ethnic communities. This has encouraged regionally-rooted identities in place of ethnic-based identities and the new national borders have become fraught with the potential for bloody conflicts based on the clash of these two types of identity.[6]

The resultant divisions have created tension and disputes between the Central Asian states in numerous ways and they encourage a loose, low-profile border regime. On the other hand, the uncertain status and permeability of these borders facilitate drug and arms trafficking, permit the passage of armed militants and terrorists from state to state, and undermine national defence based on border protection. They also encourage hot-pursuit operations across borders or pre-emptive cross-border raids by national army or air force units, which may not be coordinated with or approved by the country on the receiving end of such operations. In these circumstances even minor skirmishes can sour relations between Central Asian states. This scenario has been played out in Uzbek cross-border raids into Tajikistan.

The adverse effects of open border regimes in Central Asia are related to a growing preoccupation on the part of local governments with internal security needs and with the ties between opposition groups beyond and within national borders. This has been accompanied by an increasing tendency for Central Asian officials to relate perceived external threats to internal stability. This particularly colours thinking in Uzbekistan and may explain Tashkent's determination to 'harden' its borders, even if this is initiated on a unilateral basis.

As noted in chapter 2, in January and March 2000 Uzbek border guards for the first time unilaterally marked out stretches of border which Kazakhstan claimed as within its territory. The creation of a joint Uzbek–Kazakh border commission to demarcate this 2000-km border is unlikely to overcome tensions around this sensitive issue. Tajikistan has reportedly complained to the Uzbek authorities over alleged unilateral moves to demarcate the Tajik–Uzbek frontier. Serious strain also occurred in Uzbek–Kyrgyz relations in early 1999 over their joint border, which did not deter Uzbekistan later that year from trying to unilaterally demarcate its border with Kyrgyzstan in the Ferghana Valley.[7] More promising, however, was the conclusion of an agreement in June 2000 on demarcating the Uzbekistan–Turkmenistan joint border.

This process of hardening intra-CIS land borders may be explicable in security terms, but it inevitably results in greater restrictions on cross-border relations, which can be expected to hinder Central Asian integration, trade and economic development overall. It can also strengthen the conflictual potential of disputes over the distribution of water resources, as analysed in chapter 4, and undermine the spirit of cooperation on this key issue for the long term security of Central Asian states. The process of creating firmer borders within the CIS Central Asian region is not only driven by the insecurities of local leaders. Russia too is concerned that its internal security may be compromised by the permeability of southern frontiers. Russia has decided to begin serious efforts to create a real state border with Kazakhstan guarded by border troops, despite the fact that this border too has not yet been delimited.[8]

It is possible, however, that common borders in Central Asia could induce cooperation where economic incentives are sufficiently high. This may apply, for example, to the specific circumstances of the Caspian Sea, despite strong rivalry over access to its hydrocarbon resources. The failure to agree on the demarcation of national sectors in the Caspian Sea would threaten the development of oil and gas fields which have strategic value for all the five Caspian littoral states. Soviet-era treaties did not leave relevant criteria for a division of the Sea, despite Russian claims to the contrary, and this has pitted the littoral states against each other in demarcating national sectors, and Russia has resisted the idea of full national sectors. This has provided opportunities for Russia and Iran at various periods in the 1990s to use their position on the Caspian Sea as part of a broader bargaining agenda with their Central Asian neighbours. However, the prospects of large economic gains, the high international stakes involved and the relatively unmilitarized nature of the Sea (despite Russian control of remnants of the Soviet Caspian flotilla and Iranian naval forces) suggest that despite rivalry and the prospect of complicated negotiations the Caspian Sea could eventually be delimited through cooperative efforts. This would reduce the chances of the region remaining a source of enduring dissension in Central Asia.

As noted above, the hardening of Central Asian borders is connected with perceptions of internal security challenges and the infiltration of foreign-based opposition groups. This represents a focus by Central Asian leaders on regime maintenance rather than national defence *per se*. One result has been the strengthening of the interior troops in most of the Central Asian states and a greater focus on the risks posed by deprived regions and disenchanted minority communities. However, insensitive policies toward these communities could further exacerbate tensions, for example, between the Uzbek and Tajik governments.

In particular, the effects of repression within the volatile Ferghana Valley by any one government (Uzbek, Kyrgyz or Tajik) are unlikely to be confined to the borders of that state. The likelihood of such repression is high because of the conflict between the parts of the Ferghana Valley in each of the three states concerned and their respective national capitals, as well as a growing intolerance in these capitals of Islamic ex pression in general.[9] The proximity of the region to northern Afghanistan, which is inhabited by Uzbek and Tajik co-ethnic communities and harbours Islamic groups committed to the formation of a new Islamic state in the Ferghana Valley, threatens major instability. The incursion of Islamic insurgent groups into the region during summer 1999 and 2000 has highlighted the dangers. It is also changing the interaction between the policies of major external powers and the security dynamics of the region.

Overall it is clear that the security environment in Central Asia is deteriorating in various respects and that the potential for conflict within states is growing. The impact of cross border threats such as drug trafficking or transnational challenges, such as Islamic extremism, is only part of this equation. However, they increase the risk of direct confrontation between the states of the region, including Afghanistan. In these circumstances and as a result of the varying national strategies of the CIS Central Asian states it has been difficult to develop and sustain initiatives and structures for regional cooperation which can respond to new threats to regional security, although a variety of such initiatives have been proposed. This section has highlighted some of the pressures which could lead instead to a further fragmentation of the region and to discord between these states. Greater cooperation between the powers involved in the region may help to counteract these adverse trends and should be encouraged. This could be facilitated by the OSCE and the United Nations.

External powers, security assistance and shifting alignments in Central Asia

The prospects for increased cooperation between the powers engaged in Central Asia depend on the importance they attach to their alignments or close bilateral ties with particular states in the region and the benefits they expect from these relations. The conditions for such regional alignments have been changing since the incursions of Islamic insurgents into Kyrgyzstan and Uzbekistan in summer 1999 and 2000. So far the security assistance programmes extended by external powers to the Central Asian states reflect competitive policies more than they express common cooperative efforts.

In the Central Asian regional system the particular significance of Uzbekistan is defined by the fact that it lacks a border with Russia, has the most effective armed forces, is self-sufficient with respect to energy and in the second half of the 1990s adopted an independent, even Western-oriented foreign and security policy.[10] It is not surprising that it has been viewed as the core state for the strategic evolution of Central Asia.

In the late 1990s Russian leaders sought to restore defence cooperation with Uzbekistan through the 'troika' consultative group, on the platform of a common struggle against terrorism and Islamic extremism. The entry of Islamic insurgents into Kyrgyzstan in summer 1999 provided the direct incentive for a Russian–Uzbek military rapprochement; bilateral treaties were signed in September 1999 and June 2000. This was expedited by President Putin's readiness to raise the fight against 'terrorism' and 'religious extremism' to a front-rank priority and to brand them as responsible for conflicts from the Caucasus to Tajikistan. During a visit to Tashkent in May 2000 Putin sketched the contours of regional security arrangements under overall Russian leadership. He presented Uzbekistan as the pre-eminent country and privileged partner of Russia in Central Asia and raised the possibility of joint Russian–Uzbek 'preventive anti-terrorist actions'.

In contrast, the Uzbek President, Islam Karimov, has not been ready to commit himself to Russian patronage or to rely too much on Russian military assistance, which he regards as part of a broader Russian geopolitical agenda. In May 2000 he spoke of Uzbekistan as finding its protection 'embodied in Russia'. But he has ruled out the prospect of Russian soldiers ever fighting on the territory of Uzbekistan and has denied that Tashkent requested military assistance from Moscow in combating insurgents during summer 2000. By September that year he denounced Russian military and special services for exaggerating the Islamist threat as an argument for creating a Russian-led military bloc in Central Asia. Karimov also appeared to accept the de facto control of nearly all of Afghanistan by the Taliban and moderated his previous descriptions of the threat posed by the Taliban to Central Asia.[11]

The United States also identifies Uzbekistan strategically as a key state for stability in Central Asia, although Washington's bilateral commitment to Uzbekistan may have waned in the late 1990s and some more attention has been given to Kazakhstan. In April 2000 Secretary of State Madeleine Albright visited Almaty and Bishkek and offered security assistance in combating terrorism. The directors of the United States CIA and FBI travelled to Central Asia at the same time and held discussions primarily focusing on counter-terrorism (although FBI Director Louis Freeh discussed with Kazakh officials in addition other flashpoints causing instability in the country, such as money laundering, organized crime, corruption and drug trafficking in the region).[12] NATO officials have also raised the idea of NATO assistance for anti-terrorist efforts in Central Asia.

It is possible that the competitive dynamic between Russian and American policy in Central Asia will be reinforced through bilateral security assistance programmes to counteract the new challenges to state cohesion in Uzbekistan, Kyrgyzstan and Kazakhstan and related threats from Afghanistan, unless some common approach is developed (such as through the Euro-Atlantic Partnership Council—see chapter 10). In this competition Russia has limited high-technology resources to offer but it has the advantage that it is easier for it than for Western states to rapidly provide military assistance requested by Central Asian partner states without attention to the local state's democracy or human rights record.

In principle this would also be true for China, which shares the concerns of the Central Asian states (besides Turkmenistan) about Islamic militancy and separatist movements. China signed a military cooperation agreement with Uzbekistan in August 2000 and has offered Tashkent military equipment for conducting anti-terrorist operations as well as military training. The basis of this rapprochement would be joint action against ethnic separatism, international terrorism, religious extremism and cross-border crime. China may emerge as a more significant security partner for the Central Asian states in the future, despite their underlying strategic concerns about this huge neighbour.[13]

If priority is given to security assistance to Uzbekistan in the Central Asian policies of Russia, the United States and China this carries with it the danger of increasing tension in the Central Asian regional system overall and of deepening its lines of division. Military support for Tashkent can shift the power balance between Uzbekistan and its smaller or less populated neighbours and therefore add to the insecurities of the latter and exacerbate the differences of the Central Asian states over water resources, the ethnic distribution of populations, joint borders and so on, as previously analysed.

The fear of terrorism and armed insurgents with radical political agendas is likely overall to solidify Russian relations with Uzbekistan, Kazakhstan, Kyrgyzstan and Tajikistan. However, this will fail to address and may complicate a variety of interstate regional security concerns. Russian efforts to restore old intelligence networks, coordinate air defence systems and provide military supplies, in order to sustain a new forward policy in Central Asia, are only likely to suppress underlying tensions or conflicts between the Central Asian states. The goal of reimposing a state of hegemonic Russian 'overlay' in Central Asia, through a far-reaching agenda of reintegration (whether openly bilateral or under a CIS guise), is clearly beyond the resources of the weakened Russian state in the near or medium term, even if this prospect continues to beguile Russian nationalist politicians.

Russia is becoming more actively engaged in Central Asia in counter-terrorist plans and in the coordination of some areas of traditional military activity. But it has little chance of restoring its position of the beginning of the 1990s as the dominant security manager for the region. Equally, as argued in chapter 6, the United States has neither the will nor the access in the medium term to emerge as an alternative dominant security manager for Central Asia. For the coming decade it is also clear that neither China, Iran or Turkey has this capacity or objective.

This suggests that, despite the shifting alignments of 1999–2000, the United States and these other regionally influential states will remain part of the fluid security constellation in Central Asia, even if the security-relevant content of their bilateral relations with Central Asian states is likely to be less than that of Russia. This likelihood is reinforced by the incentives for developing Central Asian oil and gas fields and the realization of competing energy, trade and transport routes, which create enduring and significant, even strategic, interests in the region, as analysed in the chapters of this volume.

The Central Asian security complex reconsidered

The chapters in this volume allow us to evaluate better the idea of a Central Asian security complex and to address two questions raised in the introduction: is there sufficient commonality in security policy interactions across the whole of the vast region formed by the Central Asian CIS states to identify a security complex? and should the definition of such a complex be confined to the borders of these states, given the cross-border interactions which exist with a wider Central Asia?

If the full range of security-relevant interactions between the Central Asian CIS states are taken into consideration then it is reasonable to assert that they form a loose security complex. This is more the result of their common heritage (in the form of the artificiality of their borders and the effects of this on ethnic distribution and the distribution of water resources, as well as military ties from the Soviet period), which creates an interconnectedness, than any common and conscious Central Asian 'security identify' forged in the period of independence.

Indeed, the 1990s were characterized by the evolution of national security identities by all these states, which were based on distinct and separate national interests, and by the competitive dynamic between Kazakhstan and Uzbekistan. This sense of separateness was not really moderated at the end of the 1990s by their growing common fear (except in Turkmenistan) of Islamic insurgents, terrorism and other destabilizing influences from Afghanistan, since this fear has resulted in a hardening of Central Asian national borders as well as fragile efforts by the local states to coordinate their military responses to low-intensity threats.

Irrespective of the readiness of these states for cooperation with one another or the propensity for conflict between them, it is evident that their security concerns are interlocked insofar as the actions of one state to advance its security are likely also to have consequences for other parts of the complex, to a lesser or greater extent. This structural characteristic is unlikely to change as a result of variations in the roles of external powers in Central Asia. Nor is it likely to be significantly influenced by the eventual turnover of the current Central Asian leaderships.

However, it is not satisfactory to confine the scope of the Central Asian security complex, even as an analytical construct, to the borders of the CIS Central Asian states. The growth in security interactions across the borders of the Central Asian states suggests that a wider complex can

be identified which involves northern Afghanistan, the northern and eastern parts of Xinjiang and perhaps regions in southern Russia adjacent to
Kazakhstan. For example, Kazakhstan would be affected by any destabilization of Xinjiang caused by the activities of separatists and Chinese
countermeasures, even if Kazakh leaders deny that their territory is being
used by such separatists and security measures involving all member
states are discussed in the Shanghai Forum.

The existence of a wider Central Asian security complex is particularly
evident in relation to the conflict dynamics which involve parts of Afghanistan and threaten to destabilize the surrounding region. But it can
be argued that Afghanistan also constitutes the link between a Central
Asian security complex and a South-West Asian complex. Regional complexes may be viewed as linked to one another by 'knots' or 'shatter
belts'. If Afghanistan forms such a shatter belt, capable of causing major
regional security disruption, then the Ferghana Valley could be viewed
as a knot which links Tajikistan, Uzbekistan and Kyrgyzstan and also has
threads connecting it to northern Afghanistan. The Russian tendency
since 1996 to play up the direct threat posed by the Taliban militias, Russian claims since 1999 that there are strong links between Taliban commanders, Uzbek Islamists and Chechen rebels, and Russia's warning in
May 2000 that it could conduct air strikes against training camps for
these groups in northern Afghanistan—which provoked a response by
Taliban leaders that they would retaliate against Uzbekistan—all show
the dangerous potential for the escalation of crises and conflict in the
connecting zone between the Central Asian regional system and the
South-West Asian security complex.

Central Asian security: future trajectories

The foregoing chapters enable us to clarify the content and likelihood of
the four alternative scenarios for the future security situation of Central
Asia which were presented in the introduction.

The *first scenario* is premised on the existence of conflictual dynamics
within the region as well as strategic competition between external powers. As a result of these processes the region would be fragmented and
characterized by deep divisions. This situation has similarities to the evolution of events described earlier in this chapter. However, current local
and international trends have not yet led to deep divisions of this kind in
Central Asia, manifested by Central Asian states being pitted against

each other and by one or several external powers developing close patron–client relations with individual Central Asian states to the exclusion of their relations with others. In this situation strategic competition by the external powers would be replicated at the regional interstate level. At present the orientation of the Central Asian states remains diversified. The danger remains, however, that external powers will align to a greater extent with states in the region and that these alignments will create blocs and thereby lasting divisions.

The *second scenario* assumes conflictual dynamics between the external powers but cooperative dynamics among the Central Asian states. This partly corresponds to current trends in Central Asia. The Central Asian states are still able to maintain room for maneuver between external powers within a diversified foreign policy, with the exception of Tajikistan. There are cooperative trends within the region and subregional cooperation has developed to some extent, as outlined in chapter 10.

However, such cooperation remains nascent, despite numerous paper agreements and summit meetings, especially on traditional security issues. The agendas for these meetings between Central Asian leaders include serious contentious problems between them, such as those related to water resource use or economic and trade development, but in the absence of significant progress on these questions the cooperative endeavours of the Central Asian states remain fragile. It is possible that the national strategies of these countries will be moderated over time and collaborative impulses will deepen. But even if this happens it cannot be precluded that a serious crisis in the region ensuing, for example, from the destabilization of the Ferghana Valley or regions closer to Caspian oil and gas fields by armed insurgents, would result in an intervention by one or several external powers to defend their perceived interests. This second scenario, therefore, cannot be considered inherently as stable.

The *third scenario* is premised on cooperation between the external powers in circumstances where there are strong conflictual dynamics within the region. Such strong conflictual tendencies in Central Asia would make it difficult for external states to influence the course of events from outside the region. The option of intervention in response to the development of violent conflict generated within the region is not attractive to any power, even to Russia which has substantial experience in the 1990s of involvement in military quagmires in the southern CIS states.

It is true that if Russia were to re-establish a substantial local military presence in the Central Asian states, through bases and facilities, peacekeeping forces or rights of access (in addition to its military presence in Tajikistan), then it would have a greater capacity to influence or even manipulate the outcome of local conflicts as it has done for various periods in the South Caucasus and Tajikistan. However, even in this case Russia would not be well placed to address or mitigate the underlying sources of regional tensions and might wish to avoid becoming embroiled in open-ended internecine strife, especially in conditions when its resources are scarce. Moreover, this kind of extensive Russian military presence is less probable in a scenario of cooperation between the external powers.

The *fourth scenario* assumes that there is a firm readiness to cooperate both among the Central Asian states and between external powers engaged in the region. This combination would offer the preconditions for responding most effectively to regional security challenges. It would encourage the creation of a multilateral framework for international cooperation over military as well as non-military responses to these challenges for Central Asia. The OSCE and the UN could play a more prominent role in the region and help legitimize the activities of certain regional/subregional organizations. In this scenario Russia and the United States, and perhaps China also, may reach informal or tacit understandings about their respective roles in Central Asia. It is likely that the relations between external powers and local states in the region would be influenced much more strongly by international regimes, regulating a variety of functional issues and encouraging norms of cooperation.

This ideal condition is not likely to be realized for Central Asia as a whole. But it is possible that these principles of cooperation may be promoted for subregions, such as the Caspian Sea, where all the states involved come to accept that the benefits of broad cooperation over issues of security relevance (despite commercial competition) outweigh the risks of efforts to gain unilateral advantage.

These four scenarios or potential trajectories for Central Asia are useful for analysis but they should not be viewed as mutually exclusive. The future of the region may appear as a mix of these outcomes. The Central Asian states, other international actors in the region and external powers are likely to engage in different kinds of functional cooperation, despite the presence of conflictual tendencies in their relations.

Ultimately, the future of the region depends on the fragility of the states within it, their search for legitimacy and national consolidation. This means that they are vulnerable to a variety of non-traditional security threats, which are growing at present. Consequently external states can influence the direction of the nascent states more easily. However, this capacity to influence and the potential effects of their actions mean that the powers involved in Central Asia have a greater responsibility for their conduct in the region. Despite the potential for instability in the region, these powers can contribute to positive outcomes in Central Asia through engaging in and promoting structures and frameworks for security relations which encourage cooperative approaches and the harmonization of national interests. Without this kind of positive international engagement the Central Asian region is more likely to remain fractured and fragile and its states will face further impediments to national development.

Notes

1. Iranian Radio commentary on 1 May 2000 in British Broadcasting Corporation, *Summary of World Broadcasts: Former Soviet Union* (hereafter SU), SU/3831 G/4, 4 May 2000.

2. This contrasts with the earlier Soviet–US competition in Third World regions where the danger of competition, especially in regions where the interests of the powers were poorly defined or articulated, eventually resulted in tacit norms of competition and some formal crisis prevention regimes. See Roy Allison and Phil Williams, 'Superpower Competition and Crisis Prevention in the Third World' and 'Crisis Prevention: Patterns and Prospects', and Alexander George, 'Superpower Interests in Third Areas', all in Roy Allison and Phil Williams, eds, *Superpower Competition and Crisis Prevention in the Third World* (Cambridge: Cambridge University Press, 1990).

3. For further analysis of the different dimensions of non-traditional security threats for Central Asia (and the Caucasus states) see the chapters in Yu. Fedorov, R. Menon and G. Nodia, eds, *Russia, the Caucasus and Central Asia: The 21st Century Security Environment* (Armonk, N.Y.: M. E. Sharpe, 1999).

4. Statement by President Nazarbayev, reported in BBC Monitoring, *Inside Central Asia*, issue 337 (31 July–6 August 2000); and Kazakh Defence Minister Sat Tokpakbayev in *Kazakhstanskaya pravda*, 6 May 2000.

5. Statement by President Karimov, reported in *Nezavisimaya gazeta*, 27 May 2000. See also *Jamestown Monitor*, vol. vi, issue 108 (2 June 2000).

6. Saodat Olimova, 'Natsional'nye Gosudartstva i Etnicheskie Territorii' in Martha Brill Olcott and Aleksei Malashenko, eds, *Mnogomernye granitsy Tsentralnoi Azii* (Moscow: Moscow Carnegie Center, Gendal'f, 2000), pp. 14–26.

7. *Inside Central Asia*, 24 January–13 February 2000 and 31 January–6 February 2000; articles by Nick Megoran, *Eurasia Insight,* 14 December 1999, 19 December 1999 and 6 January 2000; and Kuban Mambetaliev, 'Problemy Kirgizsko-Uzbekskoy Granitsy v Osveshchenii SMI Kirgizii', *Mnogomernye granitsy Tsentralnoi Azii, op. cit.*, pp. 27–42.

8. This decision was taken in 1999 and began to be implemented the following spring, although only two joint sessions of the Russian–Kazakh commission on border delimitation had taken place. Interview of Lt-Gen. Gennadii Loginov, Senior Deputy Chief of the General Staff of the Federal Border Guards Service, *Obshchaya gazeta*, no. 1 (13 April 2000).

9. Barnett Rubin and Nancy Lubin, *Calming the Ferghana Valley: Development and Dialogue in the Heart of Central Asia*, Preventive Action Reports Vol. 4 (New York: Century Foundation Press, 1999), pp. 108–9.

10. For an assessment of Uzbekistan's regional influence see Svante Cornell, 'Uzbekistan: A Regional Player in Eurasian Geopolitics?', *European Security*, vol. 9, no. 2 (summer 2000), pp. 125–138.

11. *Jamestown Monitor*, vol. vi, issue 101 (23 May 2000); and for the agreement on bilateral military cooperation *Jamestown Monitor*, vol. vi, issue 127 (29 June 2000); *Inside Central Asia*, issue 325 (15–21 May 2000) and issue 326 (22–28 May 2000); and *Jamestown Monitor*, vol. vi, issue 178 (26 September 2000).

12. Theodore Karasik, 'Rising Russian Intelligence and Security Objectives in Central Asia', URL <http//www.cacianalyst.org>, 12 April 2000.

13. *Inside Central Asia*, issue 341 (4–19 September 2000). At the same time, in the context of counter-terrorism, the Chinese President Jiang Zemin also talked of the option of expanding cooperation between Uzbekistan and China in the security and military fields, although he suggested that this could be an outgrowth of opportunities created by the Shanghai Five group.

Index

Abduminov, Karimsher, 76
Afghanistan, 6, 21, 181; border
  security concerns, 256–57; CAEC
  and, 223, 239; in Central Asian
  security complex, 264; CIS security
  arrangements, 228; Iran and, 172,
  185–86, 189, 190, 191–92; narcotics trade, 38, 43; OSCE and,
  239–40; radical Islamic movement
  in, 53–55, 59–60, 67n7; Russian
  security concerns, 112–14, 260–61,
  264; as security threat, 26, 54–55,
  108, 112–14; 6 + 2 group, 225;
  Tajikistan and, 177; Turkey and,
  211; UN and, 239; water issues,
  14, 77–79, 84, 85
Agency for International
  Development, 83, 135
Akayev, Askar, 54, 124n50, 154
Albright, Madeleine, 261
Aliyev, Geidar, 209
Almaty Agreement (1998), 72, 181
Aral Sea Basin, 14, 41, 70; current
  water allocation, 87n10; external
  actors in, 78; population trends,
  71; water sharing, 71, 72–73,
  84–86
Armenia, 177, 200

Asian Development Bank, 82
Azerbaijan, 177, 206, 215; Turkey
  and, 200, 201, 205, 209. See also
  GUUAM
Azimov, Araz, 215

Bahçeli, Devlet, 202, 203
Baltic States, 1–2
Basmachi Revolt, 30
Baturin, Yurii, 98
Bedford, D., 73
Berezovsky, Boris, 116
Betts, Richard, 143
Bingol, Yilmaz, 63
Bin-Laden, Omar, 56
Bir, Çevik, 207, 215
Bishkek Group, 125n74, 143–44,
  154, 164, 234–35
Black Sea Cooperation Naval Task
  Group, 215
Border disputes, 39–41, 42; China,
  154–55; CIS role, 230; creation of
  ethnic states, 114; intra-regional,
  257–59; security concerns, 256–58;
  Russian concerns, 100–01, 106,
  107, 108
Brzezinski, Zbigniew, 3, 5, 212
Buzan, Barry, 5, 8, 9, 10